CATCHING A STAR

Transcultural Reflections On a Church for All People

Richard J. Perry, Jr., Editor

Lutheran University Press
Minneapolis, Minnesota

CATCHING A STAR

Transcultural Reflections On a Church for All People

Richard J. Perry, Jr., Editor

Library of Congress Cataloging-in Publication Data
Catching a star : transcultural reflections on a church for all people / Richard J. Perry, Jr., editor.
    p.cm.
  Includes bibliographic references
  ISBN 1-932688-03-x (alk. paper)
    1. Church I. Perry, Richard J., 1948-
  BV600.3.C38 2004
  260—dc22

                                                    2004048751

Lutheran University Press, PO Box 390759, Minneapolis, MN 55439
Manufactured in the United States of America

CONTENTS

"There is a river whose streams
make glad the city of God"
Psalm 46:4

"To think of life as being like
a river is a full and creative analogy."
Howard Thurman[1]

PREFACE

Catch a falling star and put it in your pocket! This book documents at heroic attempt to do just that—or more accurately, to transform a vision into reality and put that star into our collective pockets.

In our society, visionaries are distrusted and perceived as odd. More often than not, visions themselves are questioned and forced to remain ethereal fantasies rather than evolving into tangible realities.

Joseph, the dreamer, was seen as odd by his brothers who did everything in their power to be rid of him. Yet that very gift of dreaming, of vision, later saved the nation of Israel from death through starvation. The Old Testament prophets were also unpopular because of their prophecies. But when harm was intended toward them, God turned it around and used it for good. The visionary Martin Luther King, Jr. was destroyed by society, but God continues to use that human destruction for human reconstruction.

What we have come to understand is that what human beings intend for harm, God turns around and uses for good. We understand that without people of vision enabled by God to transcend the acceptable norm of their time, our contemporary society as we know it would not exist.

Our vision is just as significant as Joseph's, the prophets' and Martin's because all of these visions emanate from God and are for his glory. Our vision is a church on earth, a community where all the people of God can gather and glorify him without having to deal with imposed, exclusive, human standards of acceptability. This vision has become known as the inclusive church." It is the "falling star" we speak of above.

The visionary in this case, theologian Albert Pete" Pero, Jr., was met by laughter, fear, indifference, awe and a combination of all of these when he shared his vision with friends and colleagues. Nevertheless, people of God who shared the same God-centered spirit did catch the star, and made a spiritual, intellectual and physical commitment to "pocket it" as it was falling.

The work began in earnest in 1979, and will continue until we are all satisfied with how the vision has become established. Until then what we have is this book. All 100 participants at the Transcultural Seminar in Chicago in 1981 contributed to this book, because everything that was said or done on behalf of the seminar was a significant contribution.

We share a common vision: the revelation of the kingdom of God on earth and of a common creator. Asians, Blacks, Hispanics, Native Americans and new Whites come together to transform that common vision into a common reality.

By the help of God we saw the falling star to which Pete called our attention. By the help of God we were able to open our pockets and catch it before it landed, and with his help we will place that star in our collective pockets. That star is Jesus Christ, and our collective pockets is our faith in the one who is the Lord of us all. The acting out of that faith commands the substance of this document.

PART I tells how and when the falling star was caught.

PART II describes the composition and make—up of the star.

PART III explains how the star can be placed in our pockets and examines what needs to happen if we are to keep the star in our pockets.

PART IV is unwritten. Only you can write it.

Cheryl A. Stewart

Readers may note that the capitalization of ethnic groups varies through-out this work. This reflects the fact that this book was compiled during a transitional time in which Lutheran church bodies and agencies are us-ing a variety of editorial styles when referring to people of color.

FOREWORD

Any person facing the task of writing a tribute, which I am honored to do, inherits a responsibility of doing justice to the person and his/her ministry and vision and remain one step this side of idolatry. It is not easy. Many people, as I do, revere the person we are honoring. The Rev. Dr. Albert 'Pete" Pero, a child of God who manifests faith, strength and courage, gifts of mind and heart, vision, an indomitable spirit, a deep commitment to justice, independence of thought and critical thinking, and wisdom worthy of emulation. His spirit is exuberant and overwhelming.

Pete Pero eludes simple definition because he is a complex person. He is preacher, pastor, teacher, mentor, visionary, and prophet. Yet, in his role as a teaching theologian of the church, many of us have come to experience the depth of his vision and critical thinking. His prophetic voice challenges all forms of complacency whether in society or institutional life. Our imaginations will be stirred wondering what challenges Dr. Pero will see and the prophetic words he will speak even in retirement.

Pete, as he is affectionately known, would say that any movement of God's people, this side of heaven, is greater than any one individual. Any movement for justice is a communal movement. Movements for justice are a communal affair always surging toward the full liberation of God's people. The pursuit of justice calls for alliances such as those built at and continued since the first Transcultural Seminar. God's rainbow shines brighter when the voices of the people are organized as one in resisting the yokes of slavery.

The image of river comes to mind when I think of Pero's ministry. This metaphor is crucial in many communities. Many of our communities embrace the river and give it special meaning. Some communities see the river yielding all that it needs for life itself. In the African American community, for example, songs like "Deep River" convey the significance of river. It was the place of baptism and the last hurdle to freedom for many of our ancestors. Langston Hughes' poem, "The Negro Speaks of Rivers," captures how one community understands life and their relationship with nature and God.

I want to suggest, as we gather for this celebration, using river as a metaphor. As the Psalmist says, "There is a river whose streams make glad the city of God." The river, in this case, is the Lutheran church. Each community that constitutes the Lutheran church is a stream that deepens, widens, stirs up, overflows, and pushes the river in a new direction. As each community enters the river, God is glorified, because these streams make glad the city of God. The rainbow rising above the river becomes fuller and brighter as it dissipates the storm clouds of race, class, and gender.

This essay shares three dimensions of Pero's ministry. The first part provides a sense of Pero's own life and ministry as God's "obedient rebel."[2] It outlines how Pero was formed "in" the river, yet throughout his ministry never being "of" the river. The second part explores Pero's thinking as "brother Pete, our visionary rebel." Over twenty-five years ago, Pero shared his vision of what the Lutheran church could be, a church for all people. The next part examines "Dr. Pete the obedient rebel as theologian." An essential contribution to the murky waters of the river is the concept of self-transcendence. Finally, I want to raise the question: what is the challenge facing us in our contemporary call to be God's obedient rebels in our swim toward making the Lutheran church truly a "church for all people."

God's Obedient Rebel: Journeying Down the River

Journeying down the river brings one many experiences. There are moments of tranquility. There are moments of struggle. There are obstacles to overcome. In addition, there are moments of great excitement, especially when new streams enter the river. Pero has been formed "in" the river, yet never being "of" the river. This "in" but not "of" the river image captures how Pero sees himself. His identity is grounded in baptism thus his faith in Jesus inspires and strengthens him so much that he is strong enough to resist taking on the characteristics of the river. At the same time, his cultural identification; that is, being unapologetically African American gives him courage to do more than merely tread water or be overwhelmed by racist, classist, and sexist logs in the river.

That constitutes the uniqueness and distinction of the Lutheran church's first teaching theologian of color. In part, he has been formed in Lutheranism. He is a life long Lutheran. Since childhood, he has been educated in Lutheran institutions. He has served Lutheran congregations and served in other Lutheran institutions. He has ministered as a missionary both globally and on the North American continent. Through it all he has developed a deep sense of the nature of the river. As one of his conversation partners, W. E. B. Du Bois wrote in the essay "The Souls of White Folk," he "knows their thoughts and they know that I know."[3]

Although Pero was formed in the river of Lutheranism, he was not "of" the river. The African American community and its religious and ethical tradition formed him. He follows in the non-violent resistance tradition of African and African American men and women who have resisted racism and other forms of oppression. When one sits with Pero, one hears the joy and sorrow that emerges from his participation in the river called Lutheranism. When individuals in the river and that insidious sin of racism sought to erode his baptismal identity and cultural identification Pero is the quintessential "obedient rebel." He resisted with a faith in Jesus Christ!

What a marvelous description of one partially formed by the river. In his message and ministry, Pero has been that obedient rebel. When the currents of the river begin to freeze, Pero has been that agitator who challenges the church to face itself. In that sense, Pero encapsulates the spirit of his ancestors and Martin Luther. The church is not a static institution from in the past, but an *ecclesia semper reformanda* (ever reforming church) living in the present and future. New communities challenge and deepen the river upon their entry into it. The mainstream current learns to see itself as a dynamic flowing process. The banks of the river yield to the new "river whose streams make glad the city of God."

Brother Pete: The Visionary Obedient Rebel

That may be the reason the call to be a church for all people is often highly debated within the mainstream river. The debate hinges on two factors: the power of the mainstream culture to redirect the debate and failure of the mainstream to listen to what people of color[4] think constitutes a church for all people. In the former, the debate moves to the issue of quotas and setting conditions on how to "include" people of color. The latter reflects currents that supports racism; namely, denying the contributions of people of color to the river. Can anything good come out of these new tributaries to the river? Accordingly, including people of color together with their ideas, practices, religious worldviews, and theology in the mainstream of the river has often been a monocultural conversation. What white people decided constituted a multicultural or "inclusive" church became the dominant norm. People of color could be included as long as they "went along" with the flow of the river.

This mono-cultural conversation would be short-lived. Since the first Transcultural Seminar many of us have experienced Pero as "Brother Pete our visionary rebel." Pero's vision and word was not so much the river's word and question, how to include people of color in the journey down the river. Rather, Brother Pete's vision and word reflected the new streams entering the river, what do people of color think a church for all people looks like and how can we live that out within the river called Lutheranism. In the words of Howard Thurman, Pero understands that "It is the nature of the river to flow; it is always moving, always in process, always on the way." Our contributions make new possibilities in the *depth* and *direction* of the river.

Through his own experiences of racism, segregation, and racial discrimination, Brother Pete has walked with many individuals and communities in their struggle to survive and to be God's liberated people in the river. While some of us have been thrashing about in the river, tossed about by the currents of racism, gender, and economic oppression, brother Pete swims with us all the while saying: RESIST! Do not take on the yokes of slavery! Jesus said, "All power has been given to me!" "Organize."

Dr. Pete: Our Theological Rebel

In the midst of the raging storm that churns the river, Dr. Pete, our theological rebel, contributes a vision and its key current, self-transcendence. As an astute observer of the human spirit and behavior in the river, Dr. Pete gave back to us what many of us were doing in the river, becoming the other. This current, like any new current in a river, caused us to struggle and celebrate. What attributes, practices, symbols, and concepts, all that constitutes our total life, are particular and what is universal? Are there places where we make connections with each other? Are we even talking with each other about what constitutes our particularity and universality? Do we realize that by entering the river God is working through us to deepen the channel? Can we see the rainbow in the clouds and see the banks of discrimination eroding away?

This is the urgency of that lifeline, self-transcendence. It is an insight that begins with the self and its ability to reflect on what constitute a self. What constitutes the self is more than one's racial or ethnic identification. The self is a creation of God, a reflection of God's image. Thus, a self has the fruits of the Spirit: love, joy, peace, patience, faith, hope, and understanding. In addition, the self seeks to go beyond itself by connecting with others who also manifest these fruits of the Spirit.

Self-transcendence offers both an internal and an external critique. It drives us to be self-aware and self-critical. Self-aware in the sense that we are clear about our identity and in whom it is really lodged, Jesus Christ. Self-critical in the sense that we come to see that our own cultural identification, while an important dimension of God's creative design, in the context of our own stewardship of this blessing it is limited, especially in our encounters with the rich diversity of God's people. However, this impulse also functioned externally. We employed it in our critique of the Lutheran church, causing it after its initial feeling of disturbance, to reflect on itself and its direction. The flow of the river had to be changed. With renewed energy, many of us challenged the church to bring its praxis more in line with its beliefs and proclamation of being an inclusive church. How could the church be inclusive when the dominant culture is making decisions about people of color without people of color participating in the decision-making processes?

A movement emerged from that first Transcultural Seminar which sought to live out, experientially, the truth of Pero's vision. Many of us remember the struggle and joy of the Commission for a New Lutheran Church (CNLC) as it was challenged by people of color with a new vision of a multicultural church. The fruits of those labors continue to guide the praxis of this church. For example, the representational principle in the ELCA's Constitution opened the door for the many and varied gifts and talents of lay people and clergy to be included in every expression of the church.

The creation of the Commission for Multicultural Ministries and the various Associations (formerly known as Caucuses) were constituted as our voice to ourselves and to the global church. They created space for people of color to creatively deal with the concerns of our individual communities yet doing that in relationship with other communities. The Commission and the Associations became places where community accountability could regularly occur. In the analogy of the river, as each new stream entered the river, the river overflowed. It eroded the banks of racism by bringing new ideas and thoughts about what constitutes a church for all people.

We, too, became obedient rebels. For example, twenty-five years ago there were only one or two theologians of color. Today, just about every ELCA seminary has at least one theologian of color. Certainly, one could attribute the increased number of people of color in leadership positions within the Lutheran church, globally, to the agitation of God's obedient rebels. People of color are serving as bishops, as a seminary president, a seminary dean, and more recently as lay chairs of the ELCA's Church Council.

The impact of our entrance into the river can also be seen in its global impact. Through the support of various expressions of the ELCA, associations of teaching theologians, lay people, pastors, bishops, and staff persons have gathered on an international basis. The work, for example, of the Conference of International Black Lutherans (CIBL), the Asian Lutheran International Conference (ALIC), and the significant participation of Latino/Latina theologians in The Hispanic Initiative testifies to the vast reach of the original vision. These face-to-face dialogues are important as North American Lutherans of color build bridges with our soul mates in the South in the ministry of transforming the river.

Our Challenge Today

What is the challenge today? This Forward is being written in the midst of current discussions about restructuring the churchwide organization of the ELCA. People of color are, once again, intimately involved in directing the flow of the river. The banks of racism and racial prejudice are building up again. One wonders does the Lutheran church really want to be a church for all people? Has the Lutheran church forgotten that a river always changes? It is never the same because new streams enter at various points. Those new streams force the river to carry along large rocks that deepen the river and turn it in a new direction. There continues to emerge other voices that need to break the damns and melt the ice that block movement of the river. Women, youth, and those experiencing discrimination because of sexual orientation bring many experiences, perspectives and theological reflections that enhances our vision of being a church for all people.

The papers in this edited version of "Catching a Star" reflect where we were more than 20 years ago. Now we re-gather to celebrate the contributions of God's obedient rebel. We say to Pete: we thank God for your openness to the Holy Spirit which worked and will work through you, in your retirement, to call, gather, and enlighten us in our journey down the river. We also gather to discern directions for the future. With the passing on of the first generation of leaders of color, the new generation is called to make the vision of a church for all people its own.

The Planning Committee hopes the reader of these papers will catch the vision, internalize it, share it with others, and have the courage and hope of living it out. We, people of color share a lot in common. We have entered the river at various points in history with our unique history. Each stream carries resources that deepen the river. In this sense, each stream goes beyond itself. Our challenge may be that God is calling us to be obedient rebels, stirring and agitating the river toward God's future. In the words of Pero, our calling nurtured by faith in Jesus Christ is leading the river toward understanding that it is time to understand that "To be me is to fully become you!"

A word about this volume of papers is in order. The essays in this volume are the original essays shared at the 1981 Transcultural seminar. In some cases, however, titles and subheadings were edited while still maintaining the original intent of the writers. The reader may notice the various ways in which each ethnic community identified itself in 1981. For example, the writers identified the African American community Black, Afro-American, or African American. In most cases, the way the communities identified themselves in 1981 was retained. At the same time, each community's identification reflects the dynamic nature of that community and the church's own growth in accepting how each community chooses to name itself in 2004. Where possible current usage reflected in the current Commission for Multicultural Commission and ELCA documents was included.

Some readers may be troubled by the use of male language in some of the essays. The original essays retain the use of male language. The essays, therefore, point to their own situation. The reader is invited to enter the struggle of finding appropriate language which communicates that the church is a church for all people!

The Planning Committee expresses its deep gratitude to many partners. First, we thank the Commission for Multicultural Ministries and the Division for Congregational Ministries for supporting the publication of these papers. Second, we acknowledge the partners who contributed to underwriting this Seminar. Finally, we appreciate Kirk House Publishers for its willingness to take on this project in the midst of its other responsibilities.

Richard J. Perry, Jr.
September 2004

In October of 1981, the Lutheran Council in the USA convened a national "Transcultural Seminar" in Chicago, with the help of funding from Aid Association for Lutherans. The conference brought together 100 Lutheran leaders active in ministry with people of color throughout the United States. Their goal: to develop plans for a new community of faith, a church for all people. Since that time, this church has also been called "a church for our children."

The participants came from three church bodies (the Lutheran Church in America, the American Lutheran Church and the Association of Evangelical Lutheran Churches); five ethnic groups (Asians, Blacks, Hispanics, Native Americans, Whites)*; clergy and lay backgrounds; and national, regional and local experiences. This book is a collection of papers, summaries and proceedings relating to the discoveries they made.

Thanks are in order to all of the participants of the seminar for their contributions; to Joan Marie Hall of LCUSA for her diligent and expert typing of this book; to Ann Henry of LCUSA for proofreading assistance; and to Dorothy (Dee) Scholz for the initial gathering of materials.

Lily R. Wu, Editor

September 1985

INTRODUCTION

The primary context of this book is "non-white" traditional Lutheranism in North America, with special reference to the Lutheran churches. Addressing ourselves to the condition of this "non-white" traditional community also means addressing a middle class that is a "minority" within and controlled by a much larger white middle class.

Our immediate context is really only a symptom of our larger national and international context. It is a situation in which the values, power and self-perception of the majority dominate the minority by isolation, suppression or dispersal. It is not a situation in which wholeness and enrichment are found through the actualization or liberation of all communities and the offerings they bring to the whole.

Playing the "Religious Game"

Our society is multicultural and made up of plural elements. Yet the norms for behavior, status and acquisition of wealth and power are established and controlled by the majority culture. It follows then that survival for both minority and majority communities consists of conforming to the norms.

This consists of playing the "religious game," and implies adopting the rules of the game. Anyone choosing to express his/her own values, beliefs or concerns in a way that exposes the contradictions in a monolithic system of values and societal structure pays a penalty.

On the other hand, the society gives rewards in terms of perpetuation of the system, which just happens to perpetuate the power of those in control. There are no rewards for forcing the system to be responsive and responsible to the needs of those not in power. This situation applies equally to both church and nation.

While the inequality and oppressiveness of this system evokes some rage, that rage is easily defused by yielding enough benefits to keep people quiet. This usually consists of economic rewards that have seemed fairly good for middle class people, both for the people of color and Whites. So it has been relatively easy to prevent them from seeing the ever—increasing cost in human life and freedom that they must pay to ensure that the benefits keep coming.

Most of us have "hooked" our security to the system rather than to Christ. So we can be expected not only to remain quiet, but to participate willingly in perpetuating the status quo so that our security will not be threatened.

In a sense we are dealing with a problem of induced (to a large extent self—induced) blindness, of seeing without perceiving the violence that is happening to us. Many middle class people see that the system itself appears shaky and may be in jeopardy, and having become dependent on the system, this naturally threatens them. But they do not see that the real threat to their humanity, and therefore to their survival, is in their own willingness to "play the game" rather than judging it.

The cost of not judging the game is becoming excessively high. That cost must be measured in terms of their own loss of freedom and in the exploitation of millions still living in the "hard times" that the middle class pretends to have left behind. It is no secret anywhere in the world that in modern times the gap between rich and poor has increased dramatically.

High feelings of insecurity are complicated by a degree of guilt, a consequence of refusing to see what needs to be seen. And in the "minority" communities, feelings of both insecurity and shame are heightened further by another phenomenon: those Whites who had shown the most sensitivity and willingness to follow the cues of "minority" leaders in the protests of the 1960s have begun to perceive their own oppression more clearly, to react against it, and in some cases to experience the penalties for taking a stand for justice.

Toward Freedom: Critiquing Reality

Our Lord said, "If you are my disciples, you shall know the truth and the truth will make you free!" Seeing and perceiving the truth are related to knowing and acting out the truth. And to know the truth that is in Jesus is to be free and secure. There can never be any valid security without grace and freedom; and the man or woman who is free is secure indeed.

The greatest contribution to the life of the whole society will come through critiquing our cultural and societal reality with the "truth that is in Jesus." At the expense of irritation to some Lutherans, the *solas'* are operative here: *sola gratia* (grace alone), *sola scriptura* (Scripture alone), *sola fides* (faith alone), the principles upon which this work stands or falls,

This critiquing of our reality in the light of Jesus Christ must ultimately be done from both the minority or oppressed side as well as the majority or oppressor side, for reasons we hope to make clear. However, there is much in Scripture to suggest that the only valid critique comes from the oppressed.

It is true that the oppressed see and perceive more clearly. It is the blind who can see God's grace because they see the whole scene. It is the children who have been wise and revealed the secrets of salvation. It is the weak who have the strength to admit it, and the sinners and the broken who cry out for help.

It would be a mistake, though, to make this an absolute, suggesting that having a proper understanding is the private property of one class or another. The key to sight or to truth is revealed to those willing to hear and respond to the Master's "follow me."

In terms of our model, this means being faithful in involving ourselves—at whatever cost—in the struggle for love and justice. It means remembering that, "if anyone would gain the whole world, let him deny himself," take up his cross and go all the way like Jesus did. (And the cross of Jesus is usually the cross of our neighbors.) Not many of us, whether oppressed or oppressor, are prepared for that.

This can be unpacked more simply by relating it to "sight." It is true that the oppressed see and perceive more clearly. A perception of what it means to be free can come only from the oppressed, just as a perception of what life means can come only in confrontation with death. The oppressed have fewer illusions about themselves; they can't afford them. They know they are in trouble. True perception of others and of the world around us is possible only in direct proportion to our capacity to see ourselves correctly.

Nevertheless, to be clearly identified with, and as, the oppressed poses a temptation, too: that of neatly identifying **my** struggle and **my** context with the coming of the earthly kingdom of God.

Conversely, the oppressors need illusions about themselves and the world around them. They must stylize the truth by crassly individualizing it, spiritualizing it, or moralizing about it to justify their status and their oppressive, self—serving agendas. Therein lies their own oppression, their own inability to see Jesus, and hence their own enslavement.

What we are saying, then, is that the oppressed, whom we call the "out" people, have a gift. They are more prone to perceive honestly that they are indeed "out people" and understand what liberation is all about. The oppressor community, whom we call the "in" people, on the other hand, cannot and usually will not see clearly why the "out people" are "out," nor that they themselves, though self—styled "in people," are also "out people."

Needed: A Coalition of "In" and "Out" People

However, the gospel is for all people——both the "outs" and the "ins." All humanity is called to freedom in Jesus Christ. Jesus' words, "If you become my disciples you will know the truth and the truth will make you free," were spoken not to the twelve disciples, but to the Pharisees. What does that mean in our present context and in the struggle for liberation?

If the gospel of liberation is for all people, then it follows that all people are in need of it. None can claim no need, none can claim to have arrived. This implies that the "out" people can be tempted to pretend that the gospel is only for them. Or, in other cases, that they are already on a better, more secure path to achieving "in" status than the difficult "struggle path" molded by Jesus Christ. Only God can determine who are God's people.

Conversely, the gospel implies that some "in" people will try to pretend not to see (and in fact maybe cannot see) that they have paid an excessive price for being "in". Some other "in" people who claim to identify with the oppressed or to have "paid their dues" will be incapable of seeing how foolish they look.

In conclusion, we would have to say that the statement, "The gospel is for all people," has a dismal corollary: that all people are liars. Blind. All consequently need the discipline, the encouragement, *the sight of each other* in repentance and absolution. All need one another to keep judgment straight and unvarnished, and to keep the good news fresh and free. In short, we all need one another to keep us from the most warned—against sin in Scripture: idolatry.

This points to the need for a reference community, a coalition of all the "in" and "out" people, an inclusive church of all God's people who commit themselves to exposing the truth, proclaiming the truth, and acting out the truth in concert with each other for the life of the world! For we can see only through the eyes of Jesus. In a very real sense that means we can only see ourselves through each other's eyes. To be me is to become you.

Mainline white churches, however exclusive they may seem to people of color, are usually interested in being multicultural and/or inclusive in their membership. But while this goal is commendable and laudable to all, it has fallen short of the many creeds, pronouncements and resolutions of the mainline churches because of the many conditions set for membership. These conditions have preempted and misrepresented the theological understanding of membership in the body of Christ as explicated in the doctrine of baptism.

White denominations often contain a mixture of Asians, Blacks, Hispanics, Native Americans and others who have moved into their midst bringing with them their Christian cultural traditions, their experiences of God. But the dominant white cultural tradition of the mainline churches prevents these experiences from being shared.

This is one reason why a group of Asian, black, Hispanic, Native American and white Christian Lutherans gathered together in the spring of 1978 to come to grips with the issue of a multicultural/inclusive church from our perspective. We affirm the concerns and emphasis of others who have been excluded by the institutional church at this point.

Moreover, we hope that the findings and positions of this work will interest those who would emphasize sex, the handicapped, homosexuality, the aged, singles, youth, *et al.* as additional perspectives of inclusiveness. The recognition of the myriad of concerns that people have for inclusivity should help the reader perceive what a task it has been for me, struggling with issues related to a multicultural inclusive church over the last six years.

Starting the Process

After a series of meetings, the group charged me to write a theological document to serve as a point of departure and foundation for the work we were to undertake. This document was produced, shared and accepted by all: "Self—Transcendence: A Foundational Theological Concept for an Inclusive Church."

The theology and theory being established, we were now ready to establish the praxis and functional rationale to plan for the following process: (1) developing written materials for participants; (2) planning a mini—conference in early 1981; and (3) planning a major conference in late 1981. These three steps would have as an end purpose, **an inclusive church by 1990.**

We agreed that the aimed-for outcomes would be that:

(1) some 125 people, selected from among Asian, black, Hispanic, Native American and white Lutherans, would by the close of the major

conference have defined the issue of self—transcendence or multicultural inclusion in fairly concrete behavioral and functional terms as it applies to the life and mission of the Lutheran church;

(2) they would have defined where the church was not wholly inclusive a well as the potentials and benefits of fuller inclusiveness;

(3) they would have translated and understood the issue of self-transcendence and its implications for their own cultural situations now and for each other's vision of the future;

(4) they would assume ownership for the issue of inclusion, that is, make commitments to carry the discussion forward in their particular context and shape their agendas, wherever possible, in ways that would also move toward the goal of an inclusive church; and

(5) they would achieve a consensus on what steps were needed next—each ethnic group for its own context and for the whole church.

The steering committee proposed that five papers would be prepared and delivered to the conferences, from the Asian, Hispanic, Native American, Afro-American and white cultural perspectives. The basic outline of these papers would be:

- **our roots** —history —origins/development/major shaping factors,
- **our present**—contemporary situations,
- **our genius**—what we have to offer an inclusive church,
- **our plight**—what impedes our "flowering" and ability to offer our best in the whole church.

Other considerations were:

Epistemology: How do our perceptive symbol-generating and understanding processes work? What are our worldviews and convenient organizing principles?

Psychology: What are our community's dominant needs and "hang-ups," it strengths and beauties?

Sociological and Cultural Description: What cultural heritages are dominant and inform us? How do we relate and organize ourselves, our community and its indigenous institutions? How do we, as a community, relate to other communities and their institutions?

Theology: What roles do ancient religions have in our current faith perception and religious expression? What roles do faith and culture have in shaping our vision of reality, our sense of purpose and our choice of agendas and/or strategies?

Politics: How does the community survive, develop power, use it and broker with it for its own benefit and the benefit of all people?

The group also determined that a sixth paper was needed to provide a broad statement of rationale for the whole process, or some general unpacking of the issue of inclusion. This paper was assigned as the responsibility of the mission executives of the three judicatories. These papers are submitted here for your use (cf. Part II) and form the core of our struggle with cultural diversity and Christian unity.

We are one in Christ. There can be no meaningful discussion of unity without affirmation of our rich diversity. Only when there is an authentic "I" and an authentic "you" can there be also an authentic "we" or "us". As Christians in the United States we have to take two radical truths with seriousness: (1) the truth that some are **in-people** and others are **out-people** in both society and the church; and (2) the truth that the gospel of Jesus Christ is for both. The major mechanism for perpetuating a society of both in-people and out-people, and one in which we all participate one way or another, is to keep people divided.

Designing the Program

These tasks were spelled out in finer detail as we designed the program. We had to build understanding within and between ethnic groups. Our analysis of our own past and present contexts has led us to agree on what each group feels it has to offer and what we need and expect with regard to inclusion. To provide good material for the main conference to "chew" on, each ethnic group, as well as the entire group, had to develop a fuller and more concrete statement of the vision: What does an inclusive church look like in terms of how we treat each other and how we move together in society doing the mission of the church?

After trying various ways of breaking the tasks down into program events, it became clear that all three tasks could be accomplished if the groups at the conference could strive for a consensus among themselves regarding identity:

(a) Who are we, considering history, developmental factors, etc.? Who are we as particular ethnic groups and as Lutherans?

(b) What do we bring, as ethnic groups, to the whole church? What are, and how do we perceive, our unique strengths and what have we to share with an inclusive church?

(c) What unique needs and expectations do we, as ethnic groups, have **of** and **for** the whole church?

To mold consensus in each group in a way that would provide concrete material for subsequent work at the main conference, participants were asked to state (a), but especially (b) and (c), in terms of

economics, cultural style preferences, patterns of organizational development, distribution of power, theological expression——or similar
specific grids such as "mission strategies," worship style preferences,
communication patterns in the church, and so forth. Tasks (a), (b), and
(c) were goals for the mini—conference, which was seen as a vital part
of the process, with the main conference to be held in the fall of 1981.

Each group would agree on a way of understanding and expressing its own identity in terms of the issue of an inclusive Lutheran church.
Each group would begin to define in behavioral and/or functional terms
what it, as a group, brings and will commit to an inclusive church. Each
group would also spell out in behavioral and/or functional terms what
it needs and expects of an inclusive Lutheran church.

An Inclusive Church By 1990

This book is written in the light of the overarching statement of
purpose and goals for the whole process of planning the mini—and
main conferences, viz., an inclusive Lutheran church by 1990.

The Lutheran Church in North America, though itself begun as an
ethnic church, has become part and parcel of corporate America. Research in this book explains how our church operates according to corporate patterns of organization and power distribution. Our church basically accepts American myths such as "the melting pot," "U.S. superiority," and Horatio Alger stories. In practice, our church copies and finds
it difficult to adequately criticize systemic racist (i.e., exclusivist) modes,
thereby perpetuating racism in its own structures.

Nevertheless, the church has also displayed its conscience and
struggles against racism even as it struggles with its guilt for being racist. Its witness and effectiveness are often blunted by ambivalence as it
seeks to square standard practices with a more enlightened understanding of the ethic of Jesus.

Not all church people, but many, have come to the simplistic analysis that "they" (the minorities, poor, urban, etc.) are the problem——
even though, more often than not, 98% of Lutherans in this country are
white and live in small to medium size towns. Many ethnic communities and some Whites point out that Whites are the problem because
they run the system. One of the assumptions in planning this process,
however, was our willingness to dare to say: "ALL are the problem, for
all participate in the system." And, if all are the problem, all must be
part of the solution!

For ALL to work toward a common solution we need and believe
we have found, a common grid simple enough for everyone to under-

stand, yet touching each context profoundly at the point where needs exist. It is a grid broad enough for all to adopt as their own, yet specific enough to be translated into concrete, behavioral change agendas. We propose that the issue of inclusion is that grid. It has a biblical framework, "That they may be one..." and "Who is my neighbor?", and it touches each and everyone of us in one way or another.

This material does not purport to be the final word on the subject of church unity or on inclusivity relative to a multicultural church. But it does offer the beginning of a theological perspective from the people of color that is indispensable to the mainline white churches. We feel that this is our refundable service as people of God, to concretely express the body of Christ in a church that continues to struggle with the concept of inclusiveness.

The editors have attempted to present the material in a manner which engages a wide readership. Therefore we humbly present our positions for the usual challenge to academicians, theologians, pastors and lay people. Thus, through our documentations, arguments, methodologies, illustrations and definitions of terminology, we invite and encourage your response.

We also invite you to witness our process recorded on videotape. Copies are available on loan from the Transcultural Task Force, c/o the Rev. Dr. Lee Wesley, Lutheran Community Services, 33 Worth Street, New York, New York, 10013.

While I am privileged to take responsibility for the major theological thinking of this work, I thank God for all the participants who trusted and took ownership of my prophetic ideas and brought them to earth, managed and affirmed them. The theological reflection of all the authors appropriately and accurately reflects the indigenous cultures as well as the self—transcendent principle and nature of the culturally inclusive church. Without all of these Lutherans——Asian, black, Hispanic, Native American and white——this book would not have been possible.

Albert Pero, Jr.

PART ONE

How and When the Star was Caught
Thesis: Inclusive/Universal

SELF-TRANSCENDENCE
A Foundational Theological Concept for an Inclusive Church

By Dr. Albert P. Pero, Jr.

This material addresses itself primarily to the problems of Lutherans within a multicultural context separated by race, nationality, and sex. But it applies equally well to problems between religious denominations and other cultures separated by national boundaries. Such problems are becoming more visible if not more intense. It is becoming increasingly difficult for persons who identify with different groups (because of cultural background, age, race, color, creed, family, national origin, politics, education, etc.) to ignore one another or to coexist under conditions of imposed separation or segregation. The world is too small, communication and transportation too rapid, to live apart. Too many persons are becoming aware of their rights and deprivations, and too many others are developing humanitarian concerns, to allow segregation and inequity to continue. We no longer have a choice. People must learn to live and work together with tolerance, respect and understanding, or the human being as a species cannot survive.

Subsequently there is a growing concern and new agenda on a global level over the lack of adequate preparation of persons to live, work, and understand one another. This concern can be expressed in terms of cross-cultural existence.

It is redundant, but nevertheless necessary, to assert that there is a great stirring and unrest all over the world. Especially among people of color do we find these stirrings which in turn generate new perceptions and new articulations of reality.

Alex Haley's book "Roots" directed attention to a huge missing link in the various stages of development in civil rights in the U.S. "Roots" in a uniquely powerful fashion directed attention of the nation momentarily away from our preoccupation with power, material things, etc., and drove us to contemplate (if only in passing) questions of who we are and what we are like. This has heightened the awareness that being human – or inhuman—is something that transcends both ideology and color. It places us squarely into theological questions. These theological questions, however, are highly political and social. Often new stirrings are present a long time before the symbols and the articulations of what is being felt and what is happening emerge.

The major white institutions must be deeply concerned about the massive stirrings among the people of color at any one place in the country. The new feelings that something is wrong, the new quest for models of perception and of social, political understanding and action that seem to be developing are again coming out of the thoughts and struggles of leaders of the historic black churches.

The content of these new stirrings cannot be capsulized in a few words. At the risk of distortion, however, it deals basically with the dead—end street nature of systems of violence. It perceives that the "upward" quest of every definable segment of the nation for a "piece of the action" is on a collision course with survival itself. Such systems have delivered for a few, but the masses remain worse off than ever before—not just economically, but more importantly, with even less of a sense of worth or perception of their humanity left.

The problem, however, is that in the past years the doctrine that all segments have a prior right to a piece of the action has been uncritically bought by **everyone**. The more serious question is: "What happens to our humanity where the name of the game is not only grab more power for me/us, but where that power is perceived as salvation itself?"

Such a question will be resisted by majority and minority alike — except that the deep, undefined hunger and distress of human hearts at this moment in history is raising massive new questions which the church has a mission to amplify and for which the church has something to offer. Consequently we are faced with a definition of the basic questions of theology, namely:

1. What is the essence of identity?
2. What is the essence of community?
3. What is the essence of mission?

The ultimate answer to these questions will push us toward identifying the source of our resources, and furthermore enable us to clarify the correlation of indigeneity and universality. What some have hoped for in the past and many hope for today is the formation of a new community of diverse cultures in one organism.

There are particular questions which this new community must address corporately.

A. What have we learned and what do we continue to learn about our identity through our religious experiences as synthesized from our cultural traditions to our denominational heritage within the context of the Americas?

B. How do we know what is real and what isn't real (authentically tested?)

C. How do we conserve, celebrate, and share that which is behind the learnings which becomes the certification of new learnings? What is the praxis?

However, a more important question is, how do we get there? It is the nature of this work to deal with this question as a major foundational concept and action for our search for the key to establishing an inclusive community amidst diversity.

We call the concept "self—transcendence." Self—transcendence—what a concept! Christian theology suffers from "big words," beautiful words; but the actual meaning of the concept is not too far from the people since it comes from observing the people. Self—transcendence is not a new concept. It has been thoroughly dealt with by such scholars as Bernard Lonergan, Edward Hall, and others. Our treatment of the concept will not be approached from a philosophical viewpoint as others have done so eloquently. It will be more from a theological and sociological point of view. Self—transcendence for our purposes has to do with human beings and how they relate not just to God but more specifically to one another as the image of God. The concept is based on several texts in the scriptures dealing with the image of God and consequently our own image or identity: Colossians 1:15; I Corinthians 15: 49; Romans 8:29; II Corinthians 3:18; and Colossians 3:10.

The early Christians, as these texts point out, were in search of reality, wholeness, meaning, completeness —as we are today. It is the nature of humanity to search and strive for this perfection in life. We reach out and pull back and reach out again and again. The search for reality, for the early Christians and for us, is a reaching out, a leaving of self, reaching out to the transcendent. When it comes to unifying the separated, fragmented life, it takes Jesus Christ. For the apostles, Christ is the self—transcendent foundational model. Self—transcendence is not some meaningless abstraction or dreamed—up philosophy. No, in Christ it is the coming together, the reconciliation of all things and people, all politics and economy.

We approach the notion of self-transcendence existentially. Thereby, the concreteness of transcendence comes into focus, first of all, in terms of the self. In our lives, there is the experience of going beyond ourselves, an experience of self-transcendence. Second, transcendence comes into focus in terms of the foundational grounding of such self-transcendence. This grounding has internal and external, subjective and objective, indigenous and universal components—what it is "in here" and what it is "out there"[5] which makes self-transcendence possible or necessary. Third, it comes into focus in terms of the world. The praxis of self-transcendence brings about alterations in a world preoccupied with race, class, culture, sex and nationality. Thus, there are three basic ingredients or elements in the construction of the concept of self-transcendence as I see it:

1. A human experience of going beyond self,

2. The internal/external grounding of that experience,

3. The changing of the world from separated communities to cosmic unity through divine/human mediation.

Given such an understanding, we argue that the structure of self-transcendence can be manifested in a concrete imminent way. Indeed, Christian theologies of the future (as represented in King and Thurman) manifest some unique similarities between Christian (biblical) and Afro-American anthropologies. Therefore, in accordance with the three basic ingredients/ elements of self—transcendence, we will demonstrate

1. That Christianity and the black experience share three basic moments in the human experience of going beyond.

    A. A vision of the future accompanied by an experience of reality as history;

    B. A moment of "inner power" that is a moment of created freedom for the "new:" and,

    C. Action in the direction of the expected future.

2. That black Christians and white Christians differ in the way in which the experience of self-transcendence is grounded: black Christians grounding the experience in ecumenically becoming the "significant other" cross-culturally. White Christians grounding the experience only among themselves.

3. That Christianity and the black experience share a common commitment to transformation of the world beyond the established order of society in the direction of a future of fulfillment.

There are a variety of theologians and scholars who have led me to the exploration of this writing, chief of whom are M. L. King, Howard Thurman, John Pobee, Gustavo Gutierrez, Juergen Moltmann and Wolfhart Pannenberg. Other scholars who have assisted my thinking in this area are Bernard Lonergan, Edward T. Hall, Peter Berger, Thomas Luckmann and Reuel L. Howe and Paulo Freire.

Methodologically, we are challenged to offer a model for unity in diversity or synthesis of thesis—antithesis. The three basic elements of the concept of self—transcendence suggested will become the three basic categories of analysis of my thinking and that of the sources. It is recognized that our basic categories are used heuristically for the sake of analysis. On the one hand they are sufficiently broad as to allow for the presentation of views on the subject. On the other hand, they are sufficiently narrow as to allow for a concrete picture to emerge; subsequently, provocative to meaningful dialogue and continued research in this area in order to establish principles for a vision of inclusive community.

Theologically this study will reflect upon the religious faith (through my participation with other cultures) of those engaged in self—transcendence and will seek to express the content of this faith in the clearest and most coherent language available.

Finally, John Macquarrie posits four elements of a theological method which will be used in analysis of the subject matter of this work. They are as follows: Rationale, Description, Interpretation, and Application.

1. Rationale. In theological methods the rationale is the overriding coordinator of the various avenues of approach in the method, and assigns to each its proper degree of emphasis. In other words, an explanation of the controlling principles of the belief or practice.

2. Description. Macquarrie puts heavy emphasis on phenomenology as an analytical descriptive method. Phenomenology is a way of letting us see that which shows itself (the phenomenon) by removing (as far as possible) concealments, distortions, and whatever else might prevent us from seeing the phenomenon as it actually gives itself.

2. Interpretation. This is the deliberate and explicit task of continually reinterpreting the primordial revelation —applying the science of hermeneutics in this particular element of the theological method.

3. Application. By application is meant the coming back to the community of faith with the theological conclusions, in order that the

community of faith can better understand itself and can better order its life.

Part I

Self—Transcendence: A Human Experience of Going Beyond Self

As human beings we are related. To be human is to externalize. To be human is to go outside of myself. To be me is to fully know you. Lonergan defines authentic human existence as a process of self—transcendence; a process which he did not conjure up but which he discovered as inherent in or constituted by the operations of human knowing and loving. Lonergan states that human knowing is constituted by three operations: understanding, experience, and judgment corresponding to three levels of consciousness.

Human knowing, then, begins with experience, and experience may be manifold: seeing, hearing, smelling, touching, and tasting. What is significant and needs to be highlighted is that all these activities relate to objects. A person is never simply conscious, but is always conscious of something. The person is related to objects and therefore he/she in some way already transcends himself/herself.

Relationships are the essence of life and as such the irreducible ontology of relationships is life or death! My personal concern when I enter a foreign culture of people is whether they are going to harm me or love and affirm me. Every person is a potential enemy. Only through self—transcendence in love are we saved from this enmity toward one another.

What does this mean? This means that we all desire to know one another (to "know God even as we are known by God"). This knowing is the initial process of self—transcendence as Lonergan so clearly and thoroughly posits.[6] Thus when other cultures, races, sexes, impinge on the various senses, questions arise. As more and more data is available one achieves insight and/or understanding of the other. It is only at this point that the act of human knowing reaches fulfillment through the compound operations of experience, understanding and judgment. Seen in this way such an act of human knowing is clearly a process of self—transcendence, according to Lonergan.

Knowing, however, is NOT "praxis." A new type of question arises at this point. What does this "significant other" mean for him/her? This question of deliberation reveals in Lonergan's technical philosophical terms the level of rational self—consciousness. Here we are concerned with self, our own operations, goals. A person achieves actual positive self—transcendence when he/she is able to choose the good, not in a self—centered, comfort—seeking way, but in a way consistent with the good for others, a way that transcends his/her own self—seeking. On this level, it is possible to begin living out of values which transcend oneself. This level has gone beyond knowing or doing or loving. This is the level of actual self—transcendence. A person is now capable of loving: of truly transcending himself/ herself.

We are now ready to introduce a concrete illustrative model of self—transcendence as witnessed in the black experience. There are several reasons why I have chosen the Afro—American cultural experience as the model of self—transcendence. First, this model affirms that all Christians are concerned about the truth. The black situation has generally been neglected or badly distorted in our society. Common popular myths prevail as a result. There is the popular myth that Africa is a "dark continent" in which there has never been any culture or social development. There is also a myth that Afro—Americans have never made any significant contribution to history. Christians should not be content to let their views of the present day be shaped by a false view of the past.

Second, Christians are concerned about persons. A person finds himself/herself in relation to the past. The answer to the question "Who am I?" comes largely from our relationship to history. James Baldwin says to the white community, "I am not who you think I am," and he is right. Discovery of who the Afro—American really is can come in large part from discovering who he/she really has become in his/her historical situation. James Baldwin goes further and indicates that the white's inability to accept blacks as persons is related to their inability to accept themselves. Therefore, the study of the black situation may be revelatory in other cultures' efforts to understand themselves as persons, as well as in their effort to understand the black person as a person, if we are authentically to become part of an inclusive community.

Third, the Christian is concerned about communion or communication as he/she attempts to correlate the kerygma to cultural situations. Many attempts at communication between black and white today are phony and superficial because they are attempts to communicate as though nothing had ever happened. Honest communication must begin by facing the events that have brought our world to its present tragic state. Perhaps as we face these facts together we can begin to communicate and discover a real common life as children of God that has so long been denied.

Fourth, for the white community and others, a study of the black experience and its self—transcendence can mean the deliverance from false condescension if it brings to others the discovery that they have as much if not more to receive from the black person as he/she has to give in the process of "organic union." In short, we must, in love, understand and become each other with all our religious, political, social and economic different formulations. In order to face the present intelligently and bring about a different future, a future in which the "praxis" of faith in Christ is as much the pivotal point of life in one culture as in all Christian cultures.

Probably the most magnificent drama in the last thousand years of human history is the transportation of some ten million human beings out of the dark beauty of Africa to these American shores. It was the rape of the continent seldom, if ever, paralleled in ancient or modern history. The black person, having been snatched up out of a deep spiritist culture and brought into the white community's strange and cruel world, relied heavily in this early period upon both supernaturalism and emotionalism as a means by which he/she could adjust himself/herself to perplexing, baffling, staggering, and strange experiences in America,

> "...the slaves who had been torn from their homeland and kinsmen and their friends and whose cultural heritage was lost, were isolated and broken men, so to speak. . .not only did religion draw the Negroes into a union with their fellowmen it tended to break down barriers that isolated them morally from their white master."[7]

Though white people suppressed every attempt on the part of black people to be free, they failed to listen to the slaves' songs or their philosophy "wrapped up" in those songs. Black people not only sang to make their 15 to 16 hour work days easier. They sang with hope about their miseries, and gained existential, metaphysical and eschatological insights which were impossible for most white people to ascertain at that time. Examine if you will the following black songs:

> Didn't my Lord deliver Daniel
> And why not every -man?
> He delivered Daniel from the Lion's den,
> Jonah from the belly of the whale,
> And the Hebrew children from the fiery furnace,
> And why not every man?

> Nobody knows the trouble I've seen.
> Nobody knows but Jesus.

> Swing low, sweet chariot,
> Coming for to carry me home.
> Go down Moses

Way down in Egyptland.
Tell old Pharaoh
To let my people go.

These few excerpts from black spirituals historically typify what the Christian religion has meant to the black experience.

Authenticity cannot apply itself to the true function of the black church without taking into serious discussion the disenchantment, the destruction of all family ties, the dehumanization, the rebellion, the struggle for emancipation, and the unique ability toward self—transcendence by communing with God through song.

There are those with whom I have been in extensive dialogue who say that without music it is doubtful that the black person would have survived. It served as a cleansing agent in eradicating present difficulty through emotional expression; it lifted up a transcendent future with better possibilities than the present; and it brought the celestial down to earth. Troubles, joys, trials, power, and heaven are basic themes in most of the black spirituals. Shouting and great exultation were still basic characteristics of the black church of this period, The slave Christians were ingenious: by singing and shouting, they received self—transcendent strength to endure physical and mental suffering that few others could endure. The church was the sole institution in which power was used both creatively and self—transcendently. In many instances, the church serves today in the same capacity.

Given this cursory historical component of the black situation we in summary come back to our concept in the form of an interrogative and ask: "What has it been like to live in the black experience?" Better yet, "What is it like to be a black American?"

What is it like to engage in self—transcendence or to experience being black in America? Very few white people have tried to find out, One man did, and he received a rude shock. John Howard Griffin, a Southern white newspaperman, shaved his head, darkened the color of his skin, and lived as a black for a time in the Deep South. He found himself exposed to hatred and viciousness. He found that the new color of his skin confined him to a closed world in which there was no future, Griffin describes the impact of his experience most vividly in his book "Black Like Me."

As Frazier points out, the word prejudice means "pre—judgment in the sense that it is a judgment concerning objects and persons not based upon knowledge or experience."[8] To see the effects of segregation on the black community in America, we recommend Part V of "The Negro in the United States" by Frazier. The chapters deal with the problem of health and survival, of unemployment and poverty, of family disorganization, of crime and delinquency, of mental deficiency and insanity. Also of particular importance is Chapter 27 which deals with the nature of race prejudice and its effect on the black. In short, the white majority has built up a whole set of ideas and behavior patterns concerning the black race which are groundless. The black then suffers the consequences of this falsely based behavior.

What is it like to be black in America? Ralph Ellison suggests that the black person is the "Invisible Man." Because of prejudice, white persons do not really see black persons as persons. Instead, they see a figment of their imagination, and Ellison says, "I am invisible simply because people refuse to see me. The invisibility to which I refer occurs because of a peculiar disposition of the eyes of those with whom I come in contact." Ellison reflects on the consequences of being invisible and notes, "You are constantly being bumped against by those of poor vision. Or, again, you often doubt if you really exist."[9]

Ellison's comments point to a basic biblical conviction that to be a person depends upon being accepted as a person. This would suggest that if black people seem inferior to white people, perhaps it is because whites have denied the humanity of blacks rather than because black people are really inferior.

What is it like to be black in America? Richard Wright suggests that it requires the constant role of deception. Black people must constantly hide their true selves and present the false face that white people want to see. In order to survive, the black person's life must become a deliberate lie. As a friend advised, "When you are in front of white people, think before you act, think before you speak. Your way of doing things is all right amongst our people, but not for white people. They won't stand for it." This advice proved difficult for Richard Wright for as he put it, "it was simply impossible for me to calculate, to scheme, to act, to plot all the time. I would remember to dissemble for short periods and then I would forget and act straight and human again, not with the desire to harm anybody, but merely forgetting the artificial status of race and class."[10]

I have tried to uncover one of many basic facts that the subordinate or inferior role has not come naturally to the black person as some races have tried to suggest. Rather, it is a role that has been forced upon the black person in basic violation of his/her personality.

The black person's experience in America can be seen to have been caught between the natural desire to fulfill one's being as created by God and the unnatural need to fulfill one's being as prescribed by the white society, i.e., to be of no consequence or to become "white." So the struggle continues...

To become "white," How can that be? I thought you were black? How is it possible for you to become white if you are black? Well, it is possible. And black people have once again offered us the key to our understanding of how an inclusive community can exist in peace and harmony within a multi—cultural context of diversity.

Let us look a little deeper into the black experience. From an ontological perspective black people were forced to become white people by adapting to the white culture. While the experience was a negative one as has been described earlier, from a positive point of view black people became "de facto" white. The self—transcendent process took so well that blacks negatively adopted code names for one another like "oreo cookie," "vanilla wafer," meaning the degree to which a black had become white. The trading system in American white schools also indicates the proficiency of blacks with culturally white academic courses. Indeed we could analyze every fiber of American white culture and discover black people more capable than whites in these areas. From a world perspective, I have found black people who were, culturally speaking, British, German, Dutch, French, Spanish, Portuguese, etc.

The punch line to this, if I might add a little humor at this point, is to pick up the daily paper during the basketball season and turn to the sports section. There you find a picture of a black basketball player leaping high in the air to stuff the basketball into the basket and in so doing winning the game. The title reads "Fighting 'Irish' Wins Again By Two." On the black young man's jersey is printed the team name: "Irish." "Truly the black man has become every-man."

While others planned to destroy black people, God has once again turned it into good. For in the attempt to destroy black culture, black people have established an empirical, existential model of self—transcendence, returned to indigenous roots and must now positively initiate a continuance of self—transcendence with the added ingredient of affirmation of their roots.

Another human experience of going beyond self is found in the black woman who has been in the black experience the mother of mothers in taking care of her children and that of whites, the Housekeeper's Housekeeper. She is woman, mother, brother, father, sister, manager, economist, executive, psychologist, lover, friend, politician; indeed her self—transcendence has been so pervasive that it has engaged practically every facet of life. Indeed, she is as much cosmopolitan as cosmic.[11]

Still another human experience of going beyond is found in role playing within the movie and television industry. This role-playing is so effective today that it is thought to be one of the most formidable forces of influence on human behavior. While we could cite a host of programs and movies which substantiate this point, one contemporary movie entitled "A Force of One" has been distributed by the "Chicago Defender" as one of the most important movies of our time depicting "crossover roles."[12]

One of the most important principles of self—transcendence displayed in these illustrations is that by becoming the other person one breaks down the barriers and gaps which block a meeting of meaning, such as language, images, anxieties, defenses, purposes, which are the ontological needs of every human being.[13]

Finally, Edward T. Hall supports one position of self—transcendence. He asserts:

> Today man is increasingly placed in positions in which culture can no longer be depended upon to produce reliable readings of what other people are going to do next. He is constantly in the position of interacting with strangers, so he must take the next step and begin to transcend his culture. This cannot be done in an armchair.[14]

Indeed the human species must externalize; it is our nature. "Extensions often permit man to solve problems in satisfactory ways, to evolve and adapt at great speed without changing the basic structure of his body."[15] Therefore the understanding of a person's extensions is another component in comprehending the meaning of self—transcendence and subsequently the importance of this concept within a cross—cultural context—that meaning being a human experience of going beyond self within one's culture or cross—culturally. However, the experience itself is not sufficient for an inclusive community of peace without establishing the ground of that experience.

Part II

Self—Transcendence:
the Internal/external Grounding of that Experience

Since I have been a professor of theology at LSTC, I have become more aware of the theological shifts within our modern era. One has to run at breakneck speed to keep up only to find once you catch up that the rules of the game have been changed again. I have since learned that all the theological and ecclesiastical shifts and changes, though they be important, are not as important as what happens to the person internally. One thinks of black theology, white theology, liberation theology, African theology, the nagging questions of identity, the women's movement, and the political questions all of which threaten to tear Christian communities asunder. Conditions in life of separatism between rich, poor; oppressed, oppressor; life and death; body and soul; et al.—all signs of which a theologian called M. L. King, Jr. was aware of and offered a solution, a theological understanding which I would propose as a theological approach to grounding the experience of self—transcendence.

M. L. King, like few other theologians, not only wrote and preached his theology but externalized it in a most dramatic form. King has been designated as "the theologian for our time," because for him, action was not only an expression of theology but also a source of theology. He stood within the liberal theological tradition which has always considered experience as a valid substantial source of theology.

Since we are in need of a theology which reconciles peoples, God and people, ideologies, classes, races, and sexes, Martin Luther King is certainly one man of several others whose thought and work have made a significant contribution to such a theology of reconciliation which, as we shall see, is one of the outcomes of self—transcendence. In so doing, King set for himself a mission involving three tasks:

1. Intellectual
2. Moral
3. Political[16]

Since self—transcendence within America is a key to unity, or ecumenism within a contextual form of an inclusive community, those aspects of King's theology which characterize it as being specifically an "American theology" are of special interest to us. One such aspect was King's determination to seek resolution for theological dualisms wherever they occurred. Another trait which seems peculiarly "American" is the tendency to express theological reflection in action rather than in writing.

Specifically in his writings, he sought some type of synthesis between the concepts of the transcendence and immanence of God. Secondly, he dealt with the nature of God in relation to the problem of evil. Perhaps his most important contribution for our purposes in this area is his thinking about God and humanity in applying the philosophy of personalism to the person of God.

God was profoundly real for M. L. King. For validation of this understanding we turn to King's personal experience. He says:

> I have always believed in the personality of God, but in past
> years the idea of a personal God was little more than a meta-

physical category which I found theologically and philosophically satisfying. Now it is living reality that has been validated in the experiences of everyday life. Perhaps the suffering, frustration and agonizing moments which I have had to undergo occasionally as a result of my involvement in a difficult struggle have drawn me closer to God. Whatever the cause, God has been profoundly real to me.[17]

God, for King, was the God of the universe, the God and father of all people. And the person stood in a relationship of tension. "Man is neither villain nor hero; he is rather both villain and hero."[18] There is a somewhat Lutheran position here that the person is "simul justus et peccator"—sinner and saint simultaneously. The point here is that if one views all of humanity as God's children, then self-transcendence becomes desirable for all cultures.

The real distance between people and cultures is created by something other than diversity of sex, color, ideology, et al. It is created by the lack of agape. Eliminating distance between people and cultures is effected by, as you guessed—agape. Without it even Christianity would not be what it is. Therefore because of agape Christianity is uniquely what it is. Were this component missing, self—transcendence and Christianity would simply not be what history has shown it to be. The agape motif is thus fundamental to self—transcendence. It becomes the very grounding of the experience itself.

This grounding is first experienced in the ultimate roots of the image of God[19] whose personal identity is best described as love. And as God's creation we too possess his attributes, the fruits of the Spirit: love, joy, peace, patience, faith, hope, understanding. Herein is our identity and the personality traits of self—transcendence that we possess. We have and possess them by faith in Jesus Christ who becomes the power, source and revelation of self—transcendence.

Chapter 2: 1—11 of Philippians (TEV) is the classic revelation of Jesus' self—transcendence:

Your life in Christ makes you strong, and his love comforts you. You have fellowship with the Spirit, and you have kindness and compassion for one another. I urge you, then, to make me completely happy by having the same thoughts, sharing the same love, and being one in soul and mind. Don't do anything from selfish ambition or from a cheap desire to boast, but be humble toward one another, always considering others better than yourselves. And look out for one another's interests, not just for your own. The attitude you should have is the one that Christ Jesus had: He always had the nature of God, but he did not think that by force he should try to become equal with God. Instead of this, of his own free will he gave up all he had, and took the nature of a servant. He became like man and appeared in human likeness. He was humble and walked the path of obedience all the way to death—his death on the cross. For this reason Cod raised him to the highest place above and gave Whim the name that is greater than any other name. And so, in honor of the name of Jesus all beings in heaven, on earth, and in the world below will fall on their knees, and all will openly proclaim that Jesus Christ is Lord, to the glory of God the Father.

Christ became human in every way that we might, through faith, be saved and obtain the fruits of the Spirit for one another. It is in this spirit that we understand the apostle Paul's self—transcendence toward his fellow brothers and sisters in I Corinthians 9: 19—23.

The paradox of love as "power" which Jesus, Paul and King depicted in self—transcendence I accept also, for the powerlessness of God in this world, the world of exile and alienation, is also God's power in the world. It is in this power of love in Christ that we find the grounding of our experience of internal/external grounding. It is a love which freely becomes the significant other conquering sin, death, and the power of the demonic while synthesizing the good. With this power we are now able to transform the world.

Part III

Self—Transcendence:
the Changing of the World Separated Community to Cosmic Unity through Divine/human Mediation

The first component in transformation or change is a vision of hope in the future. The vision of the future gives rise to the third and last ingredient of self—transcendence. It is a moment of subjectivity as creative inner power and authority which transforms "dark today's into bright tomorrows;" transforming external servitude into external freedom. We warn the reader, however, that because of the overpowering increase of external freedom—the freedom to tinker with ecclesiastical forms, forms of worship, liturgy, religious lifestyles, and socio—political dispositions, that dogmatics must have its place. Therefore with this concept of inner power and authority and external freedom, it may be argued further (which I shall not take up here) that current external freedom has expanded at such a rapid rate that what is lacking, by contrast, is internal authority (not freedom), but deep personal conviction, what Kierkegaard referred to as "subjectivity is truth." Regardless of the rationale and uses, I maintain that our task here in unfolding the principle for change in the world is to find a religious vision of hope which will posit an external freedom coupled with inner power and authority in which neither is achieved at the expense of the other.

We note here that the human experience of transcending in both Pannenberg and Moltmann begins as a vision of the future, a vision accompanied by an awareness of reality as history inasmuch as life is experienced as in movement toward a goal.

M. L. King's vision is most apparent to us as a future in which all of God's people will be free and coexist in peace and love. The connection we have with the prophets, evangelists and apostles is at once a connection with God in a common vision.

The importance of lifting up this vision of hope in the future rests in the fact that most people spend their time debating a methodology or process without discussing or agreeing on the vision. Accordingly, Pannenberg speaks in this regard of mission/action which seeks to confirm the synthesis of meaning anticipated in the Christian's fore—conception. The grasping of God's promise for Thurman, King and others gives rise to movement in the direction of the expected future. Thus self—transcendence in the sources listed in this work all involve vision, internal authority, and power and praxis.

Some theologians use the concept "openness to the world" in dealing with the external future. This concept is borrowed from anthropologists and refers to the human characteristic whereby the person is able to self—transcend every present experience. Theologically speaking, that which is outside of us, namely the future of God, is also that which is inside of us, namely God. It is a future which comes into focus in the resurrection. Jesus' resurrection is freedom, life and power and victory. Thereby, self—transcendence is able to gain this vision of the totality of meaning in the future of God. No wonder Jesus, Paul and Silas, Gutierrez, Martin Luther King, Jr., Bonhoeffer and others could not be prevented from self—transcending their condition toward the transformation of the same. In God's power of self—transcendence through Christ nothing can prevent all of humanity from being caught up in the history of God and set on the road of the future of Christ in his lordship. Therefore the vision of the "Kingdom of God" is capable of mediation in the present through the Christian's vision and obedience.

Within self—transcendence falls an understanding of the ontology of the gospel, namely, that Jesus is the clearest expression of what it means to be human and second, that the value of the gospel is taking the person beyond him/herself.

Realizing that there is no single Christology, not even in the Bible, but rather many Christologies, our Christology within this work as has been elaborated is that Jesus is Messiah, preaching the kingdom of God whose modality was and is self—transcendence or living as others/in behalf of others in suffering, death and resurrection, i.e., in sacrifice. The basic work of God, therefore, is having to do with sacrifice/suffering. This M. L. King interpreted as non—violent resistance. Thus it is in suffering that we participate in God's kingdom. Not as pathological masochists but in behalf of the health of others. This sacrifice and suffering is not an act of human appeasement but a divine/human self—transcendent process in which God approaches humanity. It is God drawing close to people in the world. Jesus being crucified outside of the sanctuary, sanctified the outside. As the evangelist John put it, the Word was in the world. Thus as we understand self—transcendence in reciprocity[20] we understand through this concept that the church has no monopoly on the Word. That word both saves and opposes the church as illustrated in Jesus' cleansing the temple.

Black people know of no pompous, imperialist Christ, but rather a Christ who has become the wretched of the earth, who has become a man of sorrow, acquainted with grief.

Jesus Christ is the model for Christians and is an example in his life, death, and resurrection. Jesus never shut himself off from people in order to become religious. If Jesus was truly human, all the components of every human person had to be present in him. Through his relationship with God, Jesus totally committed himself to the process of self—transcendence, i.e., to living out of the value of self—giving love, and is thus a model for living an authentic human life. So it is that we have a tradition with Jesus as model.

Yet, Christ is more than just a model. He is the "way" and the "truth," which was expressed in his becoming us that we might become him and one another. Christian self—transcendence as it responds to the human condition is an authentic way of life in which the person finds the truth in becoming "little Christ" to his or her neighbor through Christ. Anything that is a way of life must be active. By being aware of the process of self—transcendence and by being open to the process, our separated exclusive lives can grow and mature and become an inclusive Christian community.

Christianity is a relational religion. One's relationship with God can only be expressed and tested through a love relationship with other human beings. Only through this human process can a person say that he/she is in relationship with God.

One begins to get the idea that by entering into this process of self—transcendence a person's life begins to change and grow. The same change and growth happens in society and community. Authentic human existence then, requires that a person consciously enter into the process of self—transcendence and then remain open to the process of struggle with one's own prejudices. Christian theology is integrally related to the process of self—transcendence because genuine Christianity is authentic human existence, self—transcendence or nothing at all.

Self—transcendence involves identity, vision, relationships, "praxis," as one becomes the other in sacrificial love. Second, self—transcendence is grounded in Jesus Christ and God's future which comes into focus in the resurrection whereby Cod is seen to be the author of the "New World." Third, such self—transcendence automatically alters the world from a killing world to a loving world stopping short of bloody revolution, yet pushing beyond just mere reform toward transforming the symptoms and the cause. It does so through non—violent resistance to evil with the power of the fruits of the Spirit.

Therefore to be engaged in self—transcendence means

1. in Martin Buber's terms, "experiencing the other side." Thus it means a readiness and a willingness to listen to others, to learn from them, to allow them to be our teachers.

2. a readiness and willingness to enter completely into the real life situations of people, to experience their lived reality with them in such a way that their questions become meaningful for us. Real questions today arise out of real situations of suffering and experience. Such questions— and their answers — cannot be given to a people or discovered for them but can only come by struggling for understanding with them.

3. a readiness and a willingness to give up our illusion of power, our temptation to impose what we have to offer. It means to set aside our own projects, our own programs, in order to discover with people— not for them—what their projects and programs are.

4. to meet people on their own terms, in their own time. It means to recognize that waiting, as painful as we may find it, may well be a more powerful force than acting.

5. to accept the fact that we do not possess the truth, the only right way of doing things. It means to accept our own need to grow in the truth, to be disposed to accept the message and values of others and

therefore to be continuously open to further conversion as a result of our dialogue with them. In a very real sense, it will be our own openness to conversion that will make it possible for others to be converted. If I let someone help me, maybe they will also allow me to help them, help them to remove whatever in their lives is a stumbling block to fuller human development and to growing into the mystery of God.

6. to develop deep personal relationships; it means to realize that in listening to others, in taking them seriously, in identifying with their world, we are saying "yes" to them. We are affirming them in a way that is mysteriously, tremendously salvific.

7. to be so immersed in the world of others, like Jesus in our world, that with people we can begin to ask questions which endorse and which challenge their basic view of human values, and in that context—from within—we can announce the Good News and denounce sinful structures.[21]

Such an incarnational theological model of self—transcendence. means an openness and exposure; it means a "capacity to be wounded which we see in the example of our Lord Jesus Christ and which we sum up in the word, 'non—violent resistance.'"

Let me conclude then with just a few words about the most powerful one of all times: the crucified God,—the God, who rich though He was, became poor for (our) sake, to make (us) rich out of His poverty (II Corinthians 8, 9). Dietrich Bonhoeffer declared: "Jesus does not call us to a new religion. Jesus calls us to life. To what sort of life? To participate in the weakness of God in the world" (1953: 357—358). M. L. King saw in Jesus a "strength to love."

Jesus represents the weakness of God in the world, but we prefer to worship a God of power and glory rather than one humbled before the powerful, one suffering, weak and dying. The challenge today is to return to this basic image of the suffering Jesus, to follow the example of Paul who "knew only about Jesus, and only about him as the crucified Christ" (I Corinthians 2:2). In today's parlance this might mean knowing only about a "powerless" Christ, a Christ who never abandons human beings, who prefers the marginalized, who is revolutionary but never categorizes, who is jeered and loved, who is thought to be mad but manifests a wisdom and power that astonishes all.

With such a powerless model, self—transcendence becomes really powerful in building an inclusive church.

To be me is to fully become you!

BIBLIOGRAPHY

Lonergan, Bernard J.F. Insight (New York: Harper & Row) 1978.

King, M. L. Strength to Love.

_____. Dissertation.

Hall, Edward T. Beyond Culture (New York: Anchor Books) 1957.

Howe, Reuel L. The Miracle of Dialogue (New York: The Seabury Press) 1964.

Haley, Alex. Roots.

Kraft, Charles H. Christianity in Culture (New York: Orbis Books 1979.

Moltmann, Juergen. Theology of Hope (New York: Harper & Row) 1975.

_____. The Crucified God (New York: Harper & Row) 1973.

Griffin, David Ray. God, Power and Evil: A Process Theodicy Philadelphia: The Westminster Press) 1976.

Allport, Gordon W. The Nature of Prejudice (New York: DoubledaymAnchor Books) 1958.

Thurman, Howard. Mysticism and the Experience of Love Pennsylvania: Sowers Printing Co.) 1961.

_____. The Inward Journey (New York: Harper & Row) 1961.

_____. The Growing Edge (Richmond, Indiana: Friends United Press) 1956.

Pannenberg, Wolfhart. Theology and the Philosophy of Science (Philadelphia: The Westminster Press) 1976.

_____. Jesus, God and Man (Philadelphia: The Westminster Press) 1974.

_____. Theology and the Kingdom of God (Philadelphia: The Westminster Press) 1975.

Berger, Peter L. and Luckmann, Thomas. The Social Construction of Reality (New York: Anchor Books) 1967

.

A DOCUMENTARY HISTORY
of the Transcultural Project

By the Rev. Cheryl Stewart

In the late summer of 1977, I was asked to prepare a draft of a proposal written by Albert (Pete) Pero. That proposal was for a study seminar for the black community within Lutheranism, to enable them to come to terms with what being black and Lutheran meant, in a very positive way, in the social context of the United States. This proposal laid out the theological and sociological foundations for such a venture, and also the specific strategies and steps to be undertaken.

Pete took this proposal to the mission executives of the four major Lutheran judicatories—the Association of Evangelical Lutheran Churches (AELC), the American Lutheran Church (ALC), the Lutheran Church in America (LCA), and the Lutheran Church-Missouri Synod (LC-MS)— under the auspices of the Lutheran Council in the USA (LCUSA) early in the fall of 1977. They approved the proposal for exploration.

A meeting was then planned for November 29 and 30, 1977. Participants were to include significant black church and political leaders from around the country, as well as several leading black Lutheran pastors: the Revs. Will Herzfeld, Rudy Featherstone, Massie Kennard and Lee Wesley. An ecumenical black seminar on self-transcendence was to be the culmination of the project.

It is instructive to note that when the black community was discussing the black church, black people in mainline white denominations were not generally included. Pete saw this as something not only important for black Lutheran people to come to grips with, but equally important for the black church in growing toward ecumenism.

The meeting was held as planned at the Hilton Hotel in Arlington Park, Illinois, and the participants focused the original proposal more intensely and intentionally in ecumenicity. At this point the thrust still focused on the black community and in celebrating our own unity in the midst of our diversity. The revised proposal was forwarded to the mission executives, the Rev. James Mayer (AELC), Dr. John Houck (ALC), Dr. Kenneth Senft (LCA) and the Rev. Leslie Weber (LC-MS). Their enthusiasm led to further honing and polishing of the proposal.

On January 19-21, 1978, a small group met in New York City to address the concerns of the mission executives, who felt that the scope of the proposed seminar was, simultaneously, too broad and too limited. It was too broad in its ecumenicity, and too limited in that only the black community was to be engaged.

The make-up of the original planning committee, which had met in Illinois, had already changed by this time. Rudy Featherstone and Lee Wesley were present at this meeting for the first time, joining Pete Pero, Will Herzfeld, and myself, who attended the first meeting. Together we adjusted the proposal to include people of all colors—Asians, Blacks, Hispanics, Native Americans and Whites—and to focus on Lutheranism in the United States as the social context for self-transcendence, while maintaining an indigenous and universal focus.

During the next few months, the staff committee—with the help of LCUSA's Division for Mission and Ministry through the Rev. Donald Larsen—explained to the mission executives the movement towards a comprehensive and holistic approach to an inclusive church. The committee assured them that the proposal was, indeed, now indigenous in five cultures.

This led to discussion within the Lutheran judicatory divisions among mission staff and across judicatory lines among the mission executives relative to Pete's proposal. On August 30-31, 1978, a meeting was held at the Lutheran Center in Glen Foerd, Pennsylvania. Participants from the AELC, ALC, LCA and LC-MS were invited. (However, the LC-MS representatives could not attend, and subsequently decided not to participate).

The purpose of the meeting was to examine the proposal, to identify those elements that would need further modification in order to gain and maintain support, and to identify the next steps for implementation. The planning committee again contacted the mission executives through LCUSA and informed them of the pan-Lutheran support given by the AELC, the ALC, and the LCA.

A year after the original proposal was written and approved, the constituents and ecumenical nature had shifted. Therefore a meeting was planned for early 1979 so that the mission executives could invite a special group of ethnic representatives who would determine how inclusive the seminar on transcendence would be. "We were off and running!"

Our first really transcultural meeting took place at the Kennedy O'Hare Holiday Inn in Chicago, Illinois on March 19, 1979. Asian, black, Hispanic, Native American and white representatives from the AELC, ALC, and LCA attended. The proposal was once again reviewed and amended, and the group recommended names of persons to serve on a steering committee and a staff/planning committee, which in turn were sent to the mission executives.

Lee Wesley was named chairperson to administer and orchestrate the project because of his gifts and abilities as a Lutheran process person. Up until this point, the Rev. Cheryl Stewart, on an *ad hoc* basis, had done this.

What an exciting time for all of us! On May 25, the staff/planning committee met in New York at LCUSA offices to develop a conference design and to make work assignments. Another meeting date was set for July 6, at which time concrete designs for a mini-workshop, future steering committee meetings and the major conference would be developed.

The staff/planning committee had hoped to have a meeting of the steering committee in October or November of 1979 but due to scheduling problems, that meeting was postponed until March 15-17, 1980.

In the interim, the team met in New York (October 12) and revamped the schedule of all the future meetings, moving everything back approximately six months. Contact persons were identified at that meeting to assist in coordinating and communicating with the additional ethnic communities: Asian—Edmond Yee; Hispanic—Clemente Saenz; Native American—Marlene Helgemo. Now we had a holistic representation of Lutheran constituents. The objectives for the seminar were expanded and included in the revamped proposal.

The Transcultural Seminar Steering Committee met in Kansas City in March 1980. Specifics relative to the conference papers were ironed out; the issues to be addressed by the participants were isolated; conference logistics were explored; names of potential participants were requested from the ethnic caucuses; and the process for bringing them on board was determined.

The staff team met again on April 11-12 in Arlington Heights, Illinois and worked on papers to be presented at the mini-conference. The ethnic representatives responsible for seeing that the work was done were chosen. It was agreed that each caucus would proceed in their own manner within the same parameters: *getting at the praxis of the concept of self-transcendence as a theological foundation for an inclusive church.*

Between April 1980 and May 1981 the staff team met once via a telephone conference call to determine specific dates for both the mini- and major conferences, and during the first event itself in Cincinnati, Ohio. During this time, the individual caucuses and contact persons were hard at work preparing for the conference.

Between the two TCS conferences, the steering committee met once to evaluate the Cincinnati event and to plan for the major one to be held in Chicago, Illinois. The mood of the committee was one of great excitement, mirroring the evaluations of the participants and anticipating the culmination of four years of work. This committee met once more in January 1982, following TCSII in Chicago.

The beauty and joy of my involvement in this entire process is lodged in my knowledge of the existence of this book, the videotape and the experiential proof that acknowledges and demonstrates in theory and theology the indigenous character of cultures and their experiences of God and also the universal nature of Christianity. As Pete often says, and to which assembled Lutherans have proof, "(The) water (of baptism) is thicker than (the) blood (of birth)."

As we move towards the formation of a new church, I hope we do not lose the excitement that was kindled in these past four years. We pray that in some small measure these years will be a contribution to a truly new culturally inclusive Lutheran church, as a witness to all who are a part of the body of Christ.

PART TWO

**The Composition and Make-up of the Star
(Antithesis: Exclusive/Indigious)**

CAUCUS PAPERS
Presented at the Transcultural Seminar's Mini-Conference
Cincinnati, Ohio May 7-9, 1981

Introduction

The papers presented by the caucuses at the Mini-conference of the Transcultural Seminar, May 7-9, 1981 in Cincinnati, Ohio, were highly diversified in content and in format as well. Yet, at the same time, there was a thematic thread which tied them, however loosely, together. Because of this, coupled with the instruction from the Steering Committee to consolidate them according to the format chosen by the Asian Caucus, the task of consolidation was made somewhat difficult, and this consolidated paper may appear to be rather arbitrary. Further, the possibility of misrepresenting the view(s) of a particular caucus might well become apparent. Discussion of any misinterpretations will be welcome at the Transcultural Seminar's Major Conference in Chicago, October 21-24, 1981.

This consolidation is an attempt to call attention to the major thematic similarities and/or concerns among the groups and to note the distinctiveness of each, hoping that this process will provide some meaningful grounds for further discussion in Chicago.

Identity

The Transcultural Seminar is made up of five ethnic caucuses: Asian, Black, Hispanic, Native American and White. At the Mini-conference, helpful papers on the history and perspective of the groups were presented by various individuals. The responsibility of the caucuses was to identify how each group perceived itself and how it was viewed by others, under the general headings: stereotypes and genius.

Stereotypes

A stereotype is a set of assumptions, positive and negative, which permits classification of an individual into a group. Stereotyping can be exogenous (from external origins) as well as endogenous (growing from within). Among the caucuses there was general consensus that stereotypes exogenously produced are overwhelmingly negative. Conversely, the endogenous self-image of each group was basically positive, although not without self-criticism. The White Caucus apologetically acknowledged that white persons represent the establishment in the U.S.A., have the power to control others, and are traditionally considered divinely empowered to accomplish their own goals – three distinctions that no other caucus dared to claim.

Although there was a positive self-image among all five caucuses, the people of color often defined their identity in terms of a relationship between their ancestral roots and the dominant U.S. society. This suggested, on the one hand, a bi-culturalism produced by their unique adaptation to the dominant society, and on the other hand, an identity crisis.

Genius

The term genius was used in the sense of gifts available for sharing. More specifically, it referred to the gifts each group could contribute to an inclusive church. Each group stated a wide variety of gifts, which included indigenous theologies, rich cultural heritages, familism, talents, resources and individual expertise. To generalize and single out, the greatest gift offered by the people of color was the concept of cosmic harmony which views the individual in the greater context of an all-embracing universe. This concept, in an inclusive church, may well serve as the most important addition and corrective* to Christianity. This philosophical concept of cosmic harmony was quite different from the contributions named by the White Caucus, which were more goal and action oriented.

Needs

"Need" was not a word which the White Caucus used as a heading. However, there was expressed an implicit sense of need for self-discipline in listening to and working with the people of color, as well as in utilizing the resources in the possession of whites to meet the needs of others.

The needs of the people of color fall into the following areas:

There is a need for

1. Indigenous clergy and lay leadership development.
2. Active evangelism, more ministries among the people of bilingual materials.
3. Multi-cultural theological education for everyone.

There is a need to

1. Be recognized individually as a distinct people with religio-cultural contributions to make.
2. Affirm the assumptions of the Cincinnati Mini-conference and to have the Anglo leadership to make a commitment to participate at the Chicago Major Conference.
3. Have continued dialogue on cultural transcendance.

There is a need that

1. The church live up to its overall commitments.

Interestingly, at the Mini-conference we saw the caucuses falling into two distinct groups – "in people" and "out people" – with the "in people" talking about how to assist the "out people" and perhaps to learn from them, while the "out people" loudly voiced what their needs were.

Visions

Each caucus, explicitly or implicitly, envisioned an inclusive church. The Asian, Native American and White Caucuses articulated their visions in more specific, although occasionally vague, structural terms. In addition to a list of "steps being taken toward inclusivity," the boldest statements of commitment to an inclusive church came from the White Caucus, which expressed a readiness "to render an account of these commitments at our next meeting (in October)."

Only the Asian Caucus wrote down its vision. It envisioned an inclusive church "that is free of racism, sexism, and classism," and called for "reform in theological education" in order to enable "all professional leaders to be more effective in ministering in a multi-cultural context."

Conclusion

We began this consolidation by noting that there was a thematic thread that tied the papers together. Now we conclude the process by pointing out that beneath the common theme(s) was a tapestry woven together with many colored threads. Illustrative of this was the much shared theme, familism, which in the Asian setting was undergirded by the concept of filial piety; whereas in the Chicano group (referring to Hispanic persons whose ancestry is traceable to Mexico), it was often spoken of in social and/or structural terms rather than in philosophical terms. The variations on the theme of familism could be the ultimate impetus for the growth and meaning, as well as a source of dissatisfaction and distress, in an inclusive church, depending on how this seeming strength is utilized.

Further, it should be noted that the White Caucus seemed generally to address the people of color as a whole, while the latters' papers were aimed mainly at the White Caucus and speak little to one another. If this observation is accurate, then it may well be desirable for the people of color to examine the matter of inter-ethnic relations among themselves, and for the White Caucus to recognize that each group is distinct and should be treated as such, in fact, there are even internal variations within each group.

Finally, there are within as well as without the church, many cultural streams emerging and converging. Together they could form a beautiful garden whose landscape is elegant, blossoms unique and fragrance sweet, in which the people of God could meditate in peace, dialogue together and proclaim the Gospel in harmony. This perhaps is the meaning of being inclusive.

Edmond Yee, Consolidator

September 15, 1981

* The phrase "corrective to Christianity" is urged by the consolidator. But whether or not this is an appropriate concept is open for discussion at the major conference in Chicago.

THE ASIAN AMERICANS
Their History, Community, and Culture

by Edmond Yee

The story of George Shima, an immigrant from Japan, illustrates the indignity suffered by Asian Americans personally—and shows, as well, the spirit of resistance that foreshadowed the formation of a new consciousness among Asian Americans. Since Professor Roger Daniels has so eloquently recounted the story in his book, "The Politics of Prejudice," I shall simply quote him in part:

> Shima, who was born in 1863 in pre—Meiji Japan, came to this country in 1889 with less than a thousand dollars in capital. After working first as a common laborer and then as a labor contractor, he formed a partnership with several other Issei and leased 15 acres of reclaimed land. By use of the latest techniques, both agricultural and managerial, Shima and his associates created an agricultural empire on the virgin "drowned islands" of the San Joaquin delta and were among the first to raise potatoes successfully for the market in California. As early as 1909 Shima was referred to as the "Potato King," and each year the press speculated as to his net income. By 1920 it was alleged that he controlled 85 per cent of the crop, whose total value was over $18 million... (in 1913) Shima controlled 28,800 acres actually in production and, by means of marketing agreements, handled the produce of thousands more. His working force numbered over five hundred, from engineers and boat captains (the islands

were then accessible only by water) to common laborers, and included Japanese, East Indians, and Caucasians, both native and foreign born. At his death, in 1926, a newspaper estimated his estate at $15 million; his pallbearers included David Starr Jordan, the chancellor of Stanford University, and James Rolph, Jr., the mayor of San Francisco. Shima's was surely a Horatio Alger story, without any trace of kind benefactor or boss' daughter; but when the real—life hero was a California Issei there was bound to be a bitter twist not found in dime novels. Shima, despite his millions, was still an "alien ineligible to citizenship;" and when, in 1909, he bought a house in one of the better residential neighborhoods of Berkeley, a cry of protest went up from the citizens of the quiet university town. Although obviously embarrassed, Shima stayed. He informed the protestants, who included a university of California professor, that they need not worry, since he was putting up "a high fence to keep the other children from playing with his." (1)

The prejudice which George Shima encountered was nothing new to the Asians in America. In fact, by 1909, the Asians had already experienced the profound impact of the Burlingame Treaty of 1868 and the Exclusion Act of 1882. Yet their story is generally left unmentioned on the pages of American history, and their descendants continue to suffer the stereotype image. This paper tells ever so briefly what happened to them and makes a few observations on their community and culture.

Two clarifications are needed here before any further discussion. First, the terms "Asians" or "Asian Americans" used in this paper refer to American citizens and legal residents of the U.S. whose ancestries are traceable to China, Japan, Korea and the Philippines. Second, the omission of the recent arrival of Vietnamese and other Southeast Asian immigrants and refugees is intentional. This does not mean lack of concern for these people. Their history in this country is still young, and I do not wish to draw premature conclusions which might prove to be inaccurate.

Their History

The Chinese

The United States Immigration Commission reported the arrival of the first Chinese in 1820, and a dozen or so more followed during the next the decades. This first group, consisting mainly of merchants and students, were regarded by the Americans with a mixture of curiosity and amazement. However, Chinese emigration in the real sense of the word did not begin until 1849, one year after gold was discovered at John Sutter's sawmill in Coloma, California. The number of Chinese laborers in California in that year reached 54. By the end of 1850, their number totaled approximately 4,000, and by the end of the following year, 25,000.

There were two basic reasons for such a sudden surge of movement across the hazardous Pacific Ocean: social dislocation at home, and economic opportunity abroad. Southern China, where all early immigrants originated, experienced in the middle of the 19th century national catastrophe making the already wretched lives of the ordinary citizens more unbearable, Southern China was also the home of the ill—facted T'ai—p'ing rebellion against the Ch'ing Dynasty (1644—1911). This civil insurrection lasted for fourteen years, resulting in casualties estimated to be greater than 30,000,000. While natural catastrophe and social chaos were on the rampage in China, gold was discovered in California. These events became a push—pull force in the lives of many courageous young Chinese whose singular dream was to come to the Gold Mountain (i.e., California) to make a quick fortune and then return to their homeland to rejoin their loved ones. While the dream was only realized by a very few, a great number of them continued to come; the 1860 census reported 34,933 Chinese residents in California. Evidence suggests that they never dominated the California gold mines, but that they often worked in mines abandoned by white men.

In addition to working in gold mines, these early pioneers also labored in the fishing industry and contributed greatly to the construction of the transcontinental railroad. In 1865, for example, there were 10,000 Chinese laborers on the job, recruited first in California and later in Kuangtung, China, at the peak of construction of the Central Pacific Railroad.

Despite their contributions and their relatively small number, they were attacked by laws, both state and federal, popular tribunals and mob violence, culminating with the Exclusion Act of 1882 which was aimed mainly at Chinese laborers. (2)

The Exclusion Act had two effects on the Chinese in America: 1.) It effectively shut off immigration, therefore rendering the already small Chinese community smaller during the next five decades. For example, the 1880 census reported 105,465 Chinese in the United States, whereas the 1930 total was 74,954. This number slowly increased from 1930 on due to an increase in the female population. 2.) It condemned the Chinese already in this country to a life of bachelorhood. Because of custom and of laws against them, the Chinese did not bring their women along when they came; instead, they would go back periodically to their home-land to see their families.

The Exclusion Act remained in effect for more than sixty years and was not repealed until December 17, 1943, when the United States and China became comrades—in—arms against Japan in the Pacific theater. The so—called "Act to Repeal the Chinese Exclusion Acts, to Establish Quotas, and for Other Purposes,"[3] passed by the Congress that year in-deed established a quota for the Chinese: 105 persons allowed into this country per year! The repeal was nothing but a cosmetic gesture to pla-cate the Chinese government and an attempt of the U.S. government to save itself from embarrassment. How could one comrade—in—arms have well—established discriminatory laws against the citizens of an-other friendly nation?

The quota system remained in effect until 1965. On October 3, 1965, "Congress passed a new and more liberal immigration and na-tionality act," making "sweeping changes by abolishing national—origin quotas and establishing, on principle, a first-come-first-served basis." Under the present system, "Chinese could possibly use up to 20,000 of the annual quota." (4) The immigration figures from 1970 to 1979 reveal that the annual average was 23,117. The total population projection for 1979 was 729,150.

The Japanese

When Japan went into national isolation during the Tokugawa period (1603—1867 A.D.), Japanese emigration was illegal. But West-ern intrusion into her territory beginning in 1853 and the Meiji Restora-tion (1867—68) changed the picture. Emigration after 1869 was made possible but few left their homeland for the Western Hemisphere. And for those who did, Hawaii was their first stop. In 1868, 148 Japanese contract laborers arrived in Hawaii and were mistreated by the planta-tion owners. Learning this, Japan halted emigration. It was not until 1885 that Japanese emigration to Hawaii resumed. And in the follow-ing year, Japan once again legalized emigration in general.

Three years later, in 1869, the first group of Japanese immigrants arrived in the U.S. and settled in Gold Hill, California, where they set up the Wakamatsu Tea and Silk Farm Colony. These inexperienced immi-grants, totally unaware of the intense Californian heat in the summer, soon failed.

Between 1871 and 1880, the U.S. Bureau of the Census reported 149 Japanese immigrants to the U.S. mainland. Despite the anti—Chinese sentiments raging in California, this small group of persons from Japan went about the country unmolested. This placid attitude toward the Japanese was soon to change. In 1900, for example, when 12,635 Japanese from Hawaii entered the U.S., the alarm of a Japanese invasion was, sounded in the West.

Not unlike their Chinese counterparts, the early Japanese immigrants who came to this country were propelled by the push—pull force. At home, they faced the socio-economic dislocations brought about by westernization. At the same time, they were tempted by employment opportunities which were in a way created by the passage of the Chinese Exclusion Act, in the Hawaiian sugar plantations and on the mainland. But unlike the Chinese, the Japanese entered into a country whose anti-Asian attitudes were already well-formed and discriminatory laws well established. Therefore, it is not difficult to see when 12,635 of them arrived from Hawaii, they immediately caused concern.

The years 1901-1908 were the peak period of early Japanese immigration. During this period anti-Japanese activities were numerous. The San Francisco Chronicle was one of the major agitators in the anti—Japanese movement. For example, on February 23, 1905, it proclaimed under a front—page headline: "The Japanese Invasion, the Problem of the Hour." The Chronicle continued, off and on for over a year, to publish inflammatory anti-Japanese articles.

The Japanese government which, unlike the Chinese government, always took an interest in the welfare of her overseas subjects, protested the mistreatment of her people. A protest of this nature from a weak government would have been ignored by the U.S. But Japan by this time was already an acknowledged military power. Accordingly, in December 1906, the U.S. government entered into negotiations with Japan for a Gentlemen's Agreement. The aim was to limit Japanese laborers from entering the U.S.

On March 9, 1908, the Gentlemen's Agreement was concluded, and the specific terms of this agreement may never be known. But it seems clear that under such an agreement Japan would voluntarily restrain from issuing passports to male laborers to the U.S., and the U.S. would allow Japanese laborers already in this country to "send" for their wives or fiancées. Thus, in 1910, "Picture brides" began arriving for those Japanese men who requested wives from Japan. (5) Had the U.S. government know the sex ratio (6 males to 1 female) between Japanese males and females in this country, the terms of agreement might have been different. By allowing the Japanese males to "send" for their wives and fiancées, the U.S. government unknowingly helped the Japanese community to grow.

During World War I, the anti—Japanese campaign became subdued since Japan was an ally of the United States. But, as soon as the Treaty of Versailles was signed on June 28, 1919, the anti—Japanese campaign flared up at once in California, followed by the passage of the Alien Land Act of 1920. The purpose was "to seal the loopholes in the 1913 Alien Land Law by forbidding the Japanese Issei to buy land in the name of their American—born children, the Nisei (second generation). (6)

In the meantime, the Japanese government, hoping to defuse the hostility against her subjects, enforced the "Ladies' Agreement" in 1921. This meant that the Japanese government would voluntarily halt from issuing passports to "Picture brides." This move however, did not satisfy the exclusionists. In the following year, Congress passed the Cable Act, which provided that "...any woman citizen who marries an alien ineligible to citizenship shall cease to be a citizen of the U.S." This meant that a Nisei or a Caucasian woman who married an Issei lost her citizenship; but if this marriage terminated by divorce or death, the Caucasian woman could apply to regain her citizenship, whereas the Nisei woman could not because she was "of a race ineligible to citizenship." (7)

Sensing that the tide was favorable toward the passage of an exclusion act, the Congressional steering committee, in 1923, under U.S. McClatchy opened an office in the capitol. The exclusionists succeeded on March 15, 1924, with the passage of the Immigration Exclusion Act. This act limited all immigration to the United States, but denied all immigration from Japan.[8] From 1924 to 1952, immigration from Japan stopped. Some contemporary historians view the passage of the Immigration Exclusion Act as the cause of Pearl Harbor.

On Sunday, December 7, 1941, Japan bombed Pearl Harbor. The U. S. government, under the influence of a long history of anti—Asianism and pressure from labor, within a matter of months, rounded up more than 100,000 West Coast Japanese, both citizens and aliens, and placed them in ten concentration camps across the nation. The wartime experience, observed Harry Kitano, had one positive effect: it helped the Japanese Americans to become more acculturated. But the fact remains that the incarceration of the Japanese was the apogee of white racism against the Asians in America. As the redress movement shows, the effect of this incarceration continues to be felt among Japanese Americans today.

With the repeal of the 1924 Exclusion Act in 1952, Japanese immigration to the U.S. once again resumed. The total Japanese American population projected for 1979 was 703,102.

The Koreans

The Koreans, numerically the smallest among the four Asian groups, came to Hawaii, a U.S. territory then, beginning in 1902 when Korea was under Japanese domination. Their experiences differed from other Asian groups in early immigration history. Theirs were tied closely to events taking shape in. their homeland.

Korea, traditionally under Chinese suzerainty, came under Japanese domination in 1894, when Japan defeated China at the outbreak of the Sino—Japanese War. Chinese influence on Korea was thus removed. After a number of years of political maneuvering, Japan, in 1910, set out to annex Korea and became her dictatorial ruler—though not without challenge—for the next forty years until the end of World War II.

From within, Japanese authority was challenged by the Independence Movement; and from outside the Koreans in Hawaii and America were actively financing the political activities of their compatriots at home. Some of the Koreans in the continental U.S. even went so far as to give military training to the young Koreans to prepare them to return to fight in Korea. On the political front, they likewise promoted anti—Japanese sentiment in the U.S. prior to and during the Pacific war years. One further characteristic that marked the early Korean immigrants apart from all others is that they did not bring the clan or other social organizations with them. Instead, their Christian churches which formed the center of social, spiritual, and political activities.

After the annexation, Japan forbade the Koreans to emigrate. For this reason, the number of Koreans residing in the U.S. between 1902 and 1960 was exceedingly small, escaping practically all the racial injustice which other Asians had to endure. But since 1960, their number has increased many times. This increase became particularly noticeable beginning in 1970. The annual average, for example, of Koreans coming to the U.S. from 1970 to 1979 was 24,411, making the Korean American community the second fastest growing within the Asian American community. The projected number of Koreans' in the U.S. in 1979 was 603,335.

The Pilipinos

The Chinese Exclusion Act of 1882, the Gentlemen's Agreement of 1908, the prohibition of Korean emigration of 1910 and the Immigration Exclusion Act of 1924 had an adverse impact on the Hawaiian and American labor markets. The first to feel the pinch were the Hawaiian sugar plantation owners. Thus, through the Hawaiian Sugar Planters' Association, they experimented, from 1970 to 1919, with Pilipino labor as a replacement for the Japanese. The experiment proved to be successful. Thus, there followed, a decade after 1919, a heavy influx of laborers from the Philippines.

The first major increase of Pilipino immigration experienced by the West Coast occurred during the early 1920's, and the Pilipino presence was sharply increased after 1924 when the new immigration act excluded the Japanese. The California Pilipino panic began in 1923 when 2,426 Pilipinos were admitted to the state. Hence, they faced similar hostilities that the Chinese and the Japanese had endured.

The Pilipino immigrants differed from other Asians in two aspects. First, they entered this country not as aliens but nationals. Even so, they were ineligible to citizenship. Second, as a people, they were and are geographically and racially close to the great cultures of the East, and yet, through long centuries of Spanish rule, were greatly westernized. The Pilipinos, in a sense, were hybrid orphans of the East.

By 1930, the total number of Philipinos in Hawaii and the mainland was 108,260, with more than half in Hawaii. During the early 1930's, in the fact of demand for exclusion and a labor surplus in Hawaii, the number of Philipinos entering the U.S. and her territories dropped significantly. Though they were never explicitly excluded from coming to the U.S. and Hawaii, their number was successfully limited by a quota system under the Bill of Promised Independence (the Philippines were a U.S. territory then) which was recognized by the Congress in 1935. Accordingly, for the following 11 years, the number of Pilipinos entering the U.S. was small.

Beginning in 1947, the population began to show some increase; and since 1967, the increase has been very significant, making, in fact, the Pilipino American community the fastest growing one within the Asian American community. The average annual immigration between 1970 and 1978 was 34,200. The projected total population for this group as of 1979 was 793,994.

The early Asian immigrants were young, unmarried males with high hopes of making a quick fortune in the "melting pot." Since 1965, the picture has been changed. Today's immigrants are young and old, rich and poor, educated and ignorant, professionals and laborers. They are here to stay.

The Asian American Community.

The 1980 census reveals that there are three and a half million Asian Americans in the United States. This figure represents 1.5% of the total U.S. population. However, this statistical picture is changing constantly and rapidly because of continued and increasing immigration. One recent study suggests that by the year 2080 the U.S. population will consist of 40% Asians and Hispanics. Even though the author did not give an exact statistical breakdown of the two groups, the figure does suggest a substantial increase of Asians in this country in the future. Of the three and a half million Asian Americans, approximately 7% belong to the Christian churches. And, approximately 9% of these Christian Asian Americans/Canadians belong to Lutheran churches.

What do we Lutherans know about Asian Americans? This section is meant to be a brief portrayal of the Asian American community and culture, to facilitate a better understanding of their culture and to offer a suggestion to the church in providing social and spiritual care with the community.

Community and Culture

The Asian American Community has many variations and internal values which prohibit generalization. And yet a paper of this nature automatically calls for specificity. Caught in this dilemma and at the risk of being overly simplistic, I shall make only a few observations of the characteristics of Asian Americans and of their community.

1. The Asian American community is both old and new. The well— established segment is dominated by the early immigrants and their descendents. The new element is injected into the community by the newcomers. The latter alters not only the community structure but also its social/spiritual service systems as well.

2. The Asian American community is by and large urban, with many organizations and institutions parallel to those of the Anglos. This parallel development suggests structural pluralism, and resourcefulness of the community.

3. The Asian Americans' identification with the community is both geographical and cultural (or spiritual, if you will). Little Tokyo, in Los Angeles: for instance, is to the residents both home and a cultural center, but to the Japanese Americans living outside of its boundary, it becomes: a cultural/spiritual Mecca.

4. The Asian Americans have higher educational attainment than any other group, yet according to the 1970 census data, they are restricted in both professional and economic mobility. They are underemployed and their talents are not being used to the full extent.

5. The Asian Americans, broadly speaking, fall into three types: the traditionalist—one who retains Asian culture and value systems; the marginal person—one who is (or thinks she/he is) very Westernized; the Asian American—one who believes that both cultures, Asian and Western, have something to offer and is in the process of forming his/her own culture derived from both.

The Traditionalist

An Asian American traditionalist is a person who retains, by and large, the Asian culture and value system which are derived mainly from the four major religions: Confucianism, Buddhism., Taoism and Shinto.

The traditionalists, whose values and spirituality are derived from one or two or all of the religions, do not see any particular conflict among the religions. They possess a noble attitude of religious t o l e r - ance. Their decision to continue to adhere to the Asian ways and values is by and large by choice and to a certain extent attributable to unfavorable social and racial circumstances they encounter in this country.

Since these four religio—cultural streams play an important role in shaping the values of the traditionalists, it may be instructive to examine, however briefly, the four systems for the benefit of the reader.

Confucianism

The development of this system antedated the man Confucius (551-479 B.C.) by several hundred years. Contrary to the Western common understanding that it is merely an ethical system, Confucianism is in fact a religious system which, like Christianity, has a body of scriptures known as the Confucian Classics consisting of nine books in the present canon. The Confucian canon, unlike the Christian one, is never closed. These books, like the Christian Bible, deal with a variety of subjects. For our purposes however, I shall highlight only two: the notion of God and the concept of human nature.

Within this body of scriptures, we find the Confucian notion of God as the Creator, and Lord of history as well as the concept of the will of God. Even though Confucianism has not developed any doctrine of creation similar to the ones in Genesis, the belief in God as the Creator, source and principle of all things and of the human race is clearly evident, as the following passage shows:

How vast is God,
The Ruler of humanity below!
How arrayed in terrors is God,

With many things irregular in His ordination!
Heaven gave birth to the multitudes of the people.
But the nature it confers is not to be depended on.
(Book of Poetry)

As the Lord of history, God is an active participant, being the source of all power and authority, and protecting the creation from calamity with His presence. His power, authority and protection are often manifested through the good ruler in whom He takes a special interest.

The will of God refers to the Decree of Heaven, especially to the "Mandate of Heaven," which is the divine origin of rulership. Within the Confucian culture a ruler may rule only after she/he has received the heavenly mandate that requires the ruler to be benevolent and virtuous in caring for Cod's creation. Also, a person cannot be a person of high moral character unless that person knows this will of God.

The Confucian understanding of human nature is that it is good because its goodness in each person is inherently conferred by the Creator. Mencius (c. 371-289 B.C.) in whose book this concept is found, is the proponent of this theory. His argument runs something like this: since each person has received the four seeds of humanity, righteousness, propriety and wisdom from God, all one needs to do is cultivate the seeds in order to achieve self—realization. Consequently, the Confucians place tremendous emphasis on self—cultivation. Finally, Confucianism is a diffused religion without an organized priesthood and religious institution.

Taoism

Both the philosophical and religious aspects of Taoism originated in China, and developed alongside Confucianism in remote antiquity. It developed into an organized religion only in the early centuries of the Christian era. The early Taoism developed as a reaction against Confucianism which values human relatedness, service to the state and so forth. As such, there are, as Howard Smith points out, two basic ideas that characterized the early Taoists: 1. "They despised the pomp, glory, prestige, wealth and power for which other men strove,". . . 2. They "believed that life itself is the greatest of all possessions."[9] The Tao, which harmonizes all opposites and contrast, is the central concept in this system.

As a religion, Taoism also has a body of scriptures called the Tao-tsang comprising 1,120 volumes. Unlike Confucianism which worships the monotheistic deity, the Lord—on-High, there are in a Taoist pantheon numerous deities, with the Yellow Emperor being the supreme

God. Aside from the deities, the Taoists also affirm the five-element theory as a science, and practice breath control, fasting and dieting as a means to the attainment of a pure life.

Buddhism

People usually associate reincarnation with Buddhism, a religious system that originated in India during the sixth and fifth centuries, B.C. To a certain extent, this association is correct. But Buddhism is considerably more complex and sophisticated.

Underlying this belief system is the concept "Karma," which originally meant deed or act. Every deed or act produced a result. To this concept, however, the historical Buddha made a significant addition— intention. To him a karma cannot be generated without intention. But if intention is present, then the karma will arise with or without an act or deed. According to the individual's karma he/she will undergo repeated rebirths and assume different forms of existence in this seemingly unending cycle. The ultimate aim in a person's existence, then, is to break the cycle of rebirths because life itself in the Buddhist's view is suffering.

How can an individual break this cycle? Buddhism offers a doctrine of salvation consisting of the four noble truths: "life is suffering; this suffering has a cause, which is craving for existence and sensual pleasures; this suffering can be suppressed; the way to suppress suffering is the practice of the noble eightfold path, which consists of right views, right intentions, right speech, right action, right livelihood, right effort, right mindfulness, and right concentration."[10] If the eightfold path is rightly followed, a Buddhist, in the end, will break the cycle of rebirths and realize nirvana, a Buddhist paradise.

However, this rigid discipline is suitable only for a few who are willing to enter monastic life. So as the religion developed, dissatisfaction arose. The result was the development of a new doctrine by the Mahayana school which emphasizes that salvation is to be achieved by faith in the Buddha, love for humanity through the action of compassion and charity.

Shinto

Shinto is not considered a major Asian religion, but its influence on the lives of the Japanese from time immemorial has been great. The term Shinto means "the way of gods" and was first used in the eighth century to distinguish this particular religious practice from that of Taoism, Buddhism and Confucianism.

Shinto, unlike Christianity and Buddhism, has neither a founder nor a body of scriptures. But in practice, particularly in its personal aspect, Shinto implies faith in gods, and in its communal aspect, it is a Japanese way of life, including attitudes, ideas and ways of doing things.

Within this belief system, objects regarded as gods or objects that have the kami power include wind, thunder, sun, mountains, rivers, trees, rocks, some animals, ancestral spirits, heroes, virtuous individuals and so forth. The objective that the believers seek in worship is to attain spiritual life and harmony with the gods. The elements of worship include purification, offering, prayer and sacred feast. The last, however, is usually omitted when only a simple act of worship is performed before a shrine.

The Westernized

A Westernized Asian American is a person who, consciously or otherwise, has adopted and internalized the Western culture and value system to the point where the rejection of anything Asian may occur. The question as to why such a person would accept one and reject the other is interesting but may be too difficult to understand, particularly if such an individual's position is examined from the standpoint of the "adhesion" and "prescription" principles described by Paulo Freire in *Pedagogy of the Oppressed.*

In this work, Freire describes the initial attitude of the oppressed in their struggle for liberation in this way:

> But almost always, during the initial stage of the struggle, the oppressed, instead of striving for liberation, tend themselves to become oppressors, or 'sub—oppressors.' The very structure of their thought has been conditioned by the contradictions of the concrete, existential situation by which they were shaped. Their ideal is to be men; but for them, to be men is to be oppressors. This is their model of humanity. This phenomenon derives from the fact that the oppressed, at a certain moment of their existential experience, adopt an attitude of 'adhesion' to the oppressor. (11)

Then he goes on to define prescription as "the imposition of one man's choice upon another, transforming the consciousness of the man prescribed to into one that conforms with the prescriber's consciousness." (12)

Viewed from this perspective, it becomes quite clear as to why some Asian Americans become westernized; particularly those who reside in places in this country where the community and cultural ties may not be strong in this country. The same holds true for those immigrants who lived in places in Asia where colonial influence was pervasive prior to their emigration. These people basically did not have a chance to experience or to be taught their own religio—cultural heritage. So in these cases, prescription is also omission which can be intentional and/ or attributable to ignorance of the prescribers.

The majority of missionaries, however well intentioned, of the nineteenth and early twentieth centuries were prescribers. Nowadays, opponents of cultural pluralism and those who refuse to acknowledge the pluralistic nature of the American society likewise belong to the category of prescribers. On the other hand, the prescribed are victims of the adhesion/prescription formula.

The result could have adverse consequences on both the prescribers and the prescribed. On the one hand, the prescribed will continue to reflect the image and to affirm the values of the prescribers, while neglecting their own heritage all the more. On the other hand, the prescribers, having their prescription affirmed by the prescribed, continue to prescribe their values, whereby short changing themselves by not knowing other cultures. And because they do not know other cultures, they weaken their own by not having this knowledge which they could have used to mirror, critique and strengthen what is theirs.

Moreover, the prescribed, while realizing that they are not "authentic beings," tend to be fearful to assert their own authority which could assist them to become authentic. What some of them needed in this case was some outside impetus, which was provided by the Civil Rights Movement in the early 1960's. This movement gave rise to cultural nationalism; and with this rise a new community and a new perspective within the Asian American community was born.

The Asian American

The term Asian American was coined in the 1960's by a group of young students of Asian descent. They saw the futility of accepting the assimilationist model of existence as well as the impracticality of maintaining and practicing the pure Asian culture in the context of the larger society. As a result the members of this group underwent a collective as well as individual identity crisis, which ultimately led them to search deeply into their own roots. This search in turn helped them to discover not only their own roots but a hidden page in American history also. On this very hidden page the story of American racism was written. As the story began to unfold, they realized that they were not only personally discriminated against but that people of Asian descent collectively had been excluded and incarcerated based solely on their race as well

Illustrative of American racism against the people of Asian descent are the tale of George Shima, the Exclusion Act of 1882 and incarceration of the Japanese during World War II.

With the discovery of this hidden page of history and their roots, a new consciousness was formed. The spirit of this new consciousness is both critical and transcendent —critical of their own culture and values and that of the dominant society; and transcendent of their former ethnocentricity to form a new socio—cultural order. The ingredients for this new order are derived from their Asian socio—cultural and historical cohesiveness along with their concrete, existential experience in North, America.

Conclusion

What has been outlined in this paper is by no means exhaustive. The explicit theme of this paper is suffering and discrimination, while the implicit theme is diversity among the Asian American groups, reflecting the cultural and religious richness of their heritages.

Recognizing their suffering and their diversity, our simple suggestion, for the benefit of those who wish to provide social and/or spiritual care with the Asian Americans, is: the style, content, and delivery method of any social/spiritual care must take into account the national origin, the religio—cultural orientation and inclination, the perception of the world order, and the period of immigration of the specific group.

NOTES

1. Roger Daniels, The Politics of Prejudice. Berkeley: University of California Press, 1977, p. 10.
2. William L. Tung, The Chinese in America, 1820—1973: A Chronology and Fact Book. Dobbs Ferry, New York: Oceana Publications, Inc., 1974, pp. 56—61.
3. Ibid., pp. 79, 80
4. Ibid., p. 41
5. Masako Herman, The Japanese in America, 1843—1973, Dobbs Ferry, N.Y.: Oceana Publications, Inc., 1974, p. 11
6. Ibid., p. 13
7. Ibid., p. 15
8. Ibid., p., 16
9. Howard Smith, Chinese Religions: From 1000 B.C. to the Present Day. New York: Holt, Rinehart and Winston, 1968, p. 71
10. Kenneth Ch'en, Buddhism in China: A Historical Survey, Princeton: Princeton University Press, 1973, pp. 5,6. For further detail see, Walpola Rahula, What the Buddha Taught. New York: Grove Press, Inc. 1962, Chapters 2—5.
11. Paulo Freire, Pedagogy of the Oppressed. New York: The Seabury Press, 1970, pp. 29, 30
12. Ibid., p. 31

THE ASIAN AMERICAN WOMAN
A Case of Mistaken Identity

By Fern Lee Hagedorn

On a recent "Today" program Phil Donahue interviewed a person with a unique enterprise. This man, a white American, owned a mating service called "Cherry Blossoms." He was in the business of uniting American men with overseas Asian women. This was done through, among other things the publication of a magazine that contained pictures and vital information on these brides—to—be.

Donahue also interviewed a couple that applauded this service. Through Cherry Blossoms the man had found a good old—fashioned Oriental girl who was content to treat her husband majestically, and was satisfied with her role as mother and wife. The woman was happy because she had found a handsome American man.

Finally, Donahue interviewed a rather obese man in his 50's who was searching for a young and attractive Asian woman. He felt that Asian women accepted men for who they were and that in general, Asian women didn't mind relationships between younger women and older men. How did this man come by this information? "Well," he told Donahue, "I served in the Korean war." It makes one wonder about the kinds of women he met who led him to these views.

This mating service was based on the stereotype that Asian women are subservient and submissive, and that they enjoy being sex objects. These impressions are not only reflected in this corporation, but also in the minds of many North Americans. Where do these images of Asian women come from and why do they live on even in 1981? Are Asian women really the sexy yet submissive types that many are led to believe?

Asian Americans

The Asian American population in the United States—Chinese, Japanese, Korean, Filipino, Indochinese, and Pacific—is estimated at approximately three and a half million, based on provisional totals from the 1980 Census. The fastest growing group in the U.S. is the Koreans. In the New York—New Jersey area alone, there are more than 400,000 Asian American residents. The largest concentration is in California with over 1.25 million Asian residents.

Let's explore the two myths attributed to the female portion of this population.

Asian women are subservient

You may have seen the television commercial promoting a line of international frozen vegetables produced by the Birds Eye Company. Oriental vegetables are the focus of two of these commercials, which feature an Asian couple, husband and wife, in an Asian setting. As the husband looks into the camera, he states that the product tastes authentic—as though it had been homemade by his wonderful wife. At the end of the commercial, the actress playing the wife, who hasn't uttered a word, bows politely.

Or perhaps you've caught re—runs of an old television series called "The Courtship of Eddie's Father." Mrs. Livingston, who happens to be Japanese, is a housekeeper with a soft voice and polite bow that reflects her subservient "Oriental" character.

Portrayals like these perpetuate the stereotype that Asian women are born to be submissive, especially to men. How did this image originate?

The submissive role was a traditional one in many Asian countries. In China, for example, the woman was at the bottom of the ladder in the familial and societal hierarchy and ... yet, she was perhaps the most hard working. She was taught that sons were more important than daughters since they carried on the family name.

In America, the submissive image comes from the experience of immigrant women and men performing service tasks for a livelihood.

Some of these occupations included garment workers in sweat shops; dishwashers in restaurants; chamber maids in hotels; and domestics who labored for those who "just loved those industrious Chinese."

But now, Asian women in the U.S., as well as women in general in this country, are becoming more assertive and unwilling to accept this stereotype pinned on them by society. In general, 26.3% of all Asian Americans are college graduates in comparison to 11.8% of the white population. This is just one indication that reflects' a different kind of drive in the Asian American, and it doesn't reflect a yearning to be subservient.

Asian women enjoy being sex objects

The other stereotype attributed to Asian American women is that they like being sex objects. In this case, I'm reminded of many images from the entertainment media. For example, you may be familiar with an Old Spice cologne commercial where a white man who uses Old Spice is rewarded with an Asian woman in every port. Or maybe you've caught the late movies when they've shown "Flower Drum Song," in which the main character, an Asian woman, enjoys wearing tight Chinese dresses to show off her body; or "The World of Suzy Wong," in which a Chinese woman portrays your friendly neighborhood prostitute in Hong Kong.

Or how about the movie "Sand Pebbles," starring Steve McQueen and Candice Bergen? Chinese women portray bar girls who perform strip teases on table tops. Finally, in a macho detective "Dirty Harry" movie, an Asian woman can't resist Clint Eastwood and slips into his bed in the nude awaiting his return for the night.

The Asian American woman as a prostitute is related to the myth of Asian American women being submissive and willing to debase themselves in this manner. How did this stereotype originate?

It can be traced back to a sad chapter in American history. In 1847, the first major wave of Chinese immigration entered this country. Chinese laborers comprised 90% of the workforce that completed the first major railroad in this country and labored in other areas as well. Fearing what white society called "the yellow peril," Congress in 1882 passed the Chinese Exclusion Act, a first in a series of laws to exclude Asians from entering this country. The U.S. had never before, or since, passed such laws to exclude other groups. Since this law suspended the entry of new immigrants, Chinese laborers could not bring their wives or children to the U.S. By 1890, there was only one Chinese woman for every 26 Chinese men, a grossly unbalanced ratio in part caused by this legal form of racism enacted by the U.S.

One of the inevitable conditions that arose was prostitution, since state laws prohibited Chinese or Asian people from intermarrying with Caucasians. Some young girls were sold or given away by their parents in China in hopes of avoiding starvation. Other young women arrived here with the understanding that they would be joined with a husband, but discovered to their horror that they were in bondage to what we would now call pimps. The newspapers of the day also over—sensationalized this phenomenon of Chinese prostitutes, and Asians became an undesirable population.

The image of the Asian American woman as prostitute is also perpetuated by military personnel who have engaged in recent wars in Japan, Korea and Vietnam where their only contact with native women may have been through prostitutes.

Conclusion

I've only touched the tip of the iceberg.

The Asian American woman—submissive or assertive? Sexy or sexless? How do we categorize her? And must we categorize her? I have only briefly touched on two of the major stereotypes that Asian American women are confronted with in society. Asian American women are themselves struggling to define who they are as Asians, Americans and women. Some believe the stereotypes while others want no part in them.

Listen to the words of a Japanese American woman, a poet named Joanne Miyamoto, in her poem titled "What Are You?"

When I was young
kids used to ask me
what are you?
I'd tell them what my mom told me
I'm an American
chin chin Chinaman
you're a Jap?
flashing hot inside
I'd go home
my mom would say
don't worry
he who walks alone
walks faster

people kept asking me
what are you?
and I would always answer
I'm an American

they'd say
no, what nationality
I'm an American!
that's where I was born
flashing hot inside
and when I'd tell them what they wanted to
know
Japanese
....Oh, I've been to Japan
I'd get it over with
me they could catalogue and file me
pigeon hole me
so they'd know just how
to think of me
priding themselves
they could guess the difference
between Japanese and Chinese

they had me wishing
I was an American
just like them
they had me wishing I was what I'd
been seeing in movies and on TV
on bill boards and in magazines
and I tried
while they were laws in California
    against us owning land
we were trying to be American
and laws against us intermarrying
    with white people
we were trying to be American
when they put us in concentration camps
we were trying to be American
our people volunteered to fight against
    their own country
trying to be American
when they dropped the atom bomb Hiroshima
    and Nagasaki
we were still trying

finally we made it
most of our parents
fiercely dedicated to give us

a good education
to give us everything theynever had
we made it
now they use us as an example
to the blacks and browns
how we made it
how we overcame
but there was always
someone asking me
what are you?

Now I answer
I'm an Asian
and they say
why do you want to separate yourselves
now I say
I'm Japanese
and they say
don't you know this is the greatest country
   in the world
Now I say in America
I'm part of the third world people
and they say
   if you don't like it here
   why don't you go back

—poem reprinted, from Asian Women,
published by the University of California, Berkeley, 1971.

INDOCHINESE REFUGEES
In the United States

Unlike other Asians in America, most Vietnamese Americans are classified as political refugees and have no significant historical antecedent in this country.

The rapidly expanding influx of Vietnamese to the United States was occasioned by special contemporary conditions. The sudden collapse of the South Vietnamese government in late April 1975 created an outflow of political refugees consisting of high government officials, officers of the South Vietnamese armed forces, persons who had worked for the U.S. government or for American companies, and relatives of American personnel. These 130,000 persons were evacuated on U.S. government airplanes and ships. Many also left in privately controlled vehicles, or in vehicles which had belonged to the South Vietnamese government. Evacuees were taken to the Philippines, Wake Island and Guam enroute to the United States. They were placed in rapidly prepared camps at Camp Pendleton, California; Fort Chaffee, Arkansas; Camp Eglin, Florida; and Camp Indiantown Gap, Pennsylvania. Before they were released, the evacuees had to either show they had the financial means to survive on their own, or had to be sponsored by individuals or various agencies or local groups.

Political upheavals in Southeast Asia also resulted in the establishment of **Kampuchean and Loatian communities in America.**

The governments of Kampuchea and Laos also became Communist in 1975. These two political changes also created an outflow of refugees. Most of the refugees from Kampuchea and Laos escaped across the Mekong River into Thailand. By the summer of 1977, there were 120,000 Indochinese refugees in camps in Thailand. One large group of Laotian refugees consisted of Hmong or Meo tribespeople who feared reprisal from the new Laotian government because many of their members had been recruited by the United States during the war in Vietnam to fight against Communist forces. In the spring of 1978, there were 83,000 Laotian refugees in Thai camps awaiting resettlement. The outflow of refugees has far outpaced the willingness of countries to accept them. To date, by far the largest number has entered the United States. However, today, there are still approximately 300,000 Indochinese refugees in Thailand awaiting resettlement.

The experience of the "Boat People" **is unique in Asian American history.**

The group of refugees who have received the most heartrending news coverage has been the "boat people." These refugees are persons attempting to leave Vietnam by small boats. They either drift on the South China Sea hoping to be picked up by passing ships, or they attempt to make their way to Malaysia, Indonesia and the Philippines, with the hope of being allowed to land. However, they have been refused landing in many instances. It is estimated that one million "boat people" have died at sea. The peak of the "boat people" outflow was in late 1978 and early 1979. It is estimated that two—thirds to three—quarters of the "boat people" are ethnic Chinese who were residing in Vietnam. Many of them were encouraged to leave by the current Vietnamese government which considers them to be undesirable. The Chinese in Vietnam owned many of the small retail businesses in the country. They are considered to be remnants of capitalism. Many of the "boat people" were also prey to persons who set up escape facilities in order to get some of the gold which the ethnic Chinese in Vietnam are reputed to be hoarding. Other "boat people" have left because they find it difficult to live under the political conditions which currently obtain in Vietnam. Pressure by countries in the Association of Southeast Asian Nations which are neighbors of Vietnam has caused the Vietnamese government to reduce the outflow of "boat people."

The Indochinese community in America **is rapidly expanding**

Today there are approximately 400,000 Indochinese refugees in the U.S.* Every month 14,000 are allowed to enter under special legislation.** The intention of the resettlement agencies has been to scatter the refugees as widely as possible. However, the refugees——once they are able to get on their feet——have shown a marked preference to settle in California. Interviews with the refugees indicate they prefer California because of the warm climate, because of the larger number of Asians here, and because they believe it is easier to find jobs in California. Sizeable settlements can also be found in Texas and in the Washington, D.C. area.

*Since the time this article was written, the number of Indochinese refugees living in the United States has increased to more than 748,000.

**It is no longer the case that 14,000 are allowed to enter each month. In fact, yearly admission ceilings——set by the president of the U.S. in congressional consultations——have been decreasing.

This does not mean, however, that the needs of refugees have decreased. Ministry with them is still very much a part of the Lutheran church's total ministry. Updated information about refugee work is available from Lutheran Immigration and Refugee Service, 360 Park Avenue South, New York, NY 10010.

Courtesy of the Natinoal Association for
Pacific and Asian American Telecommunications (NAPAT)

B L A C K S
Our Plight and Our Genius
The Theology and Ethics of Black Lutherans

The Rev. Dr. Albert P. Pero, Jr.

The Rev. Cheryl A. Stewart

It goes without saying that the modern individual exists in a pluralistic world, migrating back and forth between competing and complementary cultures. This pluralization of socially available cultures with all of their differences was of particular importance in the development of the black Lutheran theological component.

It is relatively easy to be a Lutheran in a social situation where one can readily admit one's "significant others" (sociologically speaking) to fellow Lutherans. The story is quite different in a situation where one is compelled to rub shoulders with a variety of "those others" (who might even happen to be of the same "ethos"), where one is saturated with communications that deny, reject or ignore Lutheran ideas, and where one has a difficult time even finding some quiet Lutheran corners in which to withdraw.

This description is among other things one of the dynamics of being black and Lutheran. While the Lutheran church has much to offer a pluralistic society, it must be big enough to accept the different lifestyle which other cultures bring with them. Once we grasp the situation to which the gospel is applied, we also must grasp the inability of people to jump out of their skins. The forces of our immediate situation even when we understand them, because we are social beings and continue to be such even when we become Christians.

Each "ethos" is immediate to God, which is to say that we reject the approach of a gospel which stresses universality apart from particularity. We submit that there is no universality apart from particularity of the gospel. The proclamation is always directed toward humanity not in general but wrapped in all of its cultural diversity.

Lutherans come to the black situation with a gospel of forgiveness and it seems to be read by some blacks as a white ideology. Subsequently, it can be misunderstood or rejected, or it can be accepted by portions of the black community in a way which seems to result in the loss or diminution of their black identity.

Some contemporary black theologians assert that the message is no good, that there is no way for Lutheran theology to make it with black theology. Some contemporary sociologists imply that Christian theology is merely a legitimizer of white values and an alienation of black people.

What about these accusations? Does the Lutheran message do this? Is there something intrinsically wrong with Lutheran theology or the gospel as presented within the classic Lutheran theological law/gospel principle? Could these accusations be true? If there is any truth to what has been said, is it because of the gospel itself or is it because of the way in which the message is brought to the situation?

The tentative hypothesis is that Lutheran theology is situational theology. That is, the law must be related to the situation of the people so that the gospel can free them to live God's life in that situation. An examination of how Lutherans correlate the gospel and the situation will supplement the witness of the church to black people, rather than replace its theological principle.

Furthermore, the Lutheran church has great resources available to speak the word of God to the black situation. But they may not have utilized them fully. Instead they may have either obscured the resources or ignored them.

This paper attempts to demonstrate the crippling effects of white American culture on the attempts of black Americans to do here what all people everywhere must do if they are to develop fully—to find an identity, a sense of worth, to relate to others, to love, to work and to create. From the perspective of Christian ethics as it concerns itself with black people, it appears that the perennial struggle within the American society results in contradictory modes of interaction with the overall situation. An ethical delineation of the areas of experience where pressures are most severe will provide a background for dealing with a necessary clarification of the black situation. The context is a meaningful struggle for survival, struggle for expression and struggle for meaning.

A further perspective will be developed by examining the prevailing attitudes and practices toward black people historically in the Lutheran Church. The twin assumptions of white supremacy and the basic inferiority of black people have been briefly traced in the church's mission work among blacks from the earliest beginnings.

A synthesis of some contemporary material dealing with the characteristics of the black situation might assist us in the analysis. It will go deeper than the surface arguments of integration versus separation. The synthesis will move toward a deeper understanding of the correlation of the gospel to the black situation. Specifically, what is the black situation and how can law and gospel be related to it? This methodology might further enable us to determine whether what has been given as gospel is in fact gospel or a misconception.

Finally, it might help us determine better criteria for Lutheran theology as transmitted to the black situation through the educational process. We trust that the criteria will evoke a need to be used in order to relate law and gospel theology to indigenous cultures effectively. The value of this investigation lies in the synthesis of historical Lutheran theology with the experience of faith among black Christians. The data further seeks criteria to assist pastors, teachers and theologians in the testing of the authenticity of the gospel which they bring to the situation.

A task of this magnitude, then, requires that we allow the sources to speak for themselves. Subsequently readers are allowed to decide for themselves whether the material has accurately stated their viewpoints and formulated an appropriate position.

Basic Understandings

Understanding the basic issues in this work is critical for understanding its rationale and scope. The issues are simultaneously contextual and universal, grappling with Lutheran identity and daring to define blackness beyond Lutheranism. What does it mean to be black and Lutheran within Christian theology? What is the coherence and function of the foundational article of the Lutheran theological system? How do black Christians relate to it?

We shall not attempt to discuss the issues and problems of Lutheran theology and identity, which are vast and formidable. But we shall venture to summarize Lutheran theology and identity, as we shall be using it in this work. The Lutheran identity, which we will advance, will be more useful for the Augsburg Confession. It will be an identity which is more closely akin to the original Lutheran coherence.

Lutheranism as a movement offers to the whole Christian church a proposal of doctrine which posits that we are justified by faith alone. Our Augsburg Confession gives witness to this doctrine, this identity. Given this proposal, instead of black Lutherans asking what a Lutheran is from a denominational point of view, we could ask: what do we have to say to the Lutherans as to the content of the gospel?

Lutheran theology can be summed up most adequately in terms of law and gospel. Law and gospel imply a dialectic process by which a person experiences the demands of the law that finally break through into freedom in the gospel. How the dynamic of the law and gospel is experienced is of the utmost importance. The result is a better understanding of the law and gospel process that can be applied to different contexts/settings with unique content.

The gospel is the story of Jesus, who was delivered for our sins and raised for our justification. This message is of ultimate concern among black people because our ultimate concern is that which determines our black being or non—being. The task of this work, then, is enabling black people to deal with this concern, doing so with all the resources of the world in which they live. What we are attempting to advance is a historical conscience correlated with a gospel perspective.

Furthermore, it has been said that the Lutheran church is a confessing church. If confession is proclamation (preaching) in crisis, then black Lutherans have established many confessions. If confession is proclaiming that "Jesus is Lord" in the face of those who with might, power, and authority in the actions, insist that he is not, then black Lutherans hold forth the banner of Lutheran proclamation in protest of racism in a profound way.

In this sense, it is important to understand ourselves as confessional Lutheran Christians. This is our primary identity, for we do not confess the Lutheran confession. Rather we confess what Lutherans confess, mainly that is "Jesus is Lord." Finally, there is really no such thing as a Lutheran Baptism or a Lutheran Eucharist, nor can we forgive sins in the name of the Lutheran church. We can do so only as servants of the Word. It is this (Word became flesh) that is provocative for this work.

It is to be expected that some Lutherans will ask: Why explicate a theology from the black experience? Is it not true that God is color-blind? That in God there is neither black nor white? This work answers these questions by stating that there can never be a theology in general. It is always theology reflected in a particular community. If "God's approval" were to be placed on white racism, classism, and sexism, Luther himself would probably call it a theology of the anti—Christ. Moreover, in the racist society, God is never color blind. To say this is analogous to saying that God is blind to justice and injustice, to right and wrong, to good and evil.

The appearance of this theological material coming from the experiences of black people with God, within and without Lutheranism, is due to the failure of white Lutheran theologians to relate the gospel of Christ to the pain and suffering of being black men and women in a white racist society of which Lutheranism is a part. It arises from a long historical struggle of black people trying to develop an inclusive church where unity in diversity is celebrated.

This material struggles with a concept called "self—transcendence." In my understanding and research, this concept retains a basic aspect of African understanding prevalent among African—Americans today. Self—transcendence is new—being in reality. It is admittedly a renewed perspective of pneumatology.

However, the Holy Spirit is not so different from our humanity. Indeed, Spirit equals humanity, properly understood. We wrestle not against flesh and blood but against those who are against love, peace, joy, patience, and understanding—the fruits of the Spirit.

Our Plight

Let us suppose that the gospel message and its implications as proclaimed by the Lutheran church have not spoken to the black situation. An examination and clarification of this situation might be beneficial to further investigate this plight, to show how Lutheran theology may be related to it.

The perennial struggle of the black person in a society whose controlling motif is economic and political power results in contradictory modes of interaction with the overall situation. A delineation, then, of the areas of experience where pressures are most severe will provide a background for clarifying the black situation in the context of the struggle for survival, for meaning, for expression and for relevant theology.

There are several reasons why an indigenous black theological perspective is relevant to the universal perspective.

First, Christians are concerned about the truth. The black situation has generally been neglected or badly distorted in our society. Common popular myths prevail as a result. There is the popular myth that Africa is a "dark continent" in which there has never been any culture or social development. There is a myth that black people have never made any significant contribution to history. Christians should not be content to let their views of the present be shaped by false views of the past.

Second, Christians are concerned about persons. People find themselves in relation to the past. The answer to the question "Who am I?" comes largely from our relationship to history. James Baldwin says to the white community, "I am not who you think I am," and he is right. Discovery of who black persons really are can come in large part from discovering who they have become in their historical situation.

Baldwin further indicates that the white man's inability to accept the black person as a person is related to his inability to accept himself. Therefore, the study of the black situation may be revelatory in the white man's effort to understand himself as a person, as well as in his effort to understand the black person as a person.

Third, Christians are concerned about communion or communication as we attempt to correlate the gospel to the black situation. Many attempts at communication between black and white today are phony and superficial because they are attempts to communicate as though history had never occurred. Honest communication must begin by facing the events that have brought our world to its present tragic state. Perhaps as we face these facts together we can begin to discover the real common life as children of God that has so long been denied.

Fourth, for the white community a study of this black historical experience can mean deliverance from false condescension. It will be so if it brings to white persons the discovery that they have as much if not more to receive from black persons as they have to give in the process of "organic union." In short, we must understand black people's past situation, with its religious, political, social and economic formulations, in order to face the present intelligently and bring about a different future. It will be a future in which faith in Christ is as much the pivotal point of life in the black community as in all communities.

Probably the most hideous drama in the last thousand years of human history is the transporting of some ten million human beings out of the dark beauty of Africa to these American shores. It was the rape of a continent seldom, if ever, paralleled in ancient or modern history.

Although African and white Europeans were brought to the English colonies during this period, the Spanish were bringing Africans to their American possessions as early as 1501. By mid—seventeenth century, indentured servitude gave way to slavery. Black folk became the logical source for slavery since whites, insisting upon their rights as Englishmen, could always appeal to the home country or vanish undetected into the white population. Black people, however, had no one to whom they could appeal, and Africa seemed to contain an inexhaustible supply of slaves. Moreover, Blacks, having come from tropical climates, did not die off as easily as Whites when put to work in the tobacco and rice fields of the South.

Slave labor forced from black people for more than two centuries was crucial in the development of industry in the western world. Black people were regarded as property. They were human beings even though they were not recognized as such. The price of this slave society was a combination of self—deception and brutality that ultimately proved as destructive for the whites as it was for the blacks.

The Protestants of North America believed that "all men are created equal and endowed by their Creator with certain inalienable rights to life, liberty and the pursuit of happiness." Such a conscience could only live with slavery and justify it by assigning Blacks a place outside the human race; hence the doctrine of inferiority. The Civil War was the final price of such a doctrine that taught the inferiority of black people.

One of the myths that accompanied this doctrine was the belief that the slave was happy and contented with his lot. This myth of happy Negroes dancing around their plantation cabins gained popularity. But the fact that many blacks escaped from slavery via the underground railroad which led to the passage of Fugitive Slave Laws, and the widespread use of slave patrols on the part of slave masters proved the opposite. Furthermore, the myth of inferiority could never be perpetuated if the slave learned to read and understand the Bible.

It is difficult to determine accurately just how many human beings were the victims of slavery. For over two hundred years in our history, slaves were bought and sold like cattle and families were broken up. Women were violated by their masters, men were denied their manhood, children were torn from their mothers, all without any recourse to protection by the law. At the time of the Civil War only one—eighth of the approximately four million Negroes in the United States were free.

During the Civil War, the dominant theme in the black community was the hope of freedom. Immediately following the war, the preoccupation turned from visions to the hard realities of the new life. By the end of the nineteenth century and in the first decades of the twentieth, a new type of subordination was forced on black people. It was grounded in segregation and accompanied by flagrant denial of their rights, often in the form of terror. This period coincided with a new period of commercialism and expansion in the United States both internally and externally. As this country became more industrialized and wealthy and as it sought both new markets and prestige abroad by an enlightened imperialism, it was often with the veneer of the "white man's burden."

From the limited historical evidence, one would probably say that the beginning of Negro religion in this country runs from 1619 up to the Civil War in 1863. The role of religion was of great importance in the black experience. Black people, having been snatched out of a deep spiritist culture and brought into the white man's strange and cruel world, relied heavily in this early period upon supernaturalism and emotionalism to adjust themselves to perplexing, baffling, staggering, and strange experiences in America.

> The slaves who had been torn from their homeland and kinsmen and their friends and whose cultural heritage was lost, were isolated and broken men, so to speak...not only did religion draw the Negroes into a union with their fellow—men, it tended to break down barriers that isolated them morally from their white master.[22]

Authenticity cannot apply itself to the true function of the black church without taking into serious discussion the black person's disenchantment, the destruction of all family ties, the dehumanization, the rebellion, the struggle for emancipation, and the unique ability to establish unity among the people in communion with God through song.

The black church having such in cohesive unity helps us understand why some whites were so suspicious of black churches such as the African Methodist Episcopal Church organized by Richard Allen.

> During the period of Reconstruction when the Blacks enjoyed a medium amount of freedom, the clergy began to emerge as political leaders. Several of them were elected to Congress. Following the Reconstruction when Negroes were barred in the South from the political life of the community, the church again became the primary stage for any kind of leadership.[23]

The church was the sole institution in which political power was used creatively. In many instances, the church serves today in the same capacity.

Our descriptive analysis leads us to ask, what has it been like to be a black American?

Being Black in America

What is it like to be black in America? Very few white men have tried to find out. One man did, and received a rude shock. John Howard

Griffin, a Southern white newspaperman, shaved his head, darkened the color of his skin and lived as a Negro for a time in the deep South. He found himself exposed to hatred and viciousness. He found that the new color of his skin confined him to a closed world in which there was no future.[24]

As Frazier points out, the word prejudice means "prejudgment in the sense that it is a judgment concerning objects and persons not based upon knowledge or experience."[25]

What is it like to be black in America? Ralph Ellison suggests that the Negro is the "invisible man." Because of prejudice, the white man does not really see the black person as a person. Instead, he sees a figment of his imagination. As Ellison says, "I am invisible simply because people refuse to see me. The invisibility of which I refer occurs because of a peculiar disposition of the eyes of those with whom I come in contact." Ellison reflects on the consequences of being invisible and notes, "You are constantly being bumped against by those of poor vision. Or again, you often doubt if you really exist."[26]

Ellison's comments point up a basic biblical conviction that to be a person depends upon being accepted as a person. This would suggest that if the black person seems inferior to people in the white community, that it is perhaps because Whites have denied the humanity of Blacks rather than because Blacks are inferior.

What is it like to be black in America? Richard Wright suggests that it requires the constant role of deception. Black people must constantly hide their true selves and present the false face that white people want to see. In order to survive, the black person's life must become a deliberate lie. As a friend advised, "When you are in front of white people, think before you act, think before you speak. Your way of doing things is all right amongst our people, but not for white people. They won't stand for it." This advice proved difficult for Richard Wright for, as he put it, "it was simply impossible for me to calculate, to scheme, to act, to plot all the time. I would remember to dissemble for short periods and then I would forget and act straight and human again, not with the desire to harm anybody, but merely forgetting the artificial status of race and class."[27]

The subordinate or inferior role has not come naturally to the black person as some races have tried to suggest. Rather, it is a role that has been forced upon black people in basic violation of their personalities.

The black person in the U.S. has been caught between the natural desire to fulfill one's being as created by God and the unnatural need to fulfill one's being as prescribed by the white society. That is, to be of no consequence or to become "white."

Over the years, black people's growing interest in sociology, history, psychology, psychiatry, theology, and so on, has been accompanied by a suspicion of their concepts and practices. This has been largely due to racism as well as the inability to analyze the situation authentically. "The hostility to modern psychiatry can, in part, be explained by its origins. Founded in Vienna at the turn of the century, it was too often dedicated to upholding the western European value system and gave very little attention to the conditions of oppressed people."[28] While much can be gleaned from Allport, Freud and others, one cannot be fully relevant to a given ethos without prior study of that ethos. "Because of its lack of contact with Asian or African life styles, the accusation of irrelevance is understandable."[29]

The Lutheran church (as we shall see later in this work) "like other institutions in this country, has been guilty of racism,"[30] consequently deserting the rich heritage of its historical correlation of the gospel to the situation. Thus,

> The training of many psychiatrists (as well as theologians) has made it impossible for them to distinguish deviant behavior from what is, in fact, different behavior. It is not sick for a black man to feel that a white policeman might shoot him for the slightest wrong move, although it probably would be considered a sign of mental imbalance in a white man.[31]

Because theology, psychiatry, sociology, and others have been unresponsive to the needs of blacks, some have moved to other mediums such as healers, advisors, and readers. Black people "view Christianity as alien," and "recognize that the Church has played a large role in their oppression. Today, many black youth are rejecting the white man's religion together with the white man's psychology."[32]

If we are to progress, present theological, sociological and psychiatric practices must be reexamined and purged of their cultural bias. If theologians are to correlate the discipline of psychology and psychiatry with their analysis of the black situation in order to determine the "proper" use of the law/gospel dialectic, they will have to take seriously Gordon Allport's analysis of the psychology of personality by examining all the "norms" from which personalities are formed.

Black behavior is labeled as "paranoid" by Whites. "Black people don't imagine they are being persecuted by whites; they are being persecuted by whites."[33] The astute theologian not only affirms this but points the accusing finger also to the white person who is guilty before God. And as we pointed out in our historical analysis, "although they (whites) have little historical evidence for the claim, whites developed a paranoid fear of potential black violence to justify their creation of an entire system of racial segregation and discrimination."[34]

"Psychologically speaking, blacks do not have the attributes of a paranoid people. To the contrary, they have been patient, generous, non-violent with faith not exclusively in Christ but, in the ultimate goodness of whites."[35] Thus according to Poussaint, "culturally determined paranoia" is a misnomer when applied to Blacks.

Even some white psychiatrists in their attempts to maintain a false sense of superiority have exaggerated theories that Blacks have self—hate and a negative sense of self—esteem.[36]

The entire criminal element within the United States can be said to be spreading like a cancer throughout the society. The black community has not been free of its tentacles. "It is an ugly fact that the American cultural experience has taught us that crime and violence is a way to success and manhood."[37] Not much research is necessary to establish the fact that television and movie folklore reinforce for the society that violence is the key to resolving problems. "The American ethos is one of self-reliance, rugged individualism and outdoing one's neighbor. There is evidence to suggest that this atmosphere encourages people to be violent; suspicious and at odds with one another."[38]

Towards Black Liberation: A Paradigm

Another black psychologist, William E. Cross, has established a paradigm toward the development of a psychology of black liberation.[39] A very brief correlation of his process should demonstrate the importance of obtaining this kind of analysis of the black situation before applying the law/gospel dynamic. The five stages of the process are:

1. *Pre—encounter.* This means the status quo of racism, a victim and a victimizer (struggle).

2. *Encounter.* This means a jolting discovery of oppression or racism as it affects a person. This also centers itself in individualism and other similar processes (struggle).

3. *Immersion—Emersion.* People in this level are potentially violent. They are concerned about control, power. One of the major facets of this stage or level of awareness is that of name—calling (new insight).

4. *Internalization.* This takes the form of nothing more than traumatic frustration (resignation——new insight).

5. *Commitment.* Commitment to long—term goals of changing oppressive systems and institutions (new interpretations).

Questions for Correlating the Law/Gospel Dynamic

Parallel Case Studies

1. How then would you counsel someone within the framework of these levels of awareness?

2. Is it possible to create the climate or situation to move a given person along the stages of development? If so, what kind of climate or situation should be created?

3. What kind of theology would you apply to each state or level of awareness? (law/gospel).

4. Who is to do the counseling?

5. What stage are you in?

6. Can you think of a congregation or individual that went through any of these five stages? (Malcolm X and Eldridge Cleaver are examples of individuals who have gone through each of the five levels of awareness.)

The following two parallel case studies constitute a brief, sketchy overview of the responses of two ministers (one black, the other white). They were encouraged to look for clues that might assist them in developing a counseling system to help in moving others along these stages of development. This material is based on the article, "The Negro—to—Black Conversion Experience" by William E. Cross. A reading of that article is essential for a fuller understanding of what follows.

Pre—encounter (struggle)

Black Pastor

I was taught through formal and informal systems of education that black was evil, bad, that my origin began with slavery; that education was the thing that could better my self—image; that assimilation was the only answer to humanity. It offended me to even think of the word black. I went through the seminary and became the ideal pastor.

White Pastor

I, too, was trained to view black people as inferior; in addition I was trained to be superior. Everything around me helped to support the fact that my ancestors were the most moral, intellectual and enlightened ones. When I graduated, I was free to work anywhere in the world.

Encounter (struggle)

But the riots in the U.S. hurled me into conflict with what I had been taught. The thing that did it for me was my being arrested for trying to prevent a black youth from looting a store. Instead, I was arrested for so—called looting with him. This incident coupled with dialogue with other Blacks caused me to reinterpret the world. Black was now beautiful. I was filled with guilt for having thought of my people in such a degrading way. I had been deceived by the system; the result: rage.

Yes, but I was shocked to see on T.V. Dr. King killed. This did not move me to action until a fellow pastor called me that evening with the comment: "He got what he deserved." This moved me to anger and to the query: "Is it right to kill a man who is non-violent in his approach to human rights?" Moreover, I was filled with guilt over the fact that I had looked upon Blacks as being less than human. I had been pro-grammed, brain-washed.

Immersion—Emersion (New insight)

It was at this point that I immersed myself into the com-munity of blackness. I read book upon book about my people. I studied black history. I became proud of myself and my people so much that I began to write black plays for the youth of my church. I joined several activist groups, demonstrating, marching in open confrontation with the police. I delighted in dehumanizing whites with such names as (honky, pig, white devil). As I matured in the movement, I learned that I must move toward power and control.

I took another call to a parish in the black community. Here I experienced much de-humanization and anger from the Blacks. They told me to go back home to the white community. I, of course, felt frustrated, rejected and lonely. But slowly I began to understand through a few Blacks con-stantly ministering to me that I must do more than just feel sorrow. I must actually prove to them that I had changed. So, I too decided to demonstrate and join in he struggle of the oppressed. This opened my eyes even more. I continued on this path until my wife challenged my constant absence from home with her own ultimatums. I subsequently decided to work with my own people with the objective of exposing their racism.

Internationalization (Resignation—new insight)

My high goals of power and control met with much opposition and traumatic frustration from my own people. I felt like dropping the entire thing. Had I not begun to teach school and there discovered a plan whereby I could change some of the conditions of others, I would have despaired.

It was not long that I discovered the victimizer could not minister to the victim. This made me reach the nadir of despair. Had it not been for my being introduced to a black historian who introduced me to the concepts of non-western philosophy, I probably would have left the ministry.

Commitment (New interpretations)

I have been committed to this plan and others which assist in changing systems of oppression to institutions of freedom.

I, too, have been involved in a plan to run for political office and if elected, change things which I find are hurting people.

While the end result of this learning paradigm is not an understanding of law/gospel, the illustration of correlating it with the model built from Luther, Westberg, Schmidt, and the proposed learning model results in a person who comes to faith, or is renewed in faith and thus enabled to live in love. When persons are Christians, they live in love in the structures of life. They call humanity to responsible living in those structures (first use of the law) but it is not until such persons recognize God's demand (a demand that cannot be fulfilled) that they are open to the gospel. If the gospel comes to such people, they come to faith and can begin to live in love.

In the meantime, Christians also experience the judgment of God upon their failures and experience the renewing power of the gospel, that is, they go through the learning model again and again. The assumption here is that the psychologist does not analyze the problem in depth. The consequence is that the psychologist ends up with both a symptomatic analysis and symptomatic solutions. The attempt here is to illustrate how this indigenous process can be used with different content and correlated to the other models of this paper.

1.   Pre—Encounter. The human situation at first glance is "racism" but the problem is worse than that. It is a situation of both black and white people confined to a situation of nomological existence: a relationship of God and humanity in law. Racism in America is a threat to practically every facet of human existence. While the nomological order of Whites governing Blacks is preserved externally, it is unable to provide a defense against internal law—breaking. There is a minimal amount of struggle and more of an acceptance of the status quo of a racist society.

2.   Encounter. The Encounter is more than a discovery of human beings oppressing one another as they engage in fear, anxiety, anger and murder. It is, theologically, an encounter with God the Judge. It is the dimension of the law which causes Anfechtung. The fanaticism for finding salvation through economic and political power leave both black and white not with a gracious God but with the continued accusation of God's law.

3.   Immersion—Emersion. At first glance the solution to the problem appears to be a faith in power—black power, white power, power of the gun, money and race. This for some is the new insight, but a deeper theological analysis portrays that this could not be its new insight theologically because basic injustices continue. It is not a wonder that the fourth stage of the Cross model begins with frustration?

4.   Internalization. This stage takes the form of frustration and despair, given the continued chaos. Theologically, this would be analyzed as the demands of God, which become so sharp that we give up. We would commit suicide were it not for the gospel. Through Christ, then, God speaks a word of salvation and liberation which summons faith from human beings caught in the problems of racism and their illusory faith solutions. Christ frees us to live within the structures of existence as the people of a forgiving Lord. Faith called into being by the word of the gospel is joyfully received by Blacks and Whites as the good news of a new identity and a new

community. It is here that faith is lived out in a tension of hope maintained by a constant renewal of the gospel.

The Black Experience

Black people are a unique people. At first, it may seem that there is nothing new about that statement; white people have always said that Blacks are different from Whites. But they have also put a value on that difference, saying that Blacks are different but also inferior.

This message has been communicated in all kinds of ways through political, religious and social media and institutions from the period of slavery to the present. It has been reinforced over and over again. Therefore, when we say that black people are unique, we need to differentiate what we are saying from what the white racist says. We are not saying that there are biological or basic personality differences between Blacks and Whites. But there is a different experience of lifestyle. Blacks have grown up and developed in a different environment.

Cobbs and Grier put it this way:

> The American black man is unique, but he has no special psychology or exceptional genetic determinants. His mental mechanisms are the same as other men. If he undergoes emotional conflict, he will respond as neurotically as his white brother. In understanding him we return to the same reference point, since all other explanations fail. We must conclude that much of the pathology we see in black people had its genesis in slavery. The culture that was born in that experience of bondage had been passed from generation to generation. Constricting adaptations developed during some long ago time continue as contemporary character traits. That they are so little altered attests to the fixity of the black—white relationship, which has seen little change since the birth of this country.[40]

So the uniqueness of Blacks comes from what has been called the black condition or the black experience.

Leronne Bennett, in his book, *The Challenge of Blackness*, defines blackness as "that universe of values and attitudes and orientations which rise like dew from the depths of our ancestral experience and pulls us toward the distant shores of our destiny."[41] The black experience is a certain dark joy, celebrating the triumph of humanity over a degrading social order. The black experience includes cultural styles, social patterns, and behavior of Blacks that have been developed in order to cope with the racism in America.

Leon W. Chestang, in a paper, "Character Development in a Hostile Environment," characterized the black experience as one of social injustice, inconsistency and personal impotence.[42] The social injustice aspect refers to denial of legal rights experienced by Blacks in the United States since the beginning. Social inconsistency refers to the disparity between what white Americans have said about America, and what they have done to Blacks despite what they have said. These inconsistencies have been captured quite well in a poem by Langston Hughes.

> I swear to the Lord
> I still can't see
> Why democracy means
> Everybody but me.

One of the clearest examples of the institutionalization of these inconsistencies can be seen in a comparison between the Dred Scott decision and the Declaration of Independence. The Declaration of Independence said:

> We hold these truths to be self—evident: that all men are created equal; that they are endowed by their creator with certain unalienable rights; that among them is life, liberty and the pursuit of happiness.

But the Dred Scott decision countered

> too clear for dispute, that the enslaved African race were not intended to be included, and formed no-part of the people who framed and adopted this declaration; for if the language, as understood in that day, would embrace them, the conduct of the distinguished men who framed the Declaration of Independence would have been utterly and flagrantly inconsistent with the principles they asserted; and instead of the sympathy of mankind . . . they would have deserved and received universal rebuke and reprobation.

The framers of the Dred Scott Decision knew that they were on sound ground with white Americans. They were well aware that the early drafts of the Declaration of Independence contained a clause objecting to the imposition of slavery in the colonies by the English. They also knew that the clause was taken out of the final version because they were afraid of alienating Southern support. America's practice has always been inconsistent with what it preached when it came to Blacks. The inconsistencies are summed up in the words, "Blacks have no rights that Whites are bound to respect."[43]

Another characteristic of the black experience is impotence, the powerlessness felt by Blacks as they try to effect change in their lives.

The eminent psychiatrist Alvin F. Poussaint offers a telling example from personal experience: in Jackson, Mississippi, while leaving his office with his black secretary one day, he heard a white policeman should "hey boy, come here." Somewhat bothered,

> I retorted, I'm no boy." He rushed at me, inflamed, and stood towering over me, snorting, "What did you say, boy?" Quickly he frisked me and demanded, "What's your name, boy?" Frightened, I replied, "Dr. Poussaint, I am a physician." He angrily chuckled and hissed, "What's your first name, boy?" When I hesitated he assumed a threatening stance and clenched his fist, as my heart palpitated, I muttered in profound humiliation, "Alvin." He continued his psychological brutality, bellowing, "Alvin, the next time I call you, you come right away, you hear." I hesitated. "You hear me, boy?" My voice trembling with helplessness, but following my instinct for self—preservation, I murmured, "Yes, sir," Now fully satisfied that I had performed in acquiescence to my boy status, he dismissed me with, "Now boy, go on and get outta here."[44]

This incident clearly illustrates the impotency of the black experience on a personal level.

There is also group impotence. A study conducted by the Urban League showed that while Blacks comprise forty percent of Chicago's population, they hold less than one percent of the decision—making positions in major institutions, including business, social welfare and education.[45] What is true of Chicago is true generally across the land. Therefore, Blacks are not only impotent as individuals, but also as a group.

James H. Cone also gives us some characteristics of the black experience, in philosophical and theological terms. He describes the experience as an existential absurdity.[46] Cone says that black persons first awaken to the face of America and feel the sharp contradiction between things the way they are and the way they ought to be. They recognize the inconsistency between their view of themselves as human beings and America's description of them as things, and their immediate reaction is a feeling of absurdity. The absurd is basically

> what a man recognizes as disparity between what he hopes for and what seems in fact to be. He yearns for some measure of an orderly and a rational world. He is oppressed by the disparity between the universe as he wishes it to be and the way he sees it.[47]

Cone speaks of the black experience in terms of oppression by a white society. Still others have simply described it as Blacks being victimized by Whites who are guilty of attitudinal and institutional racism. Racism, according to this definition, is any attitude or activity which subordinates a person because of color, and then rationalizes that subordination by attributing to that person undesirable biological, psychological, social or cultural characteristics.

This has happened with Blacks in the United States. They have been victimized by Whites who have subordinated them. This, then, is the black experience and that experience makes Blacks unique.

Many people will try to point out that this experience is not uniquely black. They say that what I am describing is an experience shared by all who are at the lowest place in our social scale. One has to concede that this is partially true. Indians, Spanish—speaking people, Asians and women, both black and white, have had this experience. But there are a number of other things that must be said about this.

First, we need to be careful lest we fall into the trap of what has been called attenuation: that is, the endemic tendency of Americans to see less and less difference between one thing and anything else. While one has to guard against making too much of differences one also has to guard against minimizing all differences.

Second, while it is true that other people in America have been and are being victimized by the system, Blacks have been victimized for a very specific reason; they have been victimized because they are black.

In addition, even though the research has been quite meager in this area, a number of studies provide "evidence of a qualitative difference" between the black and the white child, even when living conditions are held constant, that is, family income, neighborhood, and others. In fact, as the research of Deutsch and Lott, among others, points out, no matter how carefully one may seek to equate groups, qualitative differences will emerge. The white and the black child, though living on contiguous blocks, do not live in the same world.[48]

Black Character and Personality

One of the results of the black experience as we have evidenced is the impact this experience has had on black character and personality. No serious student of the situation will deny that Blacks have developed certain character traits and unique behaviors, which are uniquely black, in an effort to survive in this racist society. Gordon Allport talks about this impact on personality in the following:

What would happen to your own personality if you heard it said over and over again that you were lazy, a simple child of nature, expected to steal, and had inferior blood. Suppose this opinion were forced on you by the majority of your fellow—citizens. And suppose nothing you could do would change this opinion—because you happen to have black skin.[49]

Where did these character traits and unique behaviors come from? There have been basically two schools of thought on this question. One school has attempted to show that some of these traits resulted from the survival of Africanism among Blacks. Among those scholars are Melville J. Herskovits and W.E. B. DuBois.[50]

Other scholars reject this position and state that the behavior and character traits of Blacks result from the way Blacks were socialized into the American scene. These scholars suggest that nothing, or at best very little, of Africanism survived in American Blacks. In their view Africanism was largely erased through the process of slavery. They hold that because of contact and interaction with Whites, Blacks adopted and adapted the culture of white America so that what one sees is a manifestation of the mediation and synthesis of two cultures. Among the scholars who hold this view are E. Franklin Frazier and John Hope Franklin.

Cobbs and Grier speak rather forcefully on this point:

Traits of character and patterns of behavior that appear more often in black people than in other groups can all be traced to various aspects of life in America. Cultural anthropologists have searched intensively and interminably and have found no contemporary evidence for the persistence of African patterns of culture. The experience of slavery was unbelievably efficient in effacing the African and producing the American Negro. As a result, the cultural and characterological patterns developed by American Negroes provide a unique picture of a people whose history was destroyed and who were offered in its stead a narrow ledge of soil on which to live and grow and nurture children. All that is uniquely Negro found its origin on these shores and provides a living document of black history in America.[51]

Our research demonstrates that new tools of research are constantly being developed, and one has every reason to believe that these will be refined even more. Until scholars have used these new tools to examine the depth of the black psyche and compare it with the psyche of Africans, the question of African survivalism in character traits and behavior of Blacks will have to remain an open question.

But one thing is sure: research has shown that environment influences social functions, behavior and character traits in a powerful way. Most psycho—social theorists, while pointing out the influence of what is inherited from one's parents, also concede that environment plays an important role in the development or personality, behavior and character. Sociocultural theorists point to the same thing. In the case of Blacks, one can study the work if Allison David and John Dolland to substantiate this.[52]

What are some of the character traits and patterns of behavior that appear more often in Blacks than in other groups? Cobbs and Grier list the following: "The black family as an extended family, the ability of Blacks to divorce themselves emotionally from an object, the streak of hedonism and the capacity for joy, drinking more, dancing more, loving more."[53] While they recognize that these characteristics are often used as stereotypes, they hold that there is a grain of truth in them. These traits and behavior patterns are prevalent in Blacks because of the impact of the American ethos on their culture.

Another factor affecting black character, development and social function is the fact that they have been denied full participation in the dominant culture——despite the fact they have accepted and internalized the values of the dominant culture. Their behavior is circumscribed and conditioned. As a result, black people have developed what has been called a "duality of response." (We shall later look at this duality theologically)

Andrew Billingsley, in his book, *Black Families in White America*,[54] states the same idea in somewhat different language. He says that Blacks have been forced to live in two environments: the nurturing environment and the sustaining environment. In the former, Blacks find their being; in the latter, they are involved in matters of survival, more often than not in a hostile society.

In a nurturing environment, the factors that give Blacks their being are their families, their community, their norms, values and tradition. They receive their basic training in this environment as to how to survive in the sustaining environment. They are able to develop and operate in an expressive way. They are free to be who and what they are in relationship with their peers.

In their sustaining environment, on the other hand, they must be concerned about survival needs, goods and services, political power and economic resources. In short, they must be concerned about factors that make it possible for them to live a reasonably successful life in both environments.

To a large extent, what is said here is true of all people. The difference is that persons in the American white community are better able (though not completely) to merge the nurturing and the sustaining environment. These two are brought closer together so that persons can respond in either environment in much the same way. Blacks on the other hand must respond differently in the two environments in order to survive, Relationships in the sustaining environment are filled with risks for the black person, because any attempt to develop expressively may be rejected by Whites. At worse the individual may be excluded from that particular environment completely.

So in the sustaining environment one has to develop what scholars call instrumental relationships, in which one's real feelings must be hidden. One develops feelings of distrust and suspicion and manipulates others in order to survive. In this environment the black person operates from what has been called a depreciated character; that is, the goal is to survive, and to succeed at all costs. This may mean relating to others as things.

Another plight that Blacks face is oftentimes what is learned in the nurturing environment about how to survive in the sustaining environment can cause conflict. The nurturing environment may place a high value on one particular social response, while the sustaining environment may place a low value on it.

This becomes especially complicated when survival in the sustaining environment depends on a different behavior than the one learned in the nurturing environment. It becomes even more complicated in that if Blacks use survival tactics that Whites value highly in the sustaining environment, they will be rejected. And if they fail to use these valued behaviors, they are still penalized. Blacks find themselves in a damned—if—you—do and damned—if—you—don't situation. We will use two examples to illustrate this point. Both have direct application to those involved in the teaching of black children.

The first illustration is the characteristic of self—assertiveness and aggressiveness. In the white society, where the nurturing environment and the sustaining environment are merged, self—assertiveness and aggressiveness are well understood and are highly valued for white persons. Whites are expected to have these traits. Blacks get double signals. In the past, they knew that they had to be passive and non—aggressive in their sustaining environment in order to make it. They were taught this in their nurturing environment. However, for Blacks to be self—assertive and aggressive in the sustaining environment has in the past and even to the present, meant to be killed or to be destroyed.

Black parents knew this and began very early to teach their children to behave nicely and say "yes sir" and "no sir" when the white man talked to them. Black males especially were told to keep their self—assertiveness and aggressiveness under control, lest they get in trouble with society. Parents taught this to their children by word and action.

Even religion was used to develop non—aggressiveness and passiveness in Blacks. Blacks were not to show too much aggression, because by showing too much aggression, they would be destroyed.

Benjamin Mays[55] undertook a study on the Negros' concept of God and discovered that many Blacks have a concept of God that is compensatory, and that a growing number of Blacks conceived of a God concerned about social reconstruction. The compensatory and the social reconstruction natures of God grew in parallel up until the second World War. Although the social reconstruction God was not talked about very much, He was there. Religion however, ceased to have a social reconstruction God until the civil rights movement in the late fifties and the early sixties. That there was a God who rewarded people in the after—life then became the rule of thumb, and black intellectuals began to do something that they had not done before: to develop a skeptical understanding of God. All of this illustrates the fact that self—assertiveness and aggressiveness is a value Blacks taught their children and lived by in order to survive in the sustaining environment.

This is not as true today as it once was. But we are still confronted with a confused picture. Whites say that Blacks ought to be self—assertive and aggressive and consider it a negative character trait that they are not. One wonders if white attitudes have changed on this point.

There are a number of factors to keep in mind when we discover the way Blacks respond or behave as a result of the black experience. While Blacks share common experiences with others, they respond differently, as well as all other people do, even to the same stimuli. For instance, all Blacks have been forced in one way or another to submerge their aggressiveness. They do it in a number of different ways, depending on factors such as socioeconomic level, family life, past relationships with Whites, and geographical location.

Some suppress aggressiveness and substitute an opposing emotional attitude—compliance, docility or a "loving" attitude. Sometimes rage can be denied completely and replaced by a compensatory happy—go—lucky attitude, flippancy or—a mechanism extremely popular among Negroes ——"being cool." Or the aggression may be channeled into competitive sports, music, dance. Another legitimate means of channeling rage is to identify with the oppressor and put all one's energy into striving to be like him. It is also legitimate and safe for the oppressed to identify with someone like themselves who, for one reason or another, is free to express rage directly at the oppressor. Still another technique is to replace the rage with a chronic resentment and stubbornness toward white people—a chip on the shoulder.

The varied responses from Blacks have caused considerable confusion in both the black and the white community. This demonstrates the urgency for developing a psychological analysis from an indigenous perspective. In our analysis of the psychological aspects of the black experience we have established that, for the most part, this discipline until recently has been guilty of an irrelevant analysis of the black experience partially due to its origins and to its inability to separate itself from the racism so prevalent in America.

There is an increasing appreciation of the richness of the various cultural heritages in America on the part of black psychologists and psychiatrists. White Lutheran involvement in ending exclusionary practices in this discipline, as well as others, will convince the youth of our sincerity and prepare them to approach. Blacks in the larger society without prejudice, and to utilize their studies as foundational sources to education.

As pastors, teachers and lay people we must try to develop emotionally and psychologically healthy people in a society that is basically racist. A black perspective is indispensable to this process. "Sesame Street," the educational television program, while useful in teaching humanitarian values, needs a counterpart in theology, to assist the young to understand at the earliest age God's multi—ethnic society.

Theological and Ethical View of the Black Situation

Sobered by the failure of the old civil rights movement in the North—and made wiser by the inter—racial confrontations which have occurred over the last several years in the academic disciplines—we approach the problem of correlating the gospel to the black situation, ecclesiastically relative to the black/white relationship within the one church of Christ. Black Christians in predominantly white denominations know well that the real question is not whether these churches can become truly integrated on Sunday morning, but whether in the next twenty—five to fifty years, these churches will have any meaningful contact with black people at all! If that question can be answered affirmatively we must ask how that contact will contribute to the dignity and humanity of both black and white people in a time of revolutionary change.

It is not merely segregation or integration that is at stake today. It is rather the question of the viability of the Christian church in the United

States—and perhaps in Western civilization. It is the question of whether or not this church can any longer encompass within it the masses of nonwhite persons who make up the majority of the peoples of the earth, without undergoing radical changes in its understanding of its purpose in the world vis—a—vis robbed, subjugated, and excluded peoples; without dismantling its organizational structures for mission; and without bringing to an end its basic conformity to European theological traditions and Anglo—Saxon styles of life and structures of value.

Specifically, the Lutheran church cannot proceed through this period of crisis as a viable and relevant institution without an ability to correlate the gospel and its unique content with differing situations. This means a radical change in its spiritual and physical relationship to black Christians—most of whom are in all black churches—and to the black community as a whole.

Looking back to the seventeenth and eighteenth centuries, we are amazed by the ease with which American Christians used the institution of religion to protect a double standard of human justice that suited their economic self—interest. No amount of scholarly research and eloquence by white church historians about the "deep sympathy and solicitude" the Christian slaveholder had for his slaves, or about the zeal with which the major denominations threw themselves into the task of evangelizing the slave population after the Revolution, can make us forget that the churches themselves excluded black persons from the very freedoms they justified for white men on the basis of Christian faith.

What of Lutheranism with its confessional law/gospel approach? The Lutheran church cannot be exempt from the prevailing racist attitudes and practices toward black people in the nineteenth century. It, too, can be characterized as assuming white supremacy and inferiority of black people. This can best be empirically verified in the church—wide mission work among Blacks historically.

The Lutheran church, in its correlation of the gospel to the black situation, accepted and condoned the values, mores and life style of Protestant America in the nineteenth century, operating racist, segregated churches and schools. While we can perceive the obvious distinction of the gospel in its correlation to the black situation with such stated racist attitudes, God in forgiveness nonetheless calls upon his people to break down the barrier of separation in the face of the white supremacy assumption still operative in the world.

Therein lies the core of moral corruption in the American churches including Lutherans today and the kernel of American racism. The churches originally found it expedient to separate love and justice where black people were concerned, and that attitude prevailed in the end. It has caused many Blacks to assume that something is wrong with Lutheran theology and the gospel which it brings to their situation. But in actuality, Lutherans have misrepresented the gospel and the meaningful way in which the confessors correlated it to their situation.

What Lincoln might have said was that the war was a test to determine whether this nation or any nation, conceived in liberty and dedicated to the proposition that all men are created equal, could extend those same ideals to black men as well as to white men and still endure. That test has not yet been determinatively made. What was guaranteed to the freedman in the amendments to the Constitution and the early civil rights laws has never been satisfactorily delivered, and the nation still endures half slave and half free. We still face the test!

Likewise, church integration has always been a one—way Street. Everything black was subordinate and inferior and had to be given up for everything white. The white church, in its accommodation and bondage to white middle—class society, attempted to make the black person and the black church over in its own image. It tried to force the black community into the mold of the white society, which was conceived to be the nearest thing on earth to the kingdom of God in Heaven.

The black churches, which were "exiled" from the white Lutheran, Methodist and Baptist denominations in the late eighteenth and early nineteenth centuries, borrowed heavily from the white churches that had first evangelized them and ordained their clergy. However, these black churches were able to develop their own styles of life and their own institutions. An authentic black culture and religion were germinated. Whatever may be said of the deficiencies or excesses of their preaching and their expressions of Christianity, they were the preeminent expressions of the yearning for freedom and dignity. They were expressions of a people who had been introduced to a religion, but who had been excluded from all but the most demanding aspect of the cultural mold of that religion.

On the other hand, the black churches which remained a part of the main line white denominations were exiled from participation in the main line culture. They were obliged to substitute whatever they held of their own for a system of white cultural and religious values. Thus a system developed in the black church and community that could only be a poor facsimile of the "real" thing—a second—class culture for second—class Christians.

Although white denominations have made a lasting contribution to these churches and communities by establishing hundreds of churches, schools, and colleges throughout the nation, especially in the South, it must nevertheless be conceded that as long as these institutions remain under white control they remain unable to interpenetrate the white cultural accretion with a distinctive black ingredient as a viable component of the American ethos. At best, they were the objects of a benevolent paternalism and either atrophied or were smothered to death in the avid embrace of the great white father. In such a situation, it was inevitable that a kind of cynicism would develop on both sides.

The problem the "whitenized" black churches have today is how to recover their own self—respect by demythologizing the white cultural "bag" through which the faith was transmitted to them and in which they have curled themselves up so comfortably. In so doing, they may discover that the essence of the Christian faith not only transcends ultimately the ethnocentric culture of Whites, but that of Blacks as well; that this Christ, in whom there is neither Jew nor Greek, bond nor free, male nor female, is also neither black nor white.

Indeed, in liberating itself against the suburban captivity of the white church, the "whitenized" black churches may be able to illuminate a theme from the left wing of the Protestant Reformation. The American experience has made this theme increasingly opaque—namely, that while the church is not permitted to create its own culture alongside the secular, it does stand in a dialectical relationship to culture—more often in opposition than accommodation—as its most severe critic and reformer rather than its champion and celebrant.

This possibility rests upon what may at first appear to be a contradictory position, but is in fact a necessary concession to the perverted reality of the black person's religious situation in America. Before the "whitenized" black churches can immerse themselves into the mainstream of the church and perform their critical and reformatory role in relation to the total culture, these churches must immerse themselves in a black theology and a black culture. They have repudiated both of these in the past, but nevertheless these churches have a peculiar responsibility for them.

Is this to say that the Christian faith as viewed through the black theology model is but yet another expression of an ethnocentric religion of culture? To this question, we must today give a qualified affirmative answer. Qualified, because what we are seeking in the posture of black religion is temporary and transitional—a way of correcting the errors of the past and preparing the ground for the future. But we must insist that if the Christian church is to become a dynamic influence in the black community which will continue to be beleaguered by white racism, it must become not only a religious institution, but a community organization. It must develop and embrace a theology not only as a defense against the racism of the white church and white culture, but as a necessary alternative to black people in the flight from dehumanizing effects of whiteness. Is it any wonder that black Christians are resisting easy and unexamined black and white relationships?

This is a hard saying that will not be readily accepted by our white Christian brethren. We have accepted from their hands a religion devoid of an ethic relevant to our real situation and a culture in which we were never permitted to participate on equal terms. But now we must stand back from them to reassess our relationship to our own people and to the hostile society within which the white church continues to live in servile accommodation and for whose sake white Christians have betrayed us—their black brothers in Jesus Christ. We must stand back and be in a strategic exodus from this unequal engagement, this degrading, debilitating embrace, until we have recovered our own sense of identity, our true relationship to the people we serve, and until the white church is ready to enter into that partnership of life and mission enabled to renew the whole church of Christ.

Black Theology and the Black Church

There is need, then, for Christian theology to address itself to the experiences of black people and a black theology, "that theology which arises out of the need to articulate the significance of black presence in a hostile white world. It is black people reflecting religiously on black experience, attempting to redefine the relevance of the Christian gospel for their lives."[56]

More specifically, black theology is "the theological explication of the blackness of black people." It explains in a religious content what it is to be black in a white world, and what black people should do about this situation. The study of black theology shows black people that Christ himself was for the liberation of the oppressed (a concept that many white theologians have omitted).

From these definitions, would one say black theology is necessary? When Whites studied theology, they wrote under the assumption that Blacks did not exist as a people, but were property. Reuben Sheares states, "The role or status of Blacks in relation to the gospel or white theology was that of an outsider, perhaps lower than that of a heathen or an infidel."[57] Maybe it can be explained that white theology justified the oppression of black people. They propagated the idea that God created Blacks to be inferior to Whites.

In days of slavery Blacks were placed beyond or outside of white theology. They were not accepted in the fullness of the faith. Therefore, in order for religion to be significant to them, Blacks withdrew from the theology and the church that served to transform or convert them into sub beings. "The independent black church emerged as a protest—a protest against the racist theology and the racist ecclesiology of the church in America."[58]

The church of the slave era was an institution of survival. They were in a hostile land surrounded by a hostile people with no way out. The church gave them the hope of a better day (heaven) and a place to release the anxieties of the preceding week. "It enabled black people to survive, to function, to maintain some degree of sanity and hope: to preserve some semblance of pride and of self; to protest in the midst of a hostile environment until, in the fullness of time, alternatives, options and strategies for dealing with the questions of freedom, justice and survival became feasible."[59]

Now Blacks are emphasizing freedom on earth, and not in the hereafter. The black church no longer emphasizes survival, but liberation. Is liberation today as important as survival was in the slave era? "The biblical God is the God who is involved in the historical process for the purpose of human liberation, and to know Him is to know what He is doing in historical events as they are related to liberation of the oppressed."[60] "The purpose of black theology is to place the actions of black people toward liberation in the Christian perspective, showing that Christ himself is participating in the black struggle for freedom."[61] It also deals with the fact that God is the liberator of the oppressed. Therefore, the importance of black theology is apparent.

The greatest movement of black liberation should come out of the church, for that is where one finds the majority of black people who still believe that one can do all things with the support of God. Thus, the black church and black theology are unifying factors for the accomplishment of black liberation.

Black theology is significant not first because it is black or imaginative or ingenious—but because it is biblically, historically, and theologically authentic. Properly understood, the powerful impact of contemporary black theology, together with an appreciation of the meaning of the black experience in American history, provides one with a model for a theological revolution in this time.

Briefly stated, black theology insists that God intends for people to be free and whole, and that Jesus participated in the life of an oppressed people to help free them and to affirm God's identification with his own suffering creation. Black theology contends that God exists where people hurt; and indeed the meaning of hurt, oppression, and injustice has been experienced to an inordinate degree by people in this country and in the world who are not white.

Black theology is not new. When Richard Allen led Blacks out of St. George's Church in Philadelphia after repeated indignities against them and formed the black Bethel Church in 1794, he was acting theologically. The black churches were theological when they risked everything to form solid links in the Underground Railroad to freedom. This theology has been conceived and transmitted in the life of black people and the black church in a largely oral tradition. What is new is its relatively recent articulation by a number of mostly young black theologians.

James H. Cone insists that his material is first of all a theology of liberation, committed to freeing God's people from oppression, and that blackness is both a concrete instance of and an ontological symbol for the condition of oppression. Such an understanding is not wishful racial thinking, but is authoritatively biblical. This is illustrated in Cone's discussion of the primacy of the liberation theme in both the Old and New Testaments:

> In the Old Testament, the liberation theme stands at the center of the Hebrew view of God. Throughout Israelite history, God is known as He who acts in history for the purpose of Israel's liberation from oppression. This is the meaning of the Exodus from Egypt, the Covenant at Sinai, the conquest and settlement of Palestine, the United Kingdom and its division, and the rise of the great prophets and the second exodus from Babylon... Israel's savior is God himself, whose sovereign rule is guiding the course of human history, liberating the oppressed from the oppressors.

> The theme of liberation in the New Testament is present in the appearance of Jesus Christ, the Incarnate One who takes upon himself the oppressed condition so that all men may be what God created them to be. He is the liberator par excellence, who reveals not only who God is and what he is doing, but also who we are and what we must do about human oppression. It is not possible to encounter this man and still remain content with human captivity. . . The Christian gospel is the good news of the liberation of the oppressed from earthly bondage.[62]

Black theology is angry and urgent in ways hardly congenial to the Anglo—Teutonic theological idiom, but quite at home with the urgency of the Hebrew prophets and of Jesus Christ. It is particular, concrete and political in the very best and broadest sense of those words. It deals with the human situation right at the moment—in Memphis, in Harlem, in rural Alabama—and it identifies the oppressors by name. This happens in ways that make white people uncomfortable, but again in a tradition well known to us from the prophetic ministries of Amos and Hosea and Jesus of Nazareth.

The black experience provides a compelling analogy to the early Christian community—small, persecuted, existing in a hostile environment, racially and religiously oppressed but radically committed to freedom and human wholeness. When Jesus came to the Jews and gentiles, when Paul went later to the Greeks, both were proclaiming to nations held under the powerful domination of the Roman empire that human liberation was nevertheless possible. In the centuries immediately following the life of Christ, the struggles of the early church in Rome— urban, hidden, scorned, and persecuted—formed an experience for which the black church is a contemporary theological model.

In spite of centuries of suffering, three qualities of the black religious tradition have persisted in affirming life in the face of death and demonstrate what the church as a whole ought to be and do. These qualities are expressed by the black church in its roles as liberator, celebrant, and servant. This is our genius.

In his article "The Genius of the Black Church," William B. McClain suggests the ways in which the black church performs these roles. First, he says, is its genuine and persistent efforts toward humanizing the social order and its refusal to accept a Christian message that does not contribute directly toward that end. Second is the free and responsive character of the black worship service, exhibiting a profound joy and a genuine commitment to life instead of death. Finally, in the black church there is no priestly—prophetic dichotomy—that is, the prophetic judgment over the institutions of society has never given way completely to a purely priestly, soul—saving function. McClain concludes:

> The genius of the black church is that it has brought a people through the torture chamber of the past two centuries. It has sustained black people throughout the history of the black man in this nation with a Gospel that has been interpreted without a dichotomy of social—religious, soul— body, priestly—prophetic categories. It declares that God's humanizing activity in the world is the tearing down of old systems that dehumanize and enslave and the building up of new structure and institutions to make the ordering of life more just, peaceful, and human. Such structures and institu-

tions must be responsive to the human needs of the dispossessed, the disinherited and the powerless and accountable under God to all whom they exist to serve.[63]

The black church has not always had the concept of liberation as its watchword. A common view is that the church served merely as a source of survival for Blacks in the era when nothing more could be hoped for and that it wrongly diverted mind and imagination from this world's struggles to rewards in the world to come.

The Rev. James Lawson, however, insists that even during that earlier period the black church was extremely ingenious and creative in the methods it used for survival. In the context of black worship, for example, a code of language was developed, so that "Steal Away to Jesus" was both a folk spiritual and a political exhortation to steal away from slavery to freedom.

The central place of black Christians, both slave and free, in the Underground Railroad and the abolition of slavery, long neglected or ignored, is beginning to be acknowledged. Even though the period from about 1880 to 1940 was largely a period of accommodation by the black church to white society, there were nevertheless many exceptions. During this time the black church served as the basis upon which -many mutual benevolent societies, fraternal organizations, and cultural activities, so necessary to survive, were established.

Now, however, the option of liberation—always a dear and distant hope—is possible and real, and the black church conceives of its mission accordingly. The Rev. Reuben Sheares, II articulates this perspective.

As the black church chooses to move beyond white theology, it also becomes necessary for it to move beyond a strategy or a theology of survival. The time is already here when to survive per se is not enough. The future well—being of black people in America requires liberation beyond survival; survival plus a quality of life and being—fullness of life for everyman. Certainly it is recognized that survival can be a rather passive or drab affair, for all of its life—sustaining validity One can survive in life, without actualizing life or even having the opportunity to actualize life and self. Black people have survived; But the struggle for liberation is now upon us. The theology of survival must now flow into a theology of liberation, beyond white theology.[64]

That the liberation movement itself defines the Christian church is expressed best by the Rev. Albert Cleage, Jr., minister of the Shrine of the

Black Madonna in Detroit: "I address my remarks to those who believe in the movement but do not understand that the movement is the Christian church in the twentieth century and that the Christian church cannot truly be the church' until it also becomes the movement."[65]

God has always been a God of liberation. The truth of that was understood by the ancient Hebrews and has been experienced and proclaimed once again by black Christians in America.

The celebrative style of the black religious experience is undoubtedly rooted in its African past where all things were mythical, musical and close to the gods. This past, of course, is unique and cannot be duplicated by white Christians. To the extent, however, that the joy expressed in the black church against impossible odds is an affirmation of God's love in spite of all, is the extent the black church serves as a theological model for white Christians.

Part of the genius of the black church has always been its centrality in the lives of its people. Where the worship service is the central experience of the week rather than a polite observance at the end of it, there God is fully present and celebrated in the lives of his creatures.

Only the church that becomes a servant, however, can liberate its people and celebrate God's love. As Jesus was a "man for others," so the church must assume a servant role if it is to be the church.

The black church has served the real needs of its people in a sacrificial way from the very beginning. More recently and more visibly it has been the focus first of the civil rights movement, then of broader based coalitions in the struggle for economic empowerment, educational and employment opportunities, and a fair share in the decision—making processes.

Liberation, celebration, servanthood—these are the cornerstones of any theology worthy of the Christian faith—and the model for their realization comes to us more clearly from a non—white perspective than from a white perspective.

The question of whether or not black theology can save the white church is a question for white Christians, not black ones. Blacks have little time for and less interest in such speculation, and in the final analysis only white Christians can answer it anyway.

Several black theologians nevertheless allude to the possibility of redemption for the white church, though most often in an oblique and rather doubtful way. C. Eric Lincoln writes:

> White theology suffers mortally from the sin of omission. It
> has sent its theologians, to study in Europe where the prob-

lem isn't; or imported the best European theologians to bring us the light—but not for our darkness. In consequence, American theology has had few words to speak to our condition. White theology has not done anything for black people except to ignore them.[66]

Professor William B. McClain points out that "The white church was closed for black Christians, special services were held for them, or they were placed in 'nigger balconies.' It is a strange turn of history that the descendants of those who were seated in the 'nigger balconies' must now be the saviors (if in fact salvation is possible), for the descendants of those who created the balconies."[67] And he concludes: "The black church affirms the unity of life in the midst of seeming contradictions. When properly understood, it could lend the universality the church needs for renewal. But can niggers from the balconies become messiahs?"[68]

In writing of the National Committee of Black Churchmen, Leon W. Watts, II, raises the same question and the same possibility: "The National Committee of Black Churchmen is not an ecumenical organization alongside others. It is a movement of black churchmen committed first to the church of Jesus the Christ, then to the liberation of the black community. It may save Christianity in the western world by giving it back to the people."[69]

Finally, Reuben Sheares states the task facing white Christians as well as black:

Black people and the black church exist and function beyond white theology out of necessity and as a matter of choice, but isn't it also imperative for white churchmen and the white church to move beyond white theology? The issues of survival and the liberation of man and world confront the white church as well as the black church. It, too, shall need to disengage itself, to become a movement committed to the release of captives and the setting at liberty of those who are oppressed. For the future well being of black people, white people and all America lies beyond historic white theology.[70]

Dietrich Bonhoeffer says: "We are not Christ, but if we want to be Christians, we must have some share in Christ's large—heartedness by acting with responsibility and in freedom when the hour of danger comes, and by showing a real sympathy that springs, not from the rear but from the liberating and redeeming love of Christ for all who suffer."[71] That may be extended to say that Whites are not black (that is, oppressed), but because they are Christ's they can and must share fully in the suffering of those who are. It is at that point of redeeming love that liberation becomes possible for everyone.

We will not conclude that the black church can save the white church. That may be too much to hope for. There may be some small possibility, however, that a profound identification with the suffering and celebration expressed in the black religious experience can help Lutherans in their attempts to correlate the Kerygma to the black situation.

Toward an Authentic Correlation: Four Observations

Assuming that the task is to proclaim God's message of law and gospel, how does one move from the then and there to the here and now of the black community in particular?

Our first observation is that the essence of the black person's life itself is one of dualism, being a part of one culture while seeking to survive in the other culture. It is being black in a white culture. Life is a continuing struggle of dialectics between being and non—being. This life style in itself has profound implications for a Christian theology of law and gospel dialectics. One such implication is seen in how well the black experience fits into H. Richard Niebuhr's motif of "Christ and Culture in Paradox." Niebuhr says:

> the dualist seems to be saying that the law of life is not law but grace; that grace is not grace but law, an infinite demand made on man; that love is an impossible possibility and hope of salvation an improbable assurance. These are the abstractions; the reality is the continuing dialogue and struggle of man with God, with its questions and answers, its divine victories that look like defeats, its humandefeats that turn into victories.[72]

This typology is closely aligned with Lutheran theology and with the black experience. Thus, a commonality exists.

Our second observation is that the black frame of reference or hermeneutic is parallel to the "new hermeneutic." This is not to legitimize the black hermeneutic but rather to establish points of communication at this point. Henry Mitchell says:

> there is probably no need to seek to legitimize the black hermeneutic by the criteria of the new hermeneutic school of thought. Indeed, the process may in due season be reversed. Black proclamation may very well make the new hermeneutic more intelligible and meaningful. The black approach to proclamation, rooted in the past and matured in the present, is far more understandable to ordinary people than the abstruse

German formulations of the new hermeneutic. If the chief task of hermeneutics is to convey the revelation in its contemporary contest, then black hermeneutics far outstrip this school.[73]

A third observation is that probably no other race of people have been more involved with syncretism or acculturation than have black people in America relative to church history. At the same time, because of being exiled, it has become necessary to them to return to their own historical antecedents and thus to regain a sense of black continuity with the past. The objective is not to live in that past or repeat it, but to better comprehend present challenges and potentialities and carve out the mistakes of the historical black church.

Black people are not alone in pursuit of an authentic "psychoanalytic" function of church history. The renaissance in Luther and Calvin studies 'as well as in the area of radical revolution has encouraged such a return to "fonts." This is understandable when one perceives the rootlessness of the modern age and how it has served to emphasize the profound existential need for roots on ecclesiastical, theological, personal and cultural levels.

Segments of Lutheran theology in the nineteenth century as well as now have never really been in harmony with American denominationalism[74] let alone the black denominations (which may account for such a small number of minority members). It does not seem to see outside of its historical conditioning, namely, the assumption that there is one uniform biblical ecclesiology as witnessed by Luther and the confessors.

The Scripture is interpreted through Luther and the confessors, and these sources are approached through the medium of seventeenth century orthodoxy. This is the line of "true Lutheranism": Holy Scripture, Luther and the confessors and dogmatics. What we have here might be termed as a static and fixated understanding of history especially when we witness an alteration (through a scholastic approach) of Luther's and the confessors' evangelical theology of law and gospel.[75]

What is significant here is that rigid historical typologies are established which leave little or no room for black or other minority church histories. This kind of parochial perspective threatens to obscure theology's ecumenicity as well as its particularity or indigenous nature.

What we are suggesting as crucial to the understanding and communication of the gospel in a given situation is an indigenous understanding of the historical church of that situation and its medium for transmitting the gospel. Moreover, since church history is foremost a theological concern, our educational concern is not based solely on one nation's experience with the gospel. It is based on the experience of all races of people who have been bearers of the good news that constitutes the biblical church. To assume that the gospel is found only in the categories of historical Lutheran doctrine is not only dangerous, but when "fenced in" becomes destructive to the universality of the gospel of Jesus Christ. Whether done by the white church or black church, it is an obvious departure from the confessions' catholicity.

The dynamics of the gospel as the viva vox dei that breaks into the history of the German ethos is the same that breaks into the black ethos. The problem here is not that the gospel breaks into the indigenous areas of life but that it is harnessed and possessed by that ethos to the exclusion of others. Subsequently, it is in danger of becoming an ideology of obscurity and ultimate obliteration. This equation means that history is no longer viewed as a person's or a community's response to the word that confronts one as law and promissio calling for faith and trust. Rather it is a doctrine about God restating what he has done in the past.[76] Result: narrow sectarianism.

Our criticism, now, is that Lutherans have misread Luther's keen understanding of the word as God's present action. Therefore, many ethnic groups have been "bombarded" with the demand for right belief as formulated by Lutheran dogmaticians such as Pieper, Quenstedt, Graebner, and others.

Considering what we have said, integrity dictates that theologians must study the indigenous sources of a given ethos and listen carefully to their historical response to the word within its struggle of oppression, exploitation and dehumanization. Because of the peculiar situation of the black community, there will be shifts in theological emphasis. Is the Lutheran church big enough to allow for these shifts of emphasis?

The narrow view of church history that Lutherans possess can indeed cause great problems of meaning; that is, hermeneutics relative to the gospel. God's word is never correlated into a vacuum. It encounters a unique situation, a situation that finds its people asking questions as an outgrowth of its particular "Sitz im Leben." It, then, becomes theology's task to correlate in a coherent form the biblical -modes of speech and forms into the indigenous thought forms of that situation. According to Ebeling this kind of process would ask: What did the word mean (the descriptive task)? What does it mean (the hermeneutical task)?[77]

It has already been suggested that the Lutheran church emphasis would be entirely one of the descriptive task because its sola scriptura emphasis sacrifices, as it were, the "situation."

The challenge here is to preserve genuine Lutheran theology as expressed in the Confessions by returning to biblical theology,[78] rather than later dogmatics. Ebeling sets the stage for a further observation of effectively correlating the gospel to the black situation.

> The word of God must be left free to assert itself in an unflinchingly critical manner against distortions and fixations. But. . . theology and preaching should be free to make a translation into whatever language is required at the moment and to refuse to be satisfied with correct, archaizing repetition of pure doctrine.[79]

The general lack of fruitful contact with whites and their churches has left Blacks free to do their own thing, translating the faith into the forms of the black world, unhampered by the "captivity of white theology." Moreover, according to Roberts,

> The abundance of raw materials for black theology is overwhelming. Among the sources that may' be freighted with religious insights we may list literature, history, sermons, spirituals, folklore, art, and the testimony of some saints and sages of the black community. All these feed into a black theology that is a process of reasoning about God in the context of the black experience.[80]

In this, we are in accord with Roberts.

It is the position of Richard N. Soulen that hermeneutical history supplies the categories for illumination of all Christian worship and not merely the black church. The history of the black church and of black worship is, largely- an oral tradition. Soulen therefore points to the need to gather data and reflect theologically on forms and modes of worship in the black church to discover which aspects of black worship speak most meaningfully the language of the Christian faith. In sum, Soulen says:

> This is not for the sake of the black church alone; It is for the sake of the whole church. For not until White middle class Christians come to understand the Language and modes of black worship are they likely to understand either the black church or its people. And perhaps not until then will they truly understand themselves.[81]

While I believe that Soulen provides some helpful guidelines for intercommunication between Blacks and Whites, I do not share the belief of Roberts who feels that the acceptance of such guidelines requires a rejection of Cone's black theology. Rather it requires a radicalizing of his theology if it is to mature into a theology which has meaning for all. Mitchell states:

Just as the new hermeneutic of Ebeling and others has sought to recapture the vital message of Luther and the reformation fathers for the benefit of their sons, so must the black hermeneutic seek to look into the message of the black past and see what the black fathers could be saying to black people today.[82]

Black people read the scripture and retold the story out of the context of the great black experience stamped with their own black African culture. To a people who were not print oriented, the gospel was preached, and in the original tongue with all of its own freshness and relevance. If, as Ebeling suggests, the gospel strives for expression, how else could it escape being in some significant sense different from the gospel as it was preached in the white culture? This illustrates two very sound principles advanced by hermeneutics:

1.   One must declare the gospel in the language and culture of the people—the vernacular.

2.   The gospel must speak to the contemporary society and, its needs.

These two points can be illustrated in the fact that Blacks in America never condoned slavery. Their spirituals attest to the fact that they seized on the Moses narrative and sung, "Tell ol' Pharaoh to let my people go," as a demand for their own liberation.

As we have used it thus far "hermeneutic" is a code word for putting the gospel on a tell—it—like—it—is, nitty—gritty basis. If the goal of German hermeneutics is detheorizing the gospel and getting to people where they are—making it flexible—the typical German intellectual patterns simply have not allowed students of German hermeneutics to practice what they preached as compared to black preachers. On the other hand, if the black community and their descendants have not been prone to theorize overmuch, their culture and their congregations have had little place for abstractions.

A fourth observation is the method of closing the hermeneutical gap. On what basis may statements made two thousand years ago be relevant today? The big question is not the horizontal gap but the vertical gap. We cannot make the assumption that things have to be constant in order to make the transfer from then to now. An alternative transfer is how can we make the situation the same, not how we make the gospel relevant.

What then is humanity's problem? The problem is idolatry, imputing the value of God to something which is not God, like country, nation, ideology.

Jesus Christ moves in and says no, not your country, nation, race, family, not even you yourself, but I am your point of departure for your faith frame of reference as you face the human situation. This begins the radicalizing of black theology.

A further radicalizing of black theology would move it from the "gray" area of identification with a specific condition of a people to the condition of all people, which is that of a sin. It would move it out of the "gray" area of being accused or projecting just another "ideology" into projecting a sounder theology of God's judgment and forgiveness upon all of humanity.

The faith frame of reference is perhaps one of the major problems that confronts any theology today. While the indigenization of theology becomes a must for communicating the Gospel to a given culture, it also becomes inadequate when its "interests" rest solely in a given culture or for a given ethnic group.[83]

Indigenous Black Churches

Indigenous black churches have been in existence for centuries and they are increasing. In Africa alone, there are some six thousand indigenous churches.[84] In the U.S. they have existed since the eighteenth century. Some of these black churches have been integrated into European forms of religion, while others continue in traditional African ways. Many have adopted ideas from other parts of the world, or created their own free style of religion.

In spite of wide variations among black indigenous churches in America, they are in many ways similar. Minimal research will demonstrate attributes peculiar to them: they are led by Blacks, supported by Blacks, and directed toward black religious concerns. This might be one of many givens which accounts for Christianity being the fastest growing religion among Africans, with over a sixth of Africa's people Christian.[85] Even during slavery in the United States, black people usually worshipped separately in their own manner and with their own preachers.

As we have seen, the oldest independent churches began in the late eighteenth century as protests by educated freedmen against white churches' snobbery in the northern cities. While these churches can be categorized as indigenous they nonetheless are similar to the white churches from which they were exiled.

After the Civil War they expanded rapidly to include masses of liberated slaves. The National Baptist Conventions and the black Methodist churches have always been loose affiliations. Since the Civil War local congregations, especially in southern states, have often been much closer to the religious ethos of Africa than are the national organizations.

Even more independent are the hundreds of tiny black churches outside the major black denominations. Most of these stem from the Baptist tradition, the Holiness Movement, or Pentecostalism. Mass migration from the southern countryside to the northern cities in this century swelled not only the large, sophisticated, urban churches, but also produced a proliferation of radically indigenous, innovative, lower—class "store—front" churches. These comparatively new, urban "store-front" groups, completely free of paternalistic white supervision have sometimes returned to beliefs and practices typical of the religious underground of the West Indies. Among Blacks in the United States, store—front churches tend to be most like African and West Indian indigenous churches.[86]

In the American culture subjugation of black people came early and brutally, but Africa remained mostly self—governing until the late nineteenth century.

Most obviously, the worship of black indigenous churches around the world is distinctive. Whether in Africa, the West Indies, or the United States, most black worship is more exuberant, more physical than most white worship. The services of black indigenous churches tend to be long, joyful celebrations, like the traditional all day festivals of shrines and villages in Africa. A worship service usually starts when people arrive, which means that some of the matrons are clapping and singing long before the main service begins. Three or four hour services are not unusual, and worshippers try to have a "good time."

Everyone present in black worship is involved. Black churches tend to be small, so members can be friends. It is also typical that individuals stand to "testify" to the Lord's blessings—perhaps a miracle, more often simply God's continued protection and the privilege of worship. There are plenty of official positions in order to give tasks and status to as many members as possible. Small congregations are divided into even smaller, more intimate fellowships—committees, choirs, ushers, and other groups -—to ensure that everyone has a place in church where he can "feel at home."[87]

Pageantry is a popular element of black worship. Church leaders are expert at using elaborate gestures, movements, robes and other liturgical paraphernalia to create an atmosphere of awe. Many of the worshippers in a typical church are robed. In Africa or the United States, black women can be seen hurrying to church in their white uniforms on Sunday morning.

Physical touch is also integral to black worship. Among black Protestants, baptism has often had special importance. This is partly due to their European Baptist heritage, but also because of the water symbolism in much African religion.[88] Communion and other orthodox sacraments tend to be replaced in black churches by novel sacraments: anointing, sprinkling, holy articles to be touched.

Music, vocal and instrumental, is the staple of black worship. The songs are short, quickly mastered, and lustily sung. They are constantly revised. They carry the enthusiasm of worship: inspiring the congregation, enlivening the sermon, enabling whatever healing or ecstasy the Spirit gives. Black music is noted for its intricate rhythms, blue notes, distinctive tones and harmonies. Happy hand—clapping and foot-tapping almost invariably accompany singing, and often there is dancing, although usually quite restrained and dignified.[89]

United States spirituals are famous for their eloquence in expressing the uncanny hope of suffering black people. In Africa, too, little known composers are writing thousands of spirituals. Studies of new hymn collections in west Africa have shown that most of them shout praises to God for his saving power, even though most of the people who sing them are in church because they have some critical need. They celebrate God's victorious might, even though they are still waiting to experience it.[90] This sensuous vitality, despite objective misery is typified by the United States spiritual:

Oh, nobody knows de trouble I've seen:

Glory Hallelujah

Sometimes I'm up, sometimes I'm down,

Oh, yes, Lord,

Sometimes I'm almost to de ground,

Oh, yes, Lord,

Oh, nobody knows de trouble I've seen,

Glory Hallelujah!

Black preaching is drama. The black preacher is a storyteller; the "Amens" and "Praise the Lords" solicited from the congregation remind some observers of the call and response of African storytelling.[91] The preacher usually begins in a low key, explicating scripture verse-by-verse, then slowly gather emotional momentum with that of listeners, until their encouragements pass into ecstasy. James Baldwin, who was a child preacher, described it:

There is no music like that music, no drama like the drama
of the saints rejoicing, the sinners moaning, the tambourines

racing, and all those voices come together and crying holy unto the Lord. There is still for me, no pathos like the pathos of the multicolored, worn, somehow triumphant and trans-figured faces, speaking from the depths of a visible, tangible, continuing despair of the goodness of the Lord. I have never seen anything to equal the fire and excitement that sometimes, without warning, fills a church, causing the church, as Lead belly and so many others have testified, to "rock." Nothing that has happened to me since equals the power and the glory that I sometimes felt when, in the middle of a sermon, I knew that I was somehow, by some miracle, really carrying, as they said, "the word"—when the church and I were one. Their pain and their joy were mine, and mine was theirs – they surren-dered their pain and joy to me, I surrendered mine to them—and their cries of "Amen" and "Hallelujah" sustained and whipped on my solos until we all became equal, wringing wet, singing and dancing, in anguish and rejoicing, at the foot of the altar.[92]

Correlating the Gospel to the Black Situation

We have examined the black experience to note the observable in-dividual and collective acts connected with it, cataloguing each institu-tion actively engaged in establishing a behavior that is learned and shared by the people of that community.

The vital ethos of Afro—Christianity is now being preserved and written as a theology. Black theology is very complex and not at all easy for Whites and even some Blacks to understand, but it is essential to the correlation of the gospel to the black situation. There are doctrines, revelation, soteriology and eschatology to be developed from a law/gos-pel Lutheran perspective since Blacks can be found in the Lutheran church. Cone's brief study is only the beginning of a necessary correla-tion in formal theological expression.

Anyone who has read the work of black authors such as James Baldwin can see the failure of the white church to correlate the gospel significantly to black persons. It appears that black people are in the United States to stay just as any other ethnic cultures or ethos. There-fore, institutions are necessary. Neither a white assimilationist ethic nor the universalism ascribed to Anglo—American particularism should be allowed to prohibit black professionals from establishing valid criteria within black history to interpret the disciplines to meet the needs and problems of black communities.

Thus black particularity in theology can and should supplement and not replace white particularism. This type of pluralism will permit an appreciation of the black experience as something which is more than a mere reflection of the dominant white society or ideology and which, thus, becomes worthy of a study in its own right.

We have seen through many scholars in psychology that there is a close relationship between Christian theology and contemporary psychology. The Lutheran theological tradition is especially formed in an experiential matrix which gives it a common ground with psychological thought[93] as well as the other academic disciplines. In this section we have examined from a black perspective, a constructive, indispensable approach to correlating Lutheran theology (what we have defined as the law/gospel dialectic) and black psychology. Lutheran theology will become more relevant when utilizing black authors as sources for the Christian task of understanding the situation before correctly applying the gospel.

Our underlying purpose in analyzing the black experience is to give the reader a glimpse of the need for anthropological prolegomena (literally the word about humanity before the gospel) so that we might test the adequacy of that understanding of not only universal humankind but also indigenous humankind.

Questions are raised here about the nature and needs of not just humanity in general, but humanity as we indigenously live, move and have our being in a particular community. How, where, and in what way will the gospel be operative in, specifically, the black situation? Does the gospel, for example, bring about an ontological or psychological and sociological change? What dynamics of personality (such as guilt, fear or identity) are involved when viewed from a black perspective as in the case of Alvin Poussaint's analysis?

While many of the clergy are still experiencing the frustration of a monologue rather than dialogue with other disciplines such as psychology, our diagnosis of the problem goes one step deeper. It goes to a dialogue between cultures so that the gospel might above all things to be understood. Indigenous cultures must question what kind of understanding of humanity the gospel speaks to and what use we can make of various current theories. Where are the inadequacies? What will not stand up in the light of the gospel?

Christianity, which is indigenously expressed and lived in the black community, is not in competition at this point with the conclusions of psychology and sociology. Its concern is with how a human being responds to the threat of psychological destruction. If the threat is our universal state, then this is compatible with Christianity's understanding of original sin as our universal compulsion to justify, to vindicate, to affirm and protect ourselves and thus to get out from under the threat of oppression and destruction.

Here, however, the black Christian theologian takes issue with any discipline, whether from a black or white perspective, which would theorize that threat, maintaining that oppression or racism is an illusion. Christianity does not say that this kind of state of existence is an illusion. The oppressive state existing in the black community, perpetuated by white racism, is indeed a state of reality.[94] What is illusory are the responses to this state of reality. Salvation and redemption come, not in denying the validity of the Christian faith in Christ; that is, saving myself by my own acts, but by accepting Jesus as my savior, giving up my illusory existence and receiving in faith the unconditional verdict of God's love and grace who affirms us in the midst of oppression.

The universal nature of the gospel of Jesus is at the same time a "skandalon" to nationalism, a mediatory force between civilizations and nature to the community of faith. It is the true humanizing force in the world as it evaluates and transforms the values of societies.

Therefore, in the Christian dialogue between cultures, the nature of the gospel does not allow Germans, Africans, or any race to claim a superiority that is self—justifying. The role of the pastor is one of correlating the gospel to the situation. The role of theology is to help the indigenous community ask the right questions, which, when arising from the heart of the community, are worthy of answers. Lutheranism then has a theological task to take the law/gospel dialectic as we have defined it, correlate it on a personal or cultural level and take the "two kingdoms" doctrines on a structural or institutional (social ethics) level.

Lutherans have been taken to task by many who challenge the law/gospel and two kingdoms approach the human social problems. But, according to this research, it appears that contemporary Lutherans have misrepresented Luther and the confessors in the area. This has been primarily due to their preoccupation with the realm of redemption or the spiritual kingdom, often to the exclusion of the realm of creation, and with their demand for right belief as formulated by Lutheran dogmaticians.[95]

Theologically, the Lutheran documents witness to the fact that God—in—Christ is Lord also over the "secular" institutions of life, but practically they have failed effectively to implement this. Therefore, we join others who have insisted that we take seriously the most fundamental insight in recent ecumenical social ethics, the assertion that God acts in all human history. That is, God is said to be active in all indigenous situations including the black situation. There is no situation where it is not relevant to ask, what is God doing?[96]

Sources for the correlation of the gospel to the black situation can be found not only within the rigid historical typologies[97] of Lutheranism but the historical black church, a church institution that possesses at once syncretistic forms of Catholic, Lutheran, Reformed Muslim, and so forth, doctrines as well as its own indigenous thought forms. The diagram depicts this and points toward an area of future research in the process for developing a theology that addresses itself to an indigenous culture.

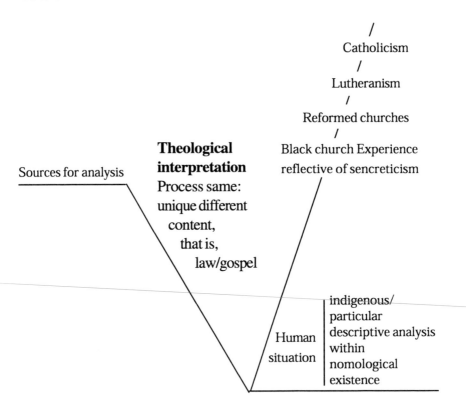

1. While the black experience can be the Christian experience of oppression sociologically and psychologically when viewed theologically, all other nations of people join their enslavement and oppression within God's nomological order of creation. This then requires more than a response of human power, but Christ's forgiveness and power.

2. Black people have always recognized as did Luther, that no one could know their condition and needs better than one living and dwelling among them, one born of themselves.

3. It appears as though the institutional church of today like that of Luther's day has used the gospel to legitimize oppression.

4. Black people have recognized the importance of education as an important socialization agency.

5. It is clearly understandable why DuBois, Washington, F. Douglass, and other leaders like Luther himself when caught in situations of overt oppression and exploitation were lifted up by the spirit of freedom they breathed. Howard Thurman to this day remains the black poet, mystic and philosopher of the black experience that espouses the unity and reverence of all life. As one perceives the life situations of men like Luther and King, one cannot but marvel at the similiarities of experience as he is transported into the depths of their realities—even into the very depths of his own soul (Anfechtung).

6. Luther and the confessors were able to articulate this "soul" in the German experience just as black leaders articulate theologically a "soul" quality in the black experience that one feels in communication with the mass of black folk.

7. The source of Christian theology is first and foremost the Scriptures deeply rooted in the black heritage. This is an African as well as an Afro—American experience. One can observe it in the slave narratives, in folktales, spirituals, novels, poems, sermons, and prayers.

8. Under the genius of the universal communality of oppression, one can observe men like Martin Luther and Martin Luther King describing an experience that takes the shape not merely of perception, but reflection upon perception. They enable the oppressed to communicate what they have been feeling so that they understand it. The theology, philosophy, psychology, and others of the black experience is a type of knowledge —- a non—knowing knowledge, that is, not rational but insightful, intuitive knowledge. It is knowing from the inside rather than from the outside. It is learning about life from living it. It is knowledge from experience rather than book knowledge. The point where thought touches life seems to be the great interests of the majority of intellectuals whose life was marked with an oppressed people. It is finally ontological existential reflection upon the realities of existence.

9. A gospel that addresses itself to the black experience as we observed in Luther's situation must tackle the Anfechtung question of meaning. This is not only the question: "Who am I?" but the question

of purpose (philosophically a theological question), which theologically is a problem of theodicy, or why is there suffering in a world in which God is defined as lovingly just? Other such crises faced by black people include the following: low—esteem, lack of self—respect, policy brutality, exploitation, dehumanization, disenfranchisement, hypertension, poor housing, and black—on—black crime. The response to racism vacillates indecisively between violence and non—violence.

10. Historically, whereas the black person was considered property to be used, a slave, an object whose death was a matter of bookkeeping; death to black people was an experience within life, as the message is born in the spirituals. Theologically, the black person 's future broke into the present life giving it significance . So there is more to heaven than what some critics call other worldliness or escapism. The meaning of Jesus' promissio brought faith and hope of an abiding existence and continued relationships with loved ones. How else may we explain the gift of laughter or the very essence of survival of the Afro—American under such conditions of oppression?

11. Black theological reflection on the black situation as we have analyzed it has not only been concerned about meaning as we witnessed during Luther's situation, but has likewise been a theology of protest or judgment. The liberation motif has demanded the willingness to die— and too often Whites have obliged Blacks with death. Nat Turner and M. L. King. Jr., both apostles of non—violence, became victims of violence. This has produced an even stronger Anfechtung experience when we realize how this generation of young people witnessed over the television screen the undisputed revelation of how cruelly sadistic man can be as a racist. Black Christians like Dr. King were beaten, chased by dogs, thrown in jail and even killed as they sought to exercise what we have theologically analyzed as the "two kingdoms" doctrine. What the oppressive institutions were willing to do to maintain a superiority position in this society was paraded before young black and white impressionable minds on national television.

12. Whatever theology one accepts in this society that has any purpose of leading humanity out of our nomological existence, one must allow for racial and national coexistence, for our destinies are found together. Together as a human race we shall nobly stand under the grace of God or foolishly fall under the judgment of God.

13. There is still a question as to how Blacks are to relate to Whites in a society where there must be coexistence in the black—white encounter. Many alternative solutions have been tried. The real question remains not merely a question of liberation from an overt oppressor like

the Roman Catholic Church of Luther's day or the white institutional church of today. Rather what does it mean to be free from the structures of a nomological existence? The alternative answer to this question can be found in the person of Jesus Christ.

14. The study of Luther and the Lutheran reformation can become as aggravating to the Roman Catholic as the study of the black experience can to the white institutional church. There is little comfort in assessing what Whites have done to Blacks in the new world, nor is there any comfort in assessing how corrupt the church was in Luther's day.

The four standards we are using to test the effectiveness of correlating the Kerygma with the black situation can be worded differently from an educational viewpoint. We offer them for additional clarity and understanding.

1. Indigenous anthropological Prolegomena

1. Context (where?). Where or in what context, does Christian education take place? Christian education takes within the indigenous Christian community. Each baptized person is ministered to by the rest of the community so that he may grow into a ministering person both within the community and in the world.

2. Source

2. When (timing). An emphasis on knowing the situation and the resources to determine what time it is in relation to God's time, situational time, the church's time, and the learner's time.

3. Church experience

3. The black church is the smaller context within the larger cultural situation, a situation that demands an organizing principle of the existential conflicts or crises derived from the indigenous prolegoma.

4. Law/gospel	4. Process (how?). How do people learn and how shall teaching learning be structured to help people learn. Evidence indicates that people learn when they are puzzled. Theologically, this correlates well with a Lutheran law/gospel dia lectic.

The first point is what we have developed in our discussion as the indigenous anthropological prolegomena (literally the word about man before the word). The question which we have posed and answered is that "Lutheran confessional theology" is a type of "situational theology" as evidenced by Luther and the confessors. It is a theology that says now one thing, now another, depending on a thorough understanding of the human situation. The assumption here is that Lutheran educational material has been prepared for Lutherans and we will be testing the relevance of the material for black Lutherans.

The second point is to question the sources of the principal foundation of Christian education. We will be looking for sources that enable the oppressed to communicate what they have been feeling so that they understand it. We will be testing whether those sources used for the principles in education represent a type of insightful knowledge, a knowing from the indigenous black community rather than from the outside. In short, we are testing how well the sources represent and analyze an ontological existential reflection upon the realities of the black existence for effective correlation of the Kerygma.

In our third point, we are operating with the concept that the organizing principle of the curriculum in Christian education should be the learner in relationship to the church's experience, especially its unique ethnic and cultural experience. The black church has had a unique historical experience with God. We will test the educational material to see whether that indigenous church experience is revealed in establishing the organizing principle.

Finally, we shall test the adequacy of the correlation of the law/gospel dialectic in the material to see whether, in fact, we have retained Luther's and the confessors' process of correlating a meaningful Christocentric message of salvation and liberation to differing indigenous situations, specifically, the black situation.

Christian Ethics in Black Lutheran Perspective

As our society grows increasingly sophisticated, the decisions we are all forced to make about right and wrong, good and evil, appear to be increasingly relative. Because of the many choices we can make, and the various implications of each choice, fewer and fewer decisions are being made in a positive way.

In a pluralistic society, different cultures have different values and standards of acceptability. For instance, a major meal may be consumed at different times of the day in different cultures: some at midday, some in the late afternoon, some in the early evening. When these cultural standards meet with each other, some confusion is bound to ensue. Each culture considers its mealtime "the best," and what becomes the basis for conflict is the timing of the major meal, not the necessity of eating itself. This may be a rather simplistic example of the general state of confusion that exists when different cultures attempt to make joint decision In response to the confusion, decisions are often made by not being made, by default.

As human beings we must all make decisions of right and wrong, good and evil. When the situation arises, as it inevitably must, wherein the question of "What ought I to do?" is asked, the problem of ethical decision making is at hand. Ethics, then, has to do with decisions of right and wrong, choices of good and evil, which affect the human being in relationship to the community. In the pluralistic society suggested above, ethical decisions may differ in different cultures. But the revelation of God and the ethical standards set up by God through revelation are all the same because Christians in all cultures know the same God and the same story of God's revelation.

There are two major revelations from/of God which all Christians hold as universal truths. The first is the revelation given to the nation of Israel in the Decalogue through Moses. These Ten Commandments were (and are) the ethical law of God because, they deal with our right relationships with one another based on our relationship with God. They show us still today that God cares about all aspects of our lives and wills only right relationships for us. The second major revelation was the word, Jesus Christ, who not only fulfilled the law fully, but also imposed a new law that summed up the law of Moses—the law of love that we also know as the gospel.

If these revelations of God are universal—and it is the conviction of the black community that they are—then a case exists for a universal ethic based on the law and the gospel. What is particular then, is how different cultures incarnate and interpret the law and the gospel. In the words of Major Jones,

> . . .whenever the oppressed black Christian, or indeed the current black person. . . attempts to answer the moral or ethical question of "What ought I to do?" he (sic) is likely to come up with a different answer derived from the same set of ethical criteria than would his (sic) counterpart who is white. If the answer to the moral questions, derived from the same set of ethical criteria, principles, models, or values, are to be altered by what one has become or what he (sic) is as a person, then to be black in pro—white America is, perhaps, to be ethical in quite a different way. . . If it is true that the basic assumptions and contentions of black theology are different from the broader scope of theology that is written from a totally white perspective, then it must also follow that Christian ethics. . .written from a white perspective would. . .be different from Christian ethics. . .written from a black frame of reference.[98]

Consequently then, just as the self—image of Blacks is different from the image imposed by Whites, so is their self—understanding and ethical orientation different from that of Whites.

God's revealed truth to black people is clear and coherent. God's truth says to black people that the oppression of any people is wrong, that the historical experience of slavery by the Israelites in Egypt was overturned by God alone, that conforming to the will of God means obeying the commands of God and imitating the life of Christ, and that black Christians must act ethically (lovingly) in a racist society because God already has liberated black people in the two major revelations cited above.

If, on the other hand, Blacks demand liberation from Whites, then they are denying the entire rootedness of the ethical traditions of faith and the fact that God does care about what happens to the creation. Black Christians have subscribed to the ethical posture of copying the life and teachings, walking in the footsteps, of Jesus Christ, and not of Whites.

In Western society where the numerical majority of God's people are white, standards of acceptability have been established based on the values of that majority. These values set the standards relative to beauty, manners and language, dress codes, cultural expressions, spiritual, intellectual and physical symbols of achievement, political and economic ideologies.

But these standards are not universal, and they are exclusive when they are used to judge all the cultures by the values of one culture. Furthermore, they are considered racist when they are enforced by overt and covert power moves against people of color.

In resisting exclusive standards of acceptability some black people have fallen prey to the perpetrator and attempted to establish other exclusive standards of acceptability. By the grace of God we have not allowed the pendulum to swing fully in the opposite direction; instead we have, as a community until recently, held onto the standards of acceptability established by God. These are universal and bridge all cultures. They are summed up in the two great commandments: love the Lord with all your heart, soul, and mind; and love your neighbor as yourself.

The contribution of the Lutheran church to articulating these universal ethical standards has been stymied by some contemporaries through the misrepresentation of the Lutheran heritage to a large extent. But the foundation still exists in the confessional nature of the denomination. Confession is declaring that God is God in the fact of those forces which declare that other subjects and objects are gods.

But we must also synchronize our creeds and deeds. The biblical and theological concept of reciprocity has much to offer us as we begin to explore once again the relationships possible within God's church on earth. At this juncture we turn to that concept with the intention of offering reciprocity as a theological and ethical principle within which our understanding of the human community will be based. This concept will also suggest alternate ways of relating to other groups/cultures within our society based on our understanding of interdependence within the body of Christ.

Reciprocity

What exactly does reciprocity mean in Christian ethics from a black perspective? The English word comes to us from the Latin 'reciprocus.' In his poetry, Tacitus uses this word as an adjective with 'mare,' the sea. In that context he writes of the "ebbing waves." Pliny uses the word to mean returning, going backwards and forwards. Today we use the word primarily to describe mutual relationships or policies in commercial dealings and in terms of corresponding advantages, licenses or privileges between countries and/or institutions. Reciprocal relations imply mutual exchange, equal returns or counteractions between two subjects.

> God is love. . .There is no room for fear in love; perfect
> love banishes fear. . .We know love because he loved us
> first.   I John 4:16b—19

Creation was the occasion that precipitated community:

The earth is the Lord's and the fullness thereof, the world
and those who dwell therein.   Psalm 24:1 (RSV)

The Psalms illustrate best the relationship between God and nature, which should be coveted in a positive way by humanity and which
should be used as a model for the relationships which humanity has
with God, with nature and with itself. The earth belongs to Yahweh (a
personal name used in a possessive phrase), and whatever grows in and
on the earth also belongs to him. This includes all the nations of the
earth, their inhabitants, all the animals and vegetation. This also implies that we use God's creations and belongings—all the worldly possessions—on a borrower's basis. As a result, God holds humanity accountable to him for the use of his creation; we must report to him on
this earth in the context of a relationship is the point of departure for
any discussion on reciprocity.

God's relationship with his creation has been one of reciprocity.
This is not to say that the creation itself was reciprocal, but rather that
the love he gave to us is reciprocal. Love flows from God to us and
among us and finally back to God, not because it is demanded of us,
but simply because God loves us. Because all was created by God in
love, there is love in all.

It is this very love that binds the created world, as we know it,
together without fear. If we were created in love, there is no need for fear
between any of the parts of the creation. As the Gospel writer says:

Perfect love banishes fear. This, then, is the configuration that our
relationship with God is supposed to take: one of unconditional love.[99]

There is no better way to introduce Christian ethics from a black
perspective than to address the universal nature of ethics from an understanding of our universal God. Because of humanity's uniqueness, that
is, being created in the image of God, we have been given more responsibility for our relationships. By being created in God's image, we are
not placed in a position to be dominators over nature, but rather to be
caretakers of God's gifts. In the past ten years, we have been looking
much more critically at our relationship with nature and consequently,
have made some significant changes. Until humanity, as part of nature
and not against nature, recognizes the authentic relationship we have
with nature, we will continue to abuse the gifts of God by setting ourselves totally apart from all of God's creation instead of recognizing
that we are a part of the total creation.

What is that authentic relationship? It is one of partnership, not of ownership; it is one of stewardship, not of harnessing; it is one of freedom, not of enslavement; it is one of reciprocity, not of abuse through misuse. This means that we will continue to be frustrated until we realize that nature will not be controlled by humanity; that we have a responsibility to use only what we need and to leave the rest (replacing and/or restoring what we have used when possible, not because of guilt or self—interest but because of unconditional love); and that we need to understand how to live in harmony with nature.

Living in harmony with nature means recognizing that we humans cannot control everything. It means allowing time to flow naturally in its cyclical fashion instead of forcing it into a linear mold.[100] It means not trying to save the shorelines of the continents from changing because they will change anyway. It means not building up large storehouses and surpluses of food to be used as a tool for bartering, but sharing extra food freely as it is needed. It means placing our faith in God as a bountiful provider instead of in money as the indication of success.

It means recognizing the context (sociological, political, and theological) within which we live, judging it positively or negatively, and working within its parameters for change. It means that although we often do "not what we ought, but what we are able," we should continually strive to do what we ought. It means rediscovering what in nature is basic for life and living in our society, and not letting what is nonessential drive us. It means not putting our trust in worldly, material possessions but trusting in the beneficence and love of God. It means being grounded in the land and creation and not in the pursuit of making a profit.

Humanity's relationship with and use of the land has always been a significant historical and faith aspect for different world religions. It is particularly so in relation to the story of the children of Israel in the Old Testament, and it has left a legacy that had implications for Christianity from the times of the early church up through the present.

Israel's faith is essentially a journeying in and out of land, and its faith can be organized around these focuses. This subject is worth our attention because contemporary problems are quite parallel. We know in our time about the hunger for rootage and the yearning for turf. We know about the destructive power of coveting and the anxiety of displacement. And we know from time to time about gifts given and promises kept. In ancient Israel and now persons and communities have been consumed by problems, most of which are about land. And so we may ask about the power of promise which is also mostly about land, a promise both glorious and problematic.[101]

It would appear that the desire on the part of some human beings to control nature has led them also to want to control other human beings. In the past, some have dared to exclude others from participating in the gift of the creation. Some have been so afraid that they have told stories and perpetrated myths of inferiority and superiority to create unnecessary separations among God's children. And worse, they have used God and God's word to reinforce and even celebrate their own injustices, inadequacies and insecurities. But repeatedly God has put his divine hand into a relationship of human beings and tried to redirect that relationship.

The biblical history of Israel should be a warning to the world. But, just as Israel did, some tend to ignore historical information, if that information directly contradicts their carefully laid plans. Relationships of inferiority and superiority, of exclusiveness and inclusiveness, of in—groups and out—groups are still being set up. Patterns and standards of acceptability contrary to God's standards and based on fleeting material values are still being established. Other human beings have been forced to let go of their cultures and values in order to he accepted.

In the beginning God created a community, a community that lived off the land, using what was essential and leaving for the less fortunate adequate supplies for the sustenance of life. Biblical history shows us time and time again how other people came along, locked up the food and put up signs saying, "PRIVATE PROPERTY—NO TRESPASSING," and then told other people what they had to do in order to earn their food.

The Lord loved his creation enough to try and re—establish his priorities a number of times. Still, human beings "bought" into what the demonic was saying and wandered farther and farther away from God. They wandered so far that the Lord decided to come in person and show us how to live according to his plan.

He chose to be born among the poor, to grow up working with his hands, to speak to those who were the outcasts of the society and to work for change for all people. He died even for those who hated him and then rose from the dead, showing that death is not the end of life, but the victory over the demonic and the beginning of a new life.

He taught that each and every person is important and, once again, left his creation moving in the direction he chose for us—loving each other as he loves us. It was in this act of dying and being raised from the dead that all of humanity was re—created in a cyclical fashion and re-united in, under, and through God's love.

Often we read in the New Testament "when the fullness of time had come. . ." This simply means that God was ready, that God's time had come (Kairos). Humanity's time, on the other hand (Chronos), tends to botch things up, particularly when humanity places itself in God's position. It is God's time and not humanity's time that ultimately will be significant. The author of Colossians 1 (13—20, NEB) wrote it in a somewhat different way:

> He rescued us from the domain of darkness and brought us away into the kingdom of his dear Son, in whom our release is secured and our sins forgiven. He is the image of the invisible God; his is the primacy over all created things. In him everything in heaven and on earth was created, not only things visible but also the invisible orders of thrones, sovereignties, authorities, and powers: the whole universe has been created through him and for him. And he exists before everything, and all things are held together in him. He is, moreover, the head of the body, the church. He is its origin, the first to return from the dead, to be in all things alone supreme. For in him the complete being of God chose to reconcile the whole universe to himself, making peace through the shedding of his blood upon the cross—to reconcile all things, whether on earth or in heaven, through him alone.

The Ethical Nature of Reciprocity

What then should reciprocity in the Christian community look like? The crux and the pivotal point of the community is that God is in the center. It is from the center that we receive life and meaning. It is the center that grounds us and sends us out to the periphery and brings us back to the center. It is around that center that community is built to revolve.

The community is composed of all shapes and sizes, colors and ages, economic classes, educational levels, languages and races. Because we are all centered in God, we are all equal before God and before one another. No one is "better" or "worse" than anyone else, and no one can do anything that is divorced from the entire community. Because we are loved by God, we love God and that love manifests itself in our love for each other. The author of the letter to the church in Ephesus states:

> Be humble and always gentle, and patient too. Be forbearing with one another and charitable. Spare no effort to make fast with bonds of peace the unity which the Spirit gives. So shall

we all at last attain to the unity inherent in our faith and our knowledge of the Son of God to mature manhood, measured by nothing less than the full stature of Christ... Let us speak the truth in love; so shall we fully grow up into Christ.

Ephesians 4: 2—3, 13, 15 (NEB)

We give to each other not because we expect anything back but because that person, or group of people, is in need and we have the resources and responsibility to fill that need. St. Paul illustrates this when writing his second letter to the Corinthians:

We must tell you, friends, about the grace of generosity which God has imparted to our congregations in Macedonia . . .Going to the limit of their resources, as I can testify, and even beyond that limit, they begged us most insistently, and on their own initiative, to be allowed to share in this generous service to their fellow—Christians. And their giving surpassed our expectations; for they gave their very selves, offering them in the first instance to the Lord, but also under God, to us.

2 Corinthians 8: 1-5 (NEB)

In Matthew 25:31—40, Jesus takes one further step when he speaks of the good and bad that must be answered for on the final day of judgment. What he is saying is that in caring for any person who has any need—be they hungry, thirsty, a stranger, naked, ill or in prison—we show not only our care for one another, we also show our care and love for God. In essence, our care for one another is not mitigated by circumstances nor is it based on good deed—doing. Rather, it is centered in God and that unconditional love which he freely gives to us. As a result we can only share and reciprocate that love and care.

What ethical configuration does this take in the Lutheran church? Martin Luther's theological legacy to the present day Lutheran church is very significant in this context. One element has been stated as follows:

Probably the best theological point of departure or exegesis in elaboration of that is the first article of the creed which says that, specifically, "I believe in God the Father Almighty,Creator of heaven and earth." The explanation of that, which is readily accepted in Lutheranism is the explanation that Luther himself gave, and that is, "I believe that God has created me and all creatures, and he has given me my body and soul, eyes and ears and all of my members and that he richly and daily sustains me and all that I need in body, mind and spirit, etc." To that end, then, we attach our faith and to that end we implement our faith. And, in so implementing that faith, it carries with it an altogether different lifestyle than what we are seen to have. The objective is to lay out the process for implementation of what we already know and believe in as the first article of creed and its explanation as it is given by Luther himself.[102]

Another important element here is Luther's affirmation of the priesthood of all believers. What Luther meant was not an individual, autonomous elevation to priesthood of all believers, not an office chosen and exclusive, but the responsibility for each Christian to fulfill a priestly (mediating) role between God and our immediate neighbor. We are responsible for praying for one another, for listening to one another, and for ministering to the physical needs of one another.

These responsibilities are manifested not solely in writing social statements, but also in not being afraid or reluctant to implement these statements. This means acting on what we believe, and not allowing xenophobia, guilt or demonic societal influences to deter us from genuinely caring about one another.

Specifically, within the love of Christ we will open our church to alternate styles of ministry and ministering. We set up standards and criteria of accountability that are pluralistic and multicultural, inclusive and nonalienating, and that allow the greatest amount of freedom and creativity within our church polity. We will be an inclusive church/community in deed as well as in creed, realizing that other cultures and experiences are as valid and instructive as the experience of the now—dominant culture.

We will realize that all people are children of God, the priesthood of all believers. Often we are tempted to divide our church, as others have attempted to divide the people of the earth, along the lines of superiority and inferiority. We tend to forget that Christ made us all brothers and sisters in himself through the sacrament of baptism. We will take care of one another because we only hurt ourselves and our God by not doing so.

Above all, under the gospel, we will not be afraid of taking risks in order to fulfill the gospel. We, as the priesthood of all believers, are called upon "to open the eyes that are blind, to bring out the prisoners from the dungeon, from the prison those who sit in darkness" (Isaiah 42:7). We do these things not because of obligation, but because we have a relationship with all people through Christ. Because Christ died for everyone, we have a relationship with all people. Our relationships will be modeled after the love of God: giving, when necessary, taking/receiving when appropriate, and judging when the situation calls for it.

Our task and mission is to share the good news, to right wrongs by showing the wrongness of an act, to expose the demonic when it "roams around like a roaring lion, seeking whom to devour" to the blinding light of the gospel. These are examples of the light that is to be shared with the prisoners of the demonic who live in the darkness of their own wrong deeds.

The risks in carrying out the task and mission of the gospel are manifold, and being an institution that remains faithful to its calling can be painful. But sometimes that very pain allows a partial and brief glimpse of the kingdom of God on earth.

Christians know that the church cannot be true to its call ing without sharing in the suffering of its Lord. When churches in their popularity and respectability have for—gotten how to live as sojourners on earth, they find that faithful obedience may be costly. Some churches are discovering that the realization of full joy of discipleship may involve loss in organizational success, prosperity, and comfortable congeniality.[103]

The leadership of the church, both lay and clergy, have of necessity a significant part to play. This- unique role is one of advocacy and is most appropriate to the servant model of ministry, the messianic task of the people:

The Spirit of the Lord God is upon me, because the Lord has anointed me to bring good tidings to the afflicted; he has sent me to bind up the broken—hearted, to proclaim liberty to the captives, and the opening of the prison to those who are bound; to proclaim the year of the Lord's favor, and the day of vengeance of our God; to comfort all who mourn.

Isaiah 61: 1—2 (RSV)

Motivated by the power of the gospel, church leaders will take the initiative and not be afraid to call their congregations back to being in harmony with God, with nature, and with the rest of humanity. Church leaders have the responsibility of leading their congregations to search for the gifts and talents of its individuals that will enable them to live in a community of genuine mutuality. Church leaders will facilitate the uncovering of the corporate gifts and talents of the congregation in order to be about the complete task of the church, to share their resources with those who are in need and to accept help from those whose resources are greater.

. . .What I ask you to do is in your own interests. You made a good beginning last year both in the work you did and in your willingness to undertake it. Now I want you to go on and finish it: be as eager to complete the scheme as you were to adopt it, and give according to your means. Provided there is an eager desire to give, God accepts what a man has; he does not ask for what he has not. There is no question of relieving others at the cost of hardship to yourselves; it is a question of equality. At the moment your surplus meets their need, but one day your need may be met from their surplus. The aim is equality; as Scripture has it, "The man who got much had no more than enough, and the man who got little did not go short."

II Corinthians 8: 10b—15 (NEB)

Church leaders have the responsibility for knowing what liberating education is all about and how to go about it. But in order for them to have these skills, the pedagogy of the church must also be educated to liberation.[104] The community that has been labeled "minority" in the constituency of the church has the resources to share this liberating education. But to tap this resource, it is necessary for our church leaders to make a total about face in the language and thinking processes.

The initial step is that of perceiving the resources as being much more than money. The next step is perceiving "minority" congregations as teachers who are able to transmit information and not simply as pupils whose purpose is to receive. They are subjects who can impact their environment and not merely as objects who are affected by the environment; but as responsible adults who are capable of making decisions about themselves and their futures.

There is another large community in our church that we don't often think of. These are the congregations whose constituency is neither economically poor nor wealthy, whose ethnicity cannot be defined in the categories used to separate "minorities" from the "majority." These are congregations isolated because of geographical location (rural/farm, mountain), age (retirees), interests and needs (leisure, arts and music). These congregations also have a certain amount of control, having had to learn how to cope in a society that judges and alienates them on the basis of subjective standards of acceptability.

Reciprocity here means inclusion of all people again, that no one survives on the periphery of the society. We are all children of God, sisters and brothers of and in Christ and congregations whose ministries relate to circumstances other than economics and race have a lot to teach and to share. In terms of those congregations already relating to mission in North America and the world, reciprocity means that a poor congregation receiving financial help from a wealthier congregation has something to share with that congregation which cannot be measured in dollars and cents. It means that we share what we have because it is not ours in the first place, but really belongs to everyone. This means that congregations receiving program support from churchwide agencies have something to give back that is worth at least as much as the gift of financial aid.

The configuration these gifts take may be varied and, perhaps, not even understandable upon measured response to the gift. But this is true reciprocity—realizing and being willing to learn from those who have historically been labeled oppressed and disenfranchised. When the "minority" people see and feel that their gifts and talents are being received with sincere joy and being shared authentically, then the church will be inclusive and about its mission—acting out God's love.

> Love is patient, love is kind and envies no one. Love is never boastful, not conceited, nor rude; never selfish, not quick to take offense. Love keeps no score of wrongs; does not gloat over another man's sins, but delights in the truth. There is nothing love cannot face; there is no limit to its faith, its hope and its endurance. Love will never come to an end.

> I Corinthians 13: 4—8 (NEB)

The ethical "ought" has now been redeemed: the gospel brings the Christian from fulfilling the demands of the law as a mandate to delighting in fulfilling the law as imitators of and empowered by Jesus Christ. In the revelation of Christ, the "you must do justice and love mercy" of the law has been replaced by the "we will do justice and love mercy" of the gospel.

BIBLIOGRAPHY

Ahlstrom, Sydney E., "Theology in America: A Historical Survey," The Shaping of American Religion. Vol. I of Religion in American Life. Edited by James W. Smith and Leland Jamison. Princeton: Princeton University Press, 1961.

Allport, Gordon W., The Nature of Prejudice. Boston, Mass.: Addison

Wesley Publishing Company, 1954.

Baldwin, James, The Fire Next Time. New York: Dial Press, 1963.

Barrett, David B., Schism and Renewal in Africa. London: n.p., 1968.

Beckman, David, "Trance: From Africa to Pentacostalism," Concordia

Theological Monthly, XLV January 1974.

Bennett, Leronne, The Challenge of Blackness. Chicago: Johnson Publishing Company, Inc., 1972.

Billingsly, Andrew, Black Families in White America. New York: Prentice Hall, Inc. 1968.

Bouman, Walter R., "The Gospel and the Smalcald Articles," Concordia Theological Monthly, XL, June, July—August 1969.

Bonhoeffer, Dietrich, Letters and Papers from Prison. New York: n.p.

Brueggemann, The Land. Philadelphia: Fortress Press, 1977.

Chestang, Leon W., "Character Development in a Hostile Environment," Occasional paper number 3, November 1973, School of Social Service Administration, n.p.

Cleage, Albert B., Jr. The Black Messiah. New York: Sheed and Ward, Inc., 1968.

Cone, James, "The Black Consciousness and the Black Church,"

Christianity and Crisis, XXX (November 2 & 16, 1970).

_____. Black Theology and Black Power. New York: Seabury Press, 1969.

Cross, William E., "The Negro—to—Black Conversion Experience: Toward A Psychology of Black Liberation," Black World (July 1971).

David, Allison and John Dolland. Children of Bondage. Washington, D.C.: American Council on Education, 1941.

Ditmanson, Harold, "New Themes in Christian Social Ethics," Lutheran World, XV, No. 1, 1968.

DuBois, W.E.B., Souls of Black Folk. New York: Premier Books, 1952.

Ebeling, Gerhard, "The Significance of the Critical Historical Method for Church and Theology in Protestantism," Word and Faith, translated by James W. Leitch, Philadelphia: Fortress Press, 1963.

Elert, Werner, The Christian Ethos, Philadelphia: Fortress Press, 1967. Law and Gospel. Philadelphia: Fortress Press, 1957.

Ellison, Ralph, Invisible Man. New York: Signet Books, 1952.

Fausset, Arthur Huff, Black Gods of the Metropolis. Philadelphia: University of Pennsylvania Press, 1944.

Fishel, K,H. and Benjamin Quarles, The Negro American. Glenview, IL: Scott Foresman and Co, 1967.

Frazier, E. Franklin, The Negro Church in America. New York: Schocken Books, 1974.

_____. The Negro in the United States. New York: MacMillan Co., 1975.

Frieri, Paulo, Pedagogy of the Oppressed. Chapters 1 & 2. Gilkey, Langdon, Part II, Chapters 3,4.

Grambs, Jean D., "The Self—Concept: Basis for Reeducation of Negro Youth," Negro Self—Concept: Implications for School

Citizenship. New York: McGraw—Hill Book Company, 1965.

Green, Hannah, I Never Promised You a Rose Garden. New York: Holt, Rinehart and Winston, 1967. Inc., 1968.

Griffin, John Howard, Black Like Me. New York: New American Library, 1961.

Headley, John M, Luther's View of Church History. New Haven, Conn: Yale University Press, 1963.

Herskovits, Melville J., The Myth of Negro Past. Boston: Beacon Press, 1941.

Jones, LeRoi, Blues People: Negro Music in White America, New York: William Morrow & Co, Inc. 1963.

Jones, Major J., Christian Ethics for Black Theology. Nashville: Abingdon Press, 1974, pps. 15—16.

Lewis, C.S., The Great Divorce. New York: MacMillan Co., 1946.

Lohff, Wenzel, "Justication and Anthropology," (translation) Concordia Theological Monthly, XLIV, January 1973.

Lincoln, Eric C., "Who's Listening?" Christianity and Crisis, XXX (November 2 & 16, 1970).

Mayer, F.E., "The Prior Distinction Between Law and Gospel and the Terminology, Visible and Invisible Church," Concordia Theological Monthly, XXV (March 1954). Study Document on Christian Action in Racial and Ethnic Relations: Its Biblical and Theological Basis. New York: Board of Social Ministry, 1965, p. 4—5.

Mays, Benjamin E, The Negro's God. New York: Atheneum, 1968.

McClain, William B, "The Genius of the Black Church," Christianity and Crisis XXX (November 2 and 16, 1970).

Meier, August and Elliot Rudwick, editors. Black Protest in the Sixties. Chicago: Chicago Quadrangle Books, Inc., 1967.

Mitchell, Henry H., Black Preaching. New York: J.B, Lippincott Company, 1970.

Mueller, W.R. and J. Jacobsen, "Samuel Beckett's Long Last Saturday to Wait or Not to Wait," in Nathan Scott, Jr., Man in Modern Theatre. Richmond, VA: John Knox Press, 1965.

Negroes in Policy—Making Positions in Chicago: A Study in Black Powerlessness. Mimeographed, Chicago: Chicago Urban League, 1968.

Niebuhr, Richard H., Christ and Culture. New York: Harper and Row, Publishers, 1951.

Oden, Thomas, The Structure of Awareness. Nashville, TN: Abingdon Press, 1969.

Poussaint, Alvin F., Why Blacks Kill Blacks. New York: Emerson Hall Publishers, Inc., 1972

Roberts, Deotis, Jr., Liberation and Reconciliation. Philadelphia: The Westminster Press, 1971.

Scharlemann, Martin H., "God's Acts as Revelation," Concordia Theological Monthly XXXII (April 1961).

Sheares, Reuben A., "Beyond White Theology," Christianity and Crisis, XXX (November 2 & 16, 1970).

Skinner, B.F, Beyond Freedom and Dignity. New York: Knopf, 1972. Soulen, Richard H, "Black Worship and Hermeneutic," The Christian Century, LXXXVI (February 11, 1970).

Thielicke, Helmut, Death and Life. Philadelphia: Fortress Press, 1970.

Tournier, Paul, Guilt and Grace: A Psychological Study. London: Hodder and Stoughton, 1962.

Turner, Harold W., African Independent Church: The Life and Faith of the Church of the Lord (Aladura). Oxford: The London Press, 1967.

Washington, Joseph R., Black Religion. Boston: Beacon Press, 1964.

_____. "How Black is Black Religion?" Quest for a Black Theology, James J. Gardiner & J. Deotis Roberts, editors, Philadelphia: Pilgrim Press, 1971.

Welbourne, Frederick Burkewood and B.A. Ogot, A Place to Feel at Home: A Study of Two Independent Churches in Western Kenya. London: Oxford University Press, 1966.

Watts, Leon W., "The National Committee of Black Churchmen," Christianity and Crisis, XXX (November 2 & 16, 1970).

B L AC K   W O M E N
and the Lutheran Church

By the Rev. Cheryl A. Stewart

An issue which should be under more fire today than ever before in the black and Lutheran community has to do with the role and future of black women who serve the church in professional capacities – pastors, executives, professors, lay associates – and of whom there are so few. In speaking of black women, we are fully aware that we are also addressing the future of the black family.

In our society black women are burdened with the additional problem of sexism. Just the simple identification of this problem can be perceived as counterproductive to the goals and objectives of the black family. But, at the same time, identifying the problem may also be seen as a faithful response in the resistance of demonic acts; in other words, naming the demon.

As a sickness in this country, sexism has been well defined. However, its form becomes even more menacing when combined with the racism with which the black family—men, women, and children—has long done battle and by which the black family has been victimized. The situation within the church, an institution like any other institution within the society, reflects the climate of the society. As long as the society's categories of male and female and of the role and respective places of women and men are accepted and adhered to, the dilemma will continue. The alternative is to use the categories supplied by our Lord himself, as demonstrated in Scripture.

There are presently seven ordained black women in all of Lutheranism. On March 21—22, 1982, a meeting planned for these women took place at the Lutheran School of Theology at Chicago. This was the first time such a meeting had occurred.

It was interesting to note that the time allotted was consumed fully with the sharing of personal odysseys to and in the ministry. One of the major concerns of the group was the lack of communication, so much so that among the seven there were some who had not previously met the others. The agenda for this meeting was to discuss identity, relationships and mission as they relate to the black community theologically and sociologically.

The future of the black family is dependent upon rebuilding the identity, relationships, and mission of black men and black women. The problems that surround us are innumerable and no one can or should implement the solutions for us. We need to remember our heritage and legacy, to recall the times when the black family stayed together regardless of the circumstances, to reclaim the values and traditions of our ancestors.

In order to contribute to this rebuilding of the black community and family, black women need to meet together in dialogue, sharing our stories and our immediate situations in life. Only in this way can we remember, recall and reclaim the fountain of wealth which we have come to call the black ethos. In so doing, we will become more equipped to offer, with our black families, our unique contribution to the ecumenical table now being prepared before us within a new Lutheran church.

HISPANICS
A Short Related History
of Mexicano and Chicano People

By Samuel Hernandez

Mexico's Earliest Civilizations

3000 B.C. -1500 B.C.

Wandering tribes of "Indians," whose ancestors had slowly migrated many centuries earlier from Eastern Asia across the Bering Strait and down the North American continent, began to settle on the land of Central and Southeastern Mexico, where they learned to cultivate maize (corn). As they grew their crops, these villagers began to invent accurate calendars, needed to measure the seasons for planting and harvesting, and a system of religion, with prayers for rain.

1000 B.C. -300 B.C. (Approximately)

The New World's first major civilization was developed by the Olmecas in the tropical lowlands of Veracruz on the Gulf Coast. Their culture spread widely, producing fine sculpture with particularly huge heads and round, mask-like faces, hieroglyphic writing, and large religious centers.

300 A.D. -1200 A.D.

The Mayan civilization, which probably began under the influence of the Olmecas, grew into a distinctive and brilliant culture. The Maya, an agricultural people unusually skilled in the arts and sciences, were governed by hereditary priests and princes. The priests were outstanding scholars, mathematicians, and astronomers. They devised an elaborate system of picture writing, invented the mathematical zero long before its use in Europe, and developed a calendar more accurate than the one used in the Old World. Their artists excelled at stone carvings and at painted frescoes. By the eighth century A.D., as many as 14 million Maya may have lived in this peaceful civilization, inhabiting small wattle or adobe houses, but using stone to build soaring 200 foot pyramids, as at Chichen Itzá.

The Maya's independent city centers were spread in a loose federation throughout southern Mexico, Guatemala, and Honduras. Around the year 900, however, the Mayan centers in the south quite suddenly collapsed, and those in Yucatan survived by adapting to the Toltec invaders.

700 A.D. -1100 A.D.

An era of cultural decline and warfare began when fierce nomadic tribes from the north, known as Chichimecas, overran the central valley of Mexico and the fertile lands of the Maya. Outstanding among the Chichimeca people were the Toltecas, who gained control of the central Mexican plateau after 900. The Toltecas rebuilt the ancient temples to serve their own bloodthirsty gods, and they placed military leaders rather than priests at the head of their society. One later group of Chichimecas settled at Texcoco, across the lake from the future site of Mexico City; their leader from about 1418 to 1470 was Nezahualcoyotl, a philosopher-poet-prince whose name meant "hungry coyote." The Chichimeca culture reached its height in the great empire built by the Aztecs, the last Chichimeca tribe to arrive in central Mexico from the north.

The Aztec Empire

1200 A. D. (approximately)

The Aztecs, a small tribe whose ancestors had come from an unidentified place in northwestern Mexico called Aztlan, reached the valley of Mexico relatively late, They wandered around the plateau and did not settle until a legendary prophecy was fulfilled.

1325 A.D.

On a marshy island in salty Lake Texcoco, the wandering Aztecs saw the sign they had been waiting for: an eagle eating a serpent while perched on a cactus. This was an omen showing them where to build a permanent settlement, their war god Huitzilopochtli had told the priests. Building on the site now covered by Mexico City, they named their city Tenochtitlan, "Near the Cactus."

1400 A.D. -1519 A.D.

From 1400 on, the Aztecs were able to use a combination of force and politics to dominate the whole valley, gradually extending their empire as far as Guatemala. As they fortified their island capital, the Aztecs became skilled engineers. Within 200 years, Tenochtitlan became the flourishing city that amazed the Spanish conquistadores. Strong dikes protected it from floods, while three causeways connected it to the lakeshore. Aqueducts brought fresh water from springs in the Chapultepec hills. There were many ornate buildings, well—kept marketplaces, and houses completed with flowering roof gardens and steam baths. Most notable were the pyramid temples dedicated to Huitzilopochtli and other gods, on whose altars thousands of human sacrifices—usually prisoners of war—were made.

In 1502, the reign of the emperor Moctezuma (1480 -1520) began. The empire that he ruled was notable for its fine sculptures, weaving, metal and feather work, and music. Almost all citizens went to school to study religion or secular occupations. Some 300,000 people lived in Tenochtitlan, one of the largest cities in the sixteenth—century world. This city was give times bigger than London for example. It was, above all, a warlike city its streets filled with soldiers whose helmets were shaped like heads of fierce animals. The military intelligence system of this empire was so efficient that Moctezuina was warned of the Spaniards' approach long before they neared his capital, and he even knew how the Spanish soldiers used guns and horses though he had never seen either.

The Spanish Conquest

1492 A.D.

Christopher Columbus (1451? -1506), sailing in the service of Spain, discovered America.

1519 A.D. -1521 A.D.

Hernan Cortes (1485 -1547) sailed from Cuba in February 1519 to find the Aztecs' rumored treasures. He landed in Yucatan and allied some enemies of the Aztecs to his cause, increasing his army's size from the original 553 Spaniards to nearly 7,000 fighting men. He received more unexpected help from the legend of Quetzalcoatl, the bearded and fair-skinned god-king whom the Aztecs expected to return from the east that very year. Moctezuma, unable to decide whether Cortes was Quetzalcoatl, offered no resistance but sent messengers to the oncoming army with fine presents and a polite request to leave his empire.

But the sight of gold and silver gifts made the conquistadores still more eager to reach the Aztec capital. They arrived in November 1519. Cortes took Moctezuma hostage and governed through him, until in the spring he had to leave with many of his soldiers to confront another Spanish expedition, sent to recall him. In Cortes' absence, the Aztecs in Tenochtitlan rebelled. When Moctezuma told the Aztecs that Cortes was their new emperor, he was stoned to death by his own people.

When Cortes returned with an even larger army, the whole city broke out in renewed fighting. Many of the Spanish soldiers, on what they named the Noche Triste (31 June 1520), were killed by Aztecs or drowned as they fled for their lives across one of the causeways to the mainland. Cortes regrouped his army and attacked again. This time the city was under the command of Cuauhtemoc (1495-1525), Moctezuma's twenty—five year old nephew. The Aztecs fought heroically for three months, but the city fell on 31 August 1521, and was razed to the ground. Cortes founded Mexico City on its ruins. Cuauhtemoc was captured, tortured and later hanged for "treason."

Colonial Mexico

1521 A.D.

The encomienda or "entrustment" system was established, under which Spanish landowners were "given in trust" certain numbers of Indians who were forced to work on their farms or in mines in return, theoretically, for being instructed in the Roman Catholic faith. In practice, it was a form of slavery; Indians who attempted to escape or rebel were branded. The great estates of the Spanish-owned haciendas were created simply by displacing the indians from their tribal villages,

1524 A.D.

The first Spanish missionaries, a group of Franciscans, arrived. They were the forerunners of many other priests who tried to Christianize and protect the Indians, but who, at the same time, made the Church extremely powerful and rich. The friar who did the most to win the Indians' trust and affection was Bartolome' de las Casas (1474-1566), a Dominican missionary and historian, who worked hard but unsuccessfully to abolish the forced labor of the encomienda.

1535 A.D.

All the Spanish lands were reorganized as the Viceroyalty of New Spain under the rule of Antonio de Mendoza (1490? -1552) who encouraged education and brought the first printing press to America, among other things. Mendoza was the first of 63 viceroys who were to represent the Spanish crown during the colonial era.

1553 A.D.

The first institution of higher learning in North America, later to be called the National University, opened in Mexico City.

1557 A.D.

A new process for mining silver made it possible to export even larger amounts of the precious metal back to Spain.

1720 A.D.

The encomienda system was offically abolished, but exploitation of the Indians continued. The colonial population had slowly developed into three distinct social groups: the Indians, who outnumbered all others; the unprivileged mestizos, people of mixed Indian and Spanish blood; and the privileged whites, who were split into two antagonistic classes—the superior Spanish-born gachupines, or "wearers of spurs," and the colonial-born Creoles, or criollos. The colonial population also included a distinct group of blacks, who later merged with the mestizos.

The Church did not solve the problems of this divided society, because its own strong political power and huge landholdings only accentuated the wide gulf between the wealthy landowners and the poor. The establishment of new industries, which might have created a middle class, was forbidden as a way of protecting royal monopolies. Mexico's mineral wealth was steadily drained off to Spain (by 1800, almost two-thirds of Spain's revenues came from New Spain). Colonial administrators were unimaginative, apathetic, or corrupt.

All these social evils increased during 300 years of colonialism, while the conquest and consolidation of new territories went on. Discontent with the Spanish government grew steadily among even the prosperous criollos, as eighteenth-century revolutionary theories spread from France to the United States. By the time Napoleon was overthrowing the Spanish royalty in the Old World, the intellectuals and merchants of Mexico were ready for their own revolt in the New Spain.

Independence

1810 A.D.

Miguel Hidalgo y Costilla (1753-1811), a Creole who was a parish priest of Dolores (in west central Mexico), became the father of Mexican Independence by a simple brave act. Hidalgo had been meeting for some time with a small group of other intellectuals to discuss independence from Spain. When this secret group was discovered by the authorities, Hidalgo knew the time had come for action. On 16 September, he summoned his parishioners to the Dolores church steps and gave his cry (grito) of liberty:

"Mexicanos! Viva Mexico! Viva independencia! Viva la Virgen de Guadalupe!" His listeners added, "Muerte a los gachupines!" ("Death to the Gachupines!")

The banner of the Virgin of Guadalupe was picked up as the flag of his followers. An Indian, Juan Diego, had in 1531 seen miraculous visions of the Virgin Mary on the hill of Tepeyacac, which was later renamed Guadalupe in honor of a shrine in Spain. Guadalupe had once been the site of a shrine to Tonantzin, Aztec goddess of fertility.

Hildalgo's ragged followers, armed with nothing more than their banner and an assortment of axes, machetes, and knives, marched off to liberate their country. Indians and mestizos deserted haciendas and silver mines to join them as the word spread. Ignacio Allende (1779-1811), a Creole officer who had been part of Hidalgo's original conspiracy, also brought some of the colonial militia into the revolutionists' ranks.

The rebel forces grew to 80,000. They overran Guanajuato, Guadalajara, and Valladolid, and defeated a royalist force at Monte de las Cruces on 30 October, but then suffered defeats. Hidalgo and other leaders, fleeing toward- the U.S., were betrayed, caught, and shot. Their heads were placed on the walls of a warehouse in Guanajuato, the scene of their first victory.

1811 A.D.

Jose Maria Morelos y Pavon (1765-1815), a young parish priest who was a mestizo, took over Hildago's role as revolutionary leader. Morelos was joined by Mariano Matamoros (d. 1814), another liberal priest. Morelos led a brilliant campaign in the south, capturing Orizaba, Oaxaca (1812), and Acapulco (1813). He called together a congress and proclaimed a republic, proposing to divide the riches of big landowners and the Church between the new government and the poor, to restore lands to dispossessed peasants, and to abolish the special privileges of the Church and army. He was defeated in battle in 1813, captured, defrocked and shot in 1815 (a year after Matamoros had met the same fate). But Morelos' policies formed the basis for the revolutionary movements that followed. Only a few leaders, notably Vicente Guerrero (1782-1831) and Guadalupe Victoria (1786?-1843), were left to carry on the fighting.

Mexican Independence

1821 A.D.

The tide turned when Agustin de Iturbide, the royalist colonel who had defeated Morelos, was sent by the viceroy to fight Guerrero. But Iturbide had begun to have his own ideas about independence, and instead of fighting he opened negotiations with Guerrero. With Guerrero's and Victoria's consent, Iturbide announced the Plan of Iguala, by which Mexico was to become an independent nation, preferably a constitutional monarchy governed by a member of the Spanish royal family. Other parts of the plan specified that all races were to be equal (opening the way for mestizos and Indians to hold office). When no Bourbon prince accepted the offer of the crown of Mexico, Iturbide's soldiers proclaimed him Emperor Agustin I, the Plan of Iguala was scrapped, and a new form of conservative government began.

1822 A.D. -1824 A.D.

A liberal revolt soon began, led by Guadalupe Victoria and Antonio Lopez de Santa Anna (1794-1876). In 1823, Iturbide was forced to abdicate and go into exile; when he returned from Europe the next year, he was captured, tried before a court of law, and shot. A republic was set up with Victoria as its first president.

Victoria was succeeded by Guerrero. Then personalismo, or personality cult, replaced liberal ideals, as a succession of political and military leaders all sought their own ends, and governments rose and fell. Nothing was done to solve the country's social problems. Santa Anna himself ruled Mexico eleven separate times between 1833 and 1855, his political affiliations swinging from liberal to clerical conservative. During his dictatorial rule, through war and through sale, Mexico lost more than half of its original territory to the United States.

The U.S.-Nexican War 1835 A.D. -1836 A.D.

In the Mexican province of Texas, conflict between Mexican officials and Anglo-American farmers (who had been given land grants by the Mexican government) grew steadily worse during the early years of the Mexican republic. A complex series of incidents (including friction caused by Mexico's law against slavery) led to open revolt by the Americans in 1835 and to their declaration of independence on March 2, 1836. A large force of Mexican soldiers, sent to subdue this Texan revolution, captured the Alamo on March 6, 1836, but was cruelly defeated six weeks later at San Jacinto. Texas became an independent republic for ten years.

1845 A.D. -1848 A.D.

The annexation of Texas by the United States in December 1845 became one of the main causes of the Mexican War. Newly-elected President James K. Polk, an aggressive expansionist, was determined to acquire California, as well. When the Mexican government refused to enter diplomatic talks about the possible sale of California and New Mexico (part of which was claimed by Texas), American empire builders and others who wanted to extend the slaveholding territories of the U.S. encouraged a war.

In March 1846, when General Zachary Taylor occupied Point Isabel at the mouth of the Rio Grande, the Mexicans, who claimed the Nueces as the boundary, believed they had been attacked. Mexican guns began to shell an American fort near Brownsville, Texas. On May 12, 1846, Congress declared war on Mexico. Taylor was already fighting. The war spread to New Mexico and to Mexico itself. American soldiers landed at Veracruz in March 1847, and, under General Winfield Scott, began a drive to Mexico City, The great fortress of Chapultepec, supposedly invincible on its rocky hill south of the city, was assaulted by the Americans and fell on September 13. The next day, the Americans entered Mexico City, where they remained until the peace treaty was signed.

Although Chapultepec fell, it became for Mexicans a symbol of pride because of the courage of Los Ninos Heroes, six military college cadets who made a suicidal last stand on its walls shouting with their dying breath, "Viva Mexico! Viva el Colegio Militar!" The Mexicans were brave, able fighters. The Americans won largely because Mexico was torn by internal strife. The presidency for example, changed hands twelve times during the war alone, and some of the Mexican states refused to help their federal government.

1848 A.D.

Secret peace talks led to the Treaty of Guadalupe Hidalgo, which was ratified by the U.S. Senate on March 10. Under its terms, Mexico ceded to the U.S. some two-fifths of its territory—including Arizona, California, New Mexico, Utah, Nevada and part of Colorado; agreed to the 1845 annexation of Texas; and agreed that the new boundary was to follow the Rio Grande, in return for a payment of $15 million. The former Mexican citizens who lived north of that new border now became full citizens of the United States unless they left their homes and moved south within a year. The treaty specifically guaranteed the civil liberties, property rights, cultural rights, and religious freedom of the new citizens.

1853 A.D.

More Mexican territory was lost by the Gadsden Purchase, by which the American government of President Franklin Pierce bought for $10 million a large strip of land (over 45,000 square miles) along the border in what is today New Mexico and Arizona. The land was sold by Santa Anna, who needed cash to pay the troops who upheld his dictatorship.

Reform and Revolution

1854 A.D.

Reform leaders met in the town of Ayutla and drew up a plan of action calling for Santa Anna's removal and a new federal constitution. Prominent among the reformers who supported this Plan of Ayutla was Benito Pablo Juarez (1806-1872), an idealistic lawyer; Juan Alvarez (1790?-1867), an Indian who had fought under Norelos; and Ignacio Comonfort (1812-1863), a general who died fighting French invaders a few years later. The subsequent Revolution of Ayutla, the most significant event in Mexican history since Independence, resulted in Santa Anna's exile in 1855.

1857 A.D.

Alvarez and then Comonfort took over the presidency. In 1857, a new constitution was written. Its clauses included land reform, free education, freedom of the press, secularization of Church property, and abolition of the army's privileges. These reforms caused an uproar among Mexican conservatives. As rebellion flared up, the government was taken over by Benito Juarez who had been acting as minister of justice. As a Zapotec Indian, Juarez was descended from a very ancient warrior tribe in southern Mexico, and had previously been governor of Oaxaca. In 1853, he had been imprisoned for opposing Santa Anna, who was then temporarily exiled in the United States.

1858 A.D.-1861 A.D.

The fierce civil struggle between reformers and conservatives, known as the War of Reform, left Mexico on the edge of ruin and bankruptcy. Juarez and his government were forced to flee to Guanajuato, Guadalajar, and finally Veracruz, but in the end they defeated the conservative elements.

1864 A.D. -1867 A.D.

New difficulties were caused almost at once by foreign powers, particularly the United States, France, Spain, and England, who intervened because Juarez's government was unable to pay Mexico's international debts. Napoleon III of France, with support from Mexican conservatives, decided to place an unemployed Austrian archduke named Maximilian (1832-1867) on the "throne" of Mexico. Maximilian, a well—meaning man, was assured that the Mexican people had elected him. He and his wife Carlota sailed for Mexico in 1864.

As French soldiers moved in to enforce Maximilian's rule, Juarez had to flee again, moving his capital to El Paso del Norte, now called Juarez. However, the Mexican people supported Juarez, the "empire" collapsed when the French soldiers were withdrawn, and Maximilian was captured and shot in May, 1867 by Juarista soldiers ("Cinco de Mayo"). Juarez, an honest and stubborn man who became a national hero, was re—elected as president in 1867 and 1871. He began the molding of modern Mexico, notably by starting free education and by developing transportation and industry.

1876 AD. -1910 A.D.

Porfirio Diaz (1830—1915), a mestizo general from Oaxaca, seized the presidency after Juarez died. Diaz ruled Mexico until 1910, longer than any other man in history. He was ambitious, pompous, and ruthless. He controlled the legislature and the press, changed the constitution so that he could remain in power, ignored Juarez's reform laws by allowing the Church to accumulate property again, and sold public lands cheaply to his favorites. As Diaz encouraged industrialization, foreign capital poured into Mexico: roads, railroads, harbors, and telegraph lines were built, but they mainly benefited the foreigners who exploited the country's natural resources.

The Mexican government and a few of the very rich got richer, but Mexico's oppressed people became poorer than ever. Education stagnated. Democracy became just an empty form. All over Mexico, Indians lost even more of their communal lands and sank deeper into peonage, the system that forced them to work on plantations to repay debts from which they could never escape. To stifle the rising discontent in the countryside, Diaz created the Rurales, a new and brutal force of federal police, who became a hated symbol of the Diaz regime.

1910 A.D.

Diaz caused a sensation by announcing that he intended to restore democratic rule, but in 1910 he was re-elected, as usual. Popular anger boiled over into revolution, led at first by aristocratic Francisco Madero (1873—1913). When Madero dared to run for election against Diaz, he was imprisoned. After Diaz' re-election, Madero was released and fled to Texas, where he proclaimed a revolution (El Plan de San Luis Potosi). On his return to Mexico, he found that several groups of rebels were already up in arms in Chihuahua under the leadership of Francisco

"Pancho" Villa (1877?-1923). Villa's rebels supported Madero and captured the town of Juarez on May 9, 1911.

At almost the same time, an independent army of rebels rose in the south in Morelos under Einiliano Zapata (1879-1919), an Indian tenant farmer who rallied peasants to the cause of agrarian reform with his cry of "Land and Liberty." Federal soldiers deserted to join the rebels they had been sent to fight. The landless Indians of many tribes—the Yaqui of Sonora, the large group of Tarahumara to their east, the Chaxnula of the southern mountain highlands in Chiapas, and the Zapotecas, among many others—joined with mestizo factory workers and liberal "Spanish" intellectuals to carry the Revolution to triumph. Mobs rioted in front of the National Palace in Mexico City. Diaz resigned on May 23, 1911, and fled to exile. Madero, elected president by an honest vote, took office in November.

1913 A.D.

Madero was unfortunately more of an idealist than an administrator, and he trusted many of the wrong people. By February 1913, when he had held office for little more than a year, Mexico City was again a battlefield. One of the government's generals, Victoriano Huerta (1854-1916), betrayed Madero and had him murdered. Huerta then maneuvered his way into the presidency, which again became a reactionary dictatorship.

1914 A.D. -1924 A.D.

Counterrevolutions appeared at once, led by Villa, Zapata, Venustiano Carranza (1859—1920), Alvaro Obregon (1880—1928), and others. For the next ten years, Mexico was in a continual state of chaotic fighting, which included intervention by American troops. More than 800,000 people died by violence or starvation and disease. From the martyred Madero to Obregon, who took office in December 1920, Mexico had ten presidents. During these years of strife, as revolutionists turned against each other, Villa and Zapata were both assassinated, as were Carranza and Obregon, in the end.

But important reforms were made in the constitution of 1917: a statement that the Mexican government owned the nation's land and minerals, opening the way for long-delayed land redistribution and the expropriation of oil fields; a labor code; a new emphasis on public education; and restoration of the ejido, the village-owned communal land. During Obregon's presidency (1920-24), there was a concerted effort to systematize the results of the Revolution and to reestablish order, The most disastrous but important decade in Mexico's history was over.

The Revolution of 1910-20 stimulated all the Mexican arts, as painters and writers took part in the political upheavals. The stirring events of Mexican history, from its earliest days to this final revolution, were recorded in the 1920s and 1930s in a series of murals by the painter Diego Rivera (1886—1957). The two other "greats" of modern Mexican art, David Alfato Siqueiros (b. 1898) and Jose Clemente Orozco (1883-1949), both joined the revolutionary troops and later also created murals on Mexican history.

North of the Border

1540 A.D. - 1848 A.D.

Under leaders like Francisco Vasquez de Coronado (in 1540) and Juan de Onate (in 1598), the ancestors of today's Mexican Americans risked their lives to explore the Southwest and make peace with the Indians living there. They had built presidios (military posts) and missions across the inhospitable region, founding Santa Fe in 1610, when the only English settlement in North America was a small fort at Jamestown. They also founded San Antonio, Albuquerque, Tucson, Los Angeles, and many other cities. Skilled miners searched for gold and silver, quicksilver, and copper. Orchards and vineyards were planted. Ranchers irrigated the dry land and multiplied the sheep and longhorn cattle originally drive up from Mexico, while their vaqueros worked as the original "cowboys." Culture and learning spread, as schools and printing presses were established.

By the early 1800s, trade with the Americanos to the northeast was conducted over the long Santa Fe Trail, but close contact and conflict with Anglo—American settlers was confined mainly to Texas. By 1848, when the Treaty of Guadalupe Hidalgo ended the U.S.—Mexican War, some 75,000 Spanish-speaking people were living in the huge region that suddenly became part of the United States.

1849 A.D. -1900 A.D.

The lure of gold, cattle, and cotton brought Anglo-Americans pouring into the Southwest as soon as the war ended, and the new settlers soon outnumbered the Mexican Americans in every state except New Mexico. Using laws, taxes, and banking practices that were foreign to the traditional Spanish ways, and often resorting to dishonesty and force, the Anglos took over the great ranches and the communally-owned grazing lands of Spanish—speaking farmers and villagers. In the gold fields of California, Mexican miners lost their claims to the forty-niners through devices like the Foreign Miners' Law of 1851.

One Sonoran miner who worked in California from 1849 to 1851 was Joaquin Murrieta. After Anglo miners raped and killed his wife Rosita, drove him from his gold claim, and then whipped him in public on a false horse—stealing charge, Murrieta vowed revenge. He became the leader of a large band of desperados, conducting a vendetta marked by daring robberies and narrow escapes. He became a legendary figure, el bandido terrible, the "Robin Hood of El Dorado." The California government offered a reward of $5,000 for him, dead or alive, and because his last name was not well known, California became unsafe for anyone whose name happened to be Joaquin. In 1853, Murrieta was surprised and shot by mounted rangers near Stockton, and his head was preserved and exhibited for many years. (Conflicting stories are told that he died of old age.)

In the San Luis Valley of Colorado in the 1860s, the Mexican-born brothers Vivian and Jose Espinoza carried on a similar guerrilla war against the Anglos, killing about thirty men in ambush before they were shot and beheaded by soldiers.

In New Mexico was another folk hero, Elfego Baca, deputy sheriff of Socorro, who once barricaded himself in an adobe hut and single-handedly fought off a mob of Texas cowboys during a night and day of gunfire.

Violent fights and murders between Mexicans and Anglos were all too common. The number of killings of Mexican Americans in the Southwest from 1850 to 1930 exceeded the number of lynchings of blacks for the same period.

1910 A.D. -1945 A.D.

The upheavals of the 1910 Revolution caused the first of many waves of immigration by Mexican citizens into the United States. Shortages of workers during the two world wars increased the American need for Mexican immigrants, who moved north by the hundreds of thousands when jobs were plentiful. But they and the American-born Chicanos were poorly paid, segregated in schools and public places, threatened by violence. They were particularly hard hit by the Depression of the 1930s, during which many of them were forcibly deported to Mexico. Their attempts to organize unions were put down by force. The fact that an unusually large number of Chicanos were decorated for heroism in World War II did not protect them from the "zoot suit riots" of Los Angeles in 1943 and other less open forms of attack.

1945 A.D. -1960 A.D.

At the end of World War II, some Chicano veterans profited from the veterans bill. The majority came home to the same socio-political and economic problems they had left. Chicanos organized veterans, social, and political groups to secure equality, with an emphasis on political patronage, involvement in education, an end to employment discrimination, and an occasional civil rights confrontation.

1962 A.D.

Cesar Chavez, messianic leader of the United Farm Workers Organizing Committee (U.F.W.O.C.) began organizing what would become the first agricultural union in the United States.

1963 A.D.

Reiess Lopez Tijerina founded the Alianza Federal de Mercedes in New Mexico, with the aim of winning back the ancient Spanish and Mexican land grants based on the conditions of the Treaty of Guadalupe Hidalgo.

Denver Chicanos demonstrated against police brutality and the killings of young Chicanos in the streets.

1965 A.D.

The long huelga, or strike, of California grape workers began in the San Joaquin Valley in 1966 with a dramatic 300—mile march from Delano to Sacramento.

Rodolfo "Corky" Gonzales founded Denver's Crusade for Justice, providing social services, cultural programs, and leadership education; organizing around educational opportunities, jobs, and land reform; and building an urban power base for Chicano community control and liberation. Chicanos demonstrated against OEO programs for failing to meet the needs of the poor.

1966 A.D. —1967 A.D.

Tijerina and his followers temporarily took over the Kit Carson National Forest, proclaiming reestablishment of the nineteenth—century Pueblo de San Joaquin de Rio de Chama. In 1967, armed Alianza members raided the county courthouse in Tierra Amarilla. The raid, an attempt to make a citizens arrest of the district attorney in reprisal for harassments, resulted in the biggest manhunt in New Mexico's history and in Tijerina's arrest.

In Texas, striking farm workers marched 400 miles from the lower Rio Grande Valley to the state capital at Austin.

Late in 1967, Jose Angel Gutierrez and other activists in Texas formed La Raza Unida, a political party to coordinate Chicano civil rights efforts in the Southwest.

Chicano youth began to mobilize in the universities, the high schools, the barrios, forming such groups as United Mexican American student (U.M.A.S.) and Los Comancheros. Thousands of barrio gangs began to address themselves politically to the Chicano movimiento instead of self—hatred turf wars.

El Paso, Texas, Chicanos boycotted the President's conference on Mexican American affairs and organized around El Plan de El Paso, a manifesto calling for equal rights. A cultural renaissance, a quest for self—identity and positive self—worth, began to burst forth.

1968 A.D.

Cesar Chavez, in the continuing strike against California's table—grape growers, fasted for twenty—five days to dramatize La Causa. The strike and the national boycott of dessert grapes by sympathetic consumers became issues in the Presidential election campaign.

Reiess Tijerina and Rodolfo Corky Gonzales took part in the Poor People's Campaign with Martin Luther King, Jr. and continued with Ralph David Abernathy after Dr. King's death.

First "blow—out" by 5,000 Los Angeles high school students. Arrests of "The Los Angeles 13," accused of organizing the blow—out, caused nationwide protests.

Chicano Liberation School started by the Crusade for Justice.

1969 A.D.

The Crusade for Justice hosted over 1,500 youths from 100 organizations at the First National Chicano Youth Conference, which adopted El Plan de Aztlan, calling for Chicano liberation.

Chicano students organized a "blow—out" across the Southwest against cultural genocide and irrelevant education.

Massive walkouts and demonstrations occurred on September 16, Mexican Independence Day, which Chicanos associate with Chicano Liberation Day called for El Plan de Aztlan.

In Los Angeles, Chicano youths organized the largest Chicano antiwar moratorium in the history of the peace movement. Police disrupted the crowds with gas, clubs, and guns, and journalist Ruben Salazar was killed by the Los Angeles deputy sheriff. Whittier Avenue was burned as Chicanos rioted in retaliation. Hundreds were injured and hundreds jailed.

NATIVE AMERICANS
A Native American Perspective

By Ramona Soto Rank

"Without their land, the people would cease to live and be. Their land is more than a place on which to live and raise a family. It is an intimate part of their way of life, The land belongs to the community, although each family may use a portion on which to build a home. The land helps to maintain the community as a cohesive unit. It is the tabernacle of their race and culture, the repository of their dead and their history and the supplier of their physical and spiritual nourishment. The land is their past, present and future."[1]

The land, historically, is the center of importance for Native American people; Indian tribes revered the land and used it to sustain their unique way of life. Their culture evolved from their environment, and the abundance of resources determined the type of homes, clothing and life style of tribal members.

In an area where there was much timber, homes were made of wood, such as the long houses of the Iroquois and the great houses of the Northwest Coast. Grass houses were known to flourish in the vast plains area where grass was plentiful. Underground homes were found in the Midwest that protected the people from harsh changes in weather.

Food and clothing of native peoples were also from the land. One example of versatility was moccasins. Moccasins were high topped in some areas in order to protect the wearer from poisonous snakes and insects. In the rough, rocky areas, moccasins were hard soled to protect the feet, Soft soled moccasins were used where the ground was easy for walking. Clothing and ornaments were made from hides, feathers and other materials native to the tribe's environment. Everything was used, nothing was wasted. All things from the creator were respected.

Religion

Respect was the foundation upon which native religion was based. Respect for nature, respect for the creator, respect for the other members of the tribe. The entire system of being for native people was derived from their sense of respect.

One of the primary symbols in native culture and religion is the symbol of the circle. The circle further symbolizes life—a cycle that has no beginning and no end, and that must be lived from birth to death and beyond. The circle, in some form, is represented in all native religious and ceremonial rites. Persons sitting within the circle are all equally important. The different perspectives that they bring to the circle are all treated with the same importance.

Native peoples were in constant communion with the creator, grandfather, the supreme force. Each day was considered a gift, a new beginning. If a person was having troubles or was not feeling well, it was said that the person was "out of balance" with the creator. Bad things were looked upon as being separated from the creator. Being "out of balance" was not a desirable state.

The entire life of native people revolved around their communion with the creator. Ceremonies were used to celebrate special events within the tribe such as the birth of a child, the first birthday of a child, puberty, a vision quest, marriage, death and other special events. We can draw similar parallels with our modern day religious ceremonies such as baptism, confirmation and communion. These rituals provided the same symbolism—communion with the creator.

History

Native peoples lived over the entire North and South American continent. There were upwards of six million people in the "New World" before the coming of the Europeans. Although similarities did exist among the various tribes, it must be remembered that each tribe was unique unto itself. Each tribe had a separate and distinct order, culture, language, and government.

European Contact

There is a great deal of discrepancy involved in describing the arrival of Europeans as the "first discovery" of the Americas. For the purposes of this discussion suffice it to say that the Europeans came to the New World. When they first came to this land, they found a vast unspoiled environment that was seemingly waiting for them. To their surprise, they also found people different from any they had previously encountered.

Europeans continued to come for many reasons—the land itself, mineral wealth, the "Fountain of Youth," the freedom of a new land, a chance for a new beginning, a way out of oppression, trade with the native people, a new land to conquer. The list goes on and on. But those who came also failed to perceive the lifestyle and customs of the people they encountered.

The native people were looked upon as savages who spoke a tongue that no one could understand. They lived in homes foreign to anything the Europeans had ever seen. Their dress was strange and they did not work in ways that were customary to the European way of life. Their total tribal structure was baffling.

Native people greeted the Europeans in a variety of ways, depending on the circumstances. The Spanish invaded territories with soldiers and found people who were amicable to them while the soldiers were present. The English found people who shared their knowledge of survival in this strange land. The French found a lucrative trade with native peoples in fur.

The European people had, of course, a history of being very protective of their religion and viewed anyone not Christian as being heathen. Since they did not take the time to become acquainted with the native people's religion and spirituality, they also branded the natives as heathen and in need of Christian conversion.

The Spanish Conquistadores were one example of the might and right of the European kingdoms. They marched North with a vast army and a contingent of Catholic priests to tame the new world and bring the heathen to Christ. They also sought the fabled Siete Ciudades de Cibol—the Seven Cities of Gold—that were alive and well in rumour.

The Pueblo Indians of the Southwest, when confronted by the Spanish soldiers with steel blades glinting in the sunlight, did indeed emulate the priest by kneeling before the cross. But knowledge of what it symbolized escaped them. The Pueblo people could not understand how this person on the cross so beloved and revered, could then have been treated so badly. Other Pueblos feared that if they treated their most honored religious person in such a way, how could they (the Pueblos) then expect to be treated?

Contact with the French in the Northern latitudes was somewhat different. The French were greeted by native people bearing gifts, as was their custom. Included in those gifts were pelts of beaver, otter and weasel. Furs were a most prized possession in Europe and were very expensive. The French immediately established a network of trade with the Indian people. Metal implements, utensils, brightly colored cloth, beads and other items made in Europe were exported to the North American continent in exchange for the abundant furs found here.

The English came to colonize America. Native peoples taught the newcomers how to survive. There was never a question of withholding life—giving survival techniques. In the mind of the native people, such information sharing was part of their culture.

The cooperation and interdependence of the newcomers with the native people continued for a while. However, in Europe circumstances were in motion that would soon bring this to an end.

The kingdoms of Europe viewed the New World as a projection of their world. The kings of Spain, France and England saw the North American continent as a new resource for wealth and a viable alternative to the overcrowded conditions of their respective countries. It was viewed as an area to colonize and to produce more power and wealth for whichever European nation could make the New World its own.

The Spanish were spurred on by the evidence of precious metals being found in the New World. If Spain could conquer the people in the New World, the wealth would be theirs. The French saw the fur trade as an economic stimulus, and also saw the possibilities of acquiring permanent land. The English looked upon the New World as another opportunity to expand their empire, through acquisition of land and colonization.

Treaties and Alliances

During this period, Indian tribes were a very strong force to be reckoned with. As Britain and France both wanted to be the dominant power in North America, it was therefore necessary to form alliances with the Indian tribes in order to become a more powerful military organization and to gain a further hold in the New World.

The French and Indian Wars are an example of European nations trying to align themselves with the most powerful Indian nations. The French and their allies were on one side while the British and their Indian allies were on the other. The stage was being set for military intervention into the framework of colonization.

Meanwhile, more and more Europeans were coming to the New World, and more land was needed to support them. Unrest and rebellion among the colonists was also beginning. The King of England was taking an unduly harsh stand with the colonists, insisting that high taxes be paid to the crown. However, the King and his forces were thousands of miles away and his ability to carry out royal edicts was diluted by the distance.

Soon the English colonists grew weary of a non—responsive government. They rebelled and formed a new independent government in the New World. It was a form of government that included several separate states that agreed to be ruled by one central government, the United States of America. Benjamin Franklin, one of the founding persons, patterned the bicameral legislature and representative government after the confederacy of the Iroquois.

In these founding years, the United States was weak militarily. Friendly alliances and compromises were necessary for survival. Treaties and agreements with Indian nations were a necessity. Those treaties with Indian nations were to be made by the central federal government to help lessen the confusion and mistrust being fostered by treaties and agreements made by the separate states. The power to make these decisions was written into the U.S. Constitution and became the "supreme law of the land." Eventually over 400 treaties with Indian nations would be signed. In doing this, the U.S. government recognized the Indian governments as separate and equal.

The time period of treaty signing can be roughly broken down into three distinct periods: 1779—1811 —when military alliances were necessary to the survival of the Europeans; 1817—1846 —when negotiations for more land for settlement were required; and finally, 1846—1864 —when the treaties of "peace and friendship" evolved because the military solution to the "Indian problem" was not working, and the western expansion had used up all available lands for settlement.

Treaties

The treaties gave certain guarantees to both sides. Indian people usually reserved those things necessary to continue their way of life such as fishing, hunting, and trapping in their usual and accustomed places. Water was needed to provide the environment and preserve the resources. Gathering of roots and herbs for medicine and food was important to the people. It was especially important to them to reserve the especially sacred areas that they knew. The U.S. government in turn promised to protect and preserve the reserved rights of the Indian nation in return for land for settlement.

Treaties will vary from tribe to tribe because of their uniqueness; however, there is always some mention of the length of the contract.

The government used language the Indian people could relate to, and nearly every treaty will contain the words "as long as the grass shall grow and the waters run." To the Indian person and to the government of that time this connoted "forever."

Unfortunately, every treaty made with Indian people has been broken from the side of the Federal government. It was not until modern times that Indian people have realized the importance of the treaties that their tribes made long ago. Treaties are legal documents and are the "supreme law of the land."

Dwindling Strength and Influence of Tribes

From 1779—1864, the "strength and influence" of tribes deteriorated. With the founding of the United States of America, European intervention into the New World from France and Spain became of decreasing importance. Trade with France was jeopardized and the U.S.A. began to acquire colonies and land from the European countries.

As the U.S. military became stronger, alliances with Indian tribes became less and less important. In fact, the military was now used by the U.S. government to keep the tribes "in line" and pacified.

The policy of the government changed from "friendly" to hostile. The Indian wars began in earnest. When Indian tribes became adamant about not moving from their homelands into unknown territory, the U.S. military was summoned to remove Indians by force. The infamous Cherokee Trail of Tears in the early 19th century would set the precedent for removal for the next century.

Reservations

When there was no more "land to the west" to move the Indian people into, a new solution for the "Indian problem" needed to be found—reservations. Pieces of land were reserved specifically for Indians by treaty that would provide for their livelihood and protection of their accustomed tribal manner. However, the reservation land was also predetermined to be land that was unfit for white settlement.

Indians owned land tribally—in common. Individual land ownership was unheard of. Indian peofle had no words or phrases in their languages that would describe "ownership of land." Remember, the land to the Indian was a sacred part of the person and a gift from the Creator.

However, from the white point of view, reservations functioned for several reasons. It provided a common place for Indians to be placed until they became "civilized" and able to live in a non—Indian society.

The reservation was a place separate from polite society so that the "heathen and savage" way of life of the Indians would not embarrass the surrounding communities. The reservations also provided the white people with jobs as Indian agents and managers for the affairs of Indian people.

Missionaries

Since the Indian nations were looked upon as heathen, savage and unfit for polite society, the missionaries of various religions found a miss-ion field "white unto harvest."

The long history of Christianizing the heathen began with the first European contact. From the time that the Spanish asked the Indian people to pay homage to their God and Savior under threat of annihilation—through the carving up of America by the Department of War and designating certain denominations to Christianize certain Indians—to the reservation days when mission life was well established—Christianity and the native people were intertwined.

On the one hand, missionary zeal destroyed many traditional Indian religions, cut a swath through clans and tribes of mistrust and disloyalty, separated families from one another and left chaos in their wake. Traditional thought and religion was branded as heathen. From the Indian point of view, missionaries accompanied soldiers either before or immediately after a major conflict. The conflict was always over land. The missionaries were looked upon as an extension of the military and another form of oppression. The job of the missionary was to placate Indian people in order to make it easier to acquire their land.

On the other hand, missionaries did accomplish some good. Missionaries during the reservation era often served as teachers and medical people. They were responsible for the teaching of many skills to Indian people. It was also the missionary who flamed the Christian conscience of America to outrage at the atrocious treatment of the native people. It was as a direct result of this that the disastrous Indian wars were halted.

Because of the process involved in selecting and pairing churches and Indian tribes, Indians on any particular reservation were a "captive audience" for the missionaries. That is why even in modern times you will find Indian people from particular tribes belonging to one denomination. It was not until the 1930's and 40's that more than one denomination could be found on reservations.

This was one of the most confusing aspects of Christianity. Indian people failed to understand the importance of denominationalism. To the Indian, all under the Creator were equal. Why did one have to pledge denominational fidelity?

Educational Impact

Further destruction of Native American culture was accomplished through government boarding schools that were set up to "civilize" the Indian children. Children ranging in age from four through the teen years were brought from the reservation to the central educational facility. Separation from parents and family was necessary to break down traditional learning patterns and obliterate what thousands of years of history had taught them. At boarding school it was against the rules to be caught speaking one's native language. All remnants of tribalism were strongly discouraged. Children had their hair cut short and soon were dressed in the fashion of the day. For any infraction in the rules, strict and swift punishment was accorded the law breaker. This included any punishment from whipping to being locked in solitary confinement for several days.

The complete eradication of "Indianness" from native people was thought to be terribly important. Since the beginning of white and Indian contact, the uppermost idea in the mind of Europeans was how to "civilize the savage." This mindset was still being encountered in the twentieth century. A new train of thought would be added—how to assimilate the native person into the mainstream.

Changing Roles

Over the years of European contact, the livelihood and lifestyle of Indian people changed drastically. The traditional roles of the male and female within the tribal structure became blurred. The male was traditionally the hunter and provider for his family. The woman was the person who took care of the home and family. Governmentally, many tribes were matriarchal, but had male leaders that were visible.

When the lifestyle of the Indian people changed, it was more easily borne by the female. The men had a much harder time of adjustment. For a period of time on the reservation, alcohol was used as a means of escape from the changing pressures surrounding their new status. It was not until fairly recent times that alcoholism among the native women has become as predominant as the male.

Dominant religions on reservations were now Christian. Old ways and native religions were outlawed. In order to continue the practice of traditional ways, native people had to go "underground."

This systematic stripping of culture from the Native American was also bound up with the U.S. government bureaucracy manifesting itself as the Bureau of Indian Affairs. The BIA was given the responsibility from Congress to complete the contract of caring and nurturing of native people and their land. However, the implementation of this system of caring was sloppy at best.

Federal Government Relationships

Because of the special relationship between Indian people and the federal government, the Indian tribes had to undergo an immeasurable amount of legalisms, rules, regulations, red tape, administrative edicts and resolutions in their daily life. The following is a list of some of the major pieces of legislation that pertain only to Indian people.

Early 1700s to 1799—INDIAN TRADE AND INTERCOURSE ACT
    provided for government trade with various Indian tribes.

1830—INDIAN REMOVAL ACT
    gave the U.S. government jurisdiction to remove Indian tribes from their traditional homes to other lands.

1887—GENERAL ALLOTNENT ACT
    gave Indian people the ability to own land individually. All land previously owned in common through the tribe was subdivided into shares, and surplus land was sold.

1924—INDIAN CITIZENSHIP ACT
    made American citizens of native peoples.

1934—INDIAN REORGANIZATION ACT
    reorganized tribal governments so that they had constitutions, by—laws, and elected representatives.

1953—HOUSE CONCURRENT RESOLUTION—TERMINATION ACT
    severed trust responsibility for some "advanced" tribes.

1972—INDIAN EDUCATION ACT
    earmarked special funds for Indian education.

1972 -—MINOMINEE RESTORATION ACT
    passed to undo the tragedy of House Concurrent Resolution on. Termination. The Minominee tribe of Wisconsin was restored to its previous trust status.

1975—INDIAN SELF-DETERMINATION AND EDUCATIONAL ASSISTANCE ACT
    marked a new era of "Indian self—determination." Indians would have charge of their own destiny.

1978—INDIAN CHILD WELFARE ACT
    stopped the removal of native children from their homes and their placement into non-native foster homes without jurisdiction from the tribes being considered.

Indian Self-Determination – Rhetoric or Reality?

It becomes apparent that dealings with native people have been complex and paradoxical. The U.S. government waxes and wanes between "freeing" the native people to pursue their own potential to "preserving and protecting" their culture. Sentiment for and against native people also waxes and wanes in popularity. In the midst of this great conflict, not of their own making, native people stand.

It is presently popular to speak of Indian self-determination. It has been a long time in coming to native people. But "self-determination" is only coming the full cycle. Indian people prior to European contact did have their own self-determination.

The native people of today are still very much the descendants of these peoples. They still believe strongly that this land remains their land and that the responsibility the creator gave them thousands of years ago to maintain, protect and respect the land is still the same today. Times have changed, issues have changed, but traditional native philosophy has not.

Despite the hardships, atrocities, cultural genocide and all other acts of civil and hostile forces that have come upon them, the native people have remained, for the most part intact, with the phrase on their lips, "We shall endure."

Indian people shall endure even as the land endures, the gift from the creator to them.

BIBLIOGRAPHY

1. Pratson, John Frederick, Land of the Four Directions. Old Greenwich, Connecticut: The Chatham Press, Inc., 1970.

2 Terrell, John Upton, The Arrow and the Cross. Santa Barbara, California: Capra Press, 1979.

3. Josephy, Alvin, The American Heritage Book of Indians. New York: American Heritage Publishing Co., Inc., Simon & Shuster, 1961.

4. Prucha, Francis Paul, Americanizing the American Indians. Cambridge, Massachusetts: Harvard University Press, 1973.

5. Kickingbird, Kirke, Indians and the U.S. Government. Washington, D.C Institute for the Development of Indian Law, 1978. Catholicism

6. Kickingbird, Kirke, The Federal Indian Trust Relationship. Washington Institute for the Development of Indian Law, 1978.

7. Smith, Jane F. and Kvasnicka, Robert M. Indian White Relationships, A Persistent Paradox. Washington, D.C.: Howard University Press, 1976.

8. Brandon, William, The Last Americans. New York: McGraw—Hill Book Company, 1974.

THE ALC
Involvement in Native American Affairs

By Terry Tafoya and Roy De Boer

We would first like to say that we respect and admire the efforts of the ALC and its representatives in providing resources and support to Native American groups and organizations. We recognize that in doing so a tightwire is walked in providing support but not control. . .helping the needy without dictating the way in which the needy live their lives. The present—day tribal governments may not be all we would have them be (and certainly the same could be said about city, state, and federal government in this country), but they are the legal bodies that represent reservation members. Modern tribal government exists as a result of a whole chain of events resulting from various acts authorized by Congress.

Know then, that among many of the Indian tribes of the Pacific Northwest, there were hereditary families who were directly responsible for specific duties necessary to carry on the functions of any society. For example, one family might be in charge of roads and transportation. This does not mean that the one family would keep roads clear, but that the family would see to it that enough person power was generated within the community to get the job done. Another family might act as "police." Thus functions of society were delegated to many different families within a tribe. When modern tribal governments were established by the Indian Reorganization Act in 1934, which established a "corporate structure" similar to what one would find in Safeco or Sea—First Bank, there was a concentration of power and authority into the hands of a corporate board, usually called a Tribal Council.

It must be understood that the above brief example of how government traditionally existed is only one of many that can be used. Out of the many, many native tribes of the Pacific Northwest, other models of government existed as well.

Perhaps the most consistent factor is the concept of tribal leader as public servant. Among the people east of the mountains in the plateau area, a chief was one who was wealthy and caring enough to be able to support his people, taking in the poor, the widows and orphans who needed help. This a fundamental gift of Indian people to those of European ancestry. . . rather than the concept of a King, someone who was served by his subjects, the Chief existed to serve his people. It should be recognized that this is also one of the teachings of Christ...but the secularization, the incorporation of this into everyday government, came from American Indians.

From a historical perspective: In 1493 Pope Alexander VI issued his Inter Caetera bull which laid down the basic Christian attitude toward the New World.

> Among other works well pleasing to the Divine Majesty and cherished in our heart, this assuredly ranks highest, that in our times especially the Catholic faith and the Christian religion be exalted and everywhere increased and spread, that the health of souls be cared for and that barbarous nations be overthrown and brought to the faith itself.[11]

This idea of Pope Alexander VI of overthrowing "barbarous nations" of the Americas and utilizing Christianity as the tool to do so has been an integral part of American society. Christianity was synonymous with civilization in the minds of the federal government of not only the United States, but other nations as well. In 1568, the Society of Jesus established a school in Havana, Cuba for the Indians of Florida. In 1617, Moor's Charity School was founded as a training school for the education of youth of native tribes, of English youth, and others in Connecticut. This was the school that would become Dartmouth College. In 1802, Congress appropriations to "promote civilization among the savages." In 1819, the Congress authorized the Early Civilization Fund to support Indian Agencies to have Christian missionaries "civilize" and "Christianize" Native Americans. In 1869, President Grant inaugurated his Peace Policy, where military personnel were replaced by men of various religious denominations to review and establish policies on reservations.

Over and over again, a central theme of federal relationships with American Indians is an attempt to "remake" Indians into a darker hue of white people, replacing "barbarous nations" with "civilized" citizens of the U.S. A great deal of tragedy has resulted from this. As the American Indian Policy Review Commission Report states:

By replacing land with cash payments for land forever lost, by making tribal governments dependent on uncertain and frequently inadequate congressional appropriations, by attacking traditional authorities and subverting native leaders who were not compliant, federal agents deprived the tribes of the economic, cultural, and political resources for building or sustaining viable independent communities. The agents, moreover, complained that their Indian wards had flunked the civilization test and failed to become decorously self—supporting citizens. The Government then proceeded to elaborate a policy for dealing with Indians as dependent paupers. (2)

In 1887 the Dawes Allotment Act split up ownership of land in many tribes from being a tribal possession (if one can even say this, since among many native philosophies, one cannot own land, but rather, the land to being assigned to ownership of individual families, along the order of New England farmers. It is significant that before the Dawes Act was passed, that this had been previously experimented with here in Washington State, among the Nisqually people. The land on reservations that had been promised to the tribes "for as long as the grass shall grow, and the rivers flow," that was not assigned to Indian tribal members (remember that this time period is the one in which native population had declined to its lowest point, roughly a quarter of a million, compared to over 1 million today) was then opened for settlement by non—Indians...the land rush of your history books. In the words of D'Arcy McNickle:

> In brief summary: The preceding 100 years had wrought incalculable damage to Indians, their property, and their societies. Tribes had been moved about like livestock until, in some cases, the original homeland was no more than a legend in the minds of old men and women. Children had been removed from the family, by force at times, and kept in close custody until they lost their mother tongue and all knowledge of who they were, while parents often did not know where the children had been taken or whether they even lived. Tribal religious practices, when they were not proscribed outright, were treated as obscenities. Land losses, as noted, were catastrophic (Indian tribes who had owned about 140 million acres of land in 1887, lost some 90 million acres of land-before the Dawes policy was abandoned two generations later), while the failure of Government to provide economic tools and training for proper land use left the remaining holdings untenable

or leased to white farmers at starvation rates. The bureaucratic structure had penetrated the entire fabric of Indian life, usurping the tribal decision-making function, demeaning local leadership, obtruding into the family—and yet was totally oblivious of its inadequacies and its inhumanity. (3)

Reform movements to support Indian tribes were centered around the belief—or perhaps dogma would be a more accurate term—that it was inevitable that Indians were the "vanishing race" and Indian languages and cultures would disappear as we would be assimilated into American society. Thus the Indian Reorganization Act that returned a significant amount of power and authority to tribes still did so in a way that did not respect traditional leadership, but rather sought to establish a local government set up in an industrial manner. Problems with the BIA and tribes were interpreted by outside "authorities" as being managerial in nature, rather than conflicts of a cultural and philosophic nature.

This is why the analogy of walking a tightwire was used in the beginning of this statement, in terms of what the ALC does in supporting native efforts. Indian people still have tremendous need. But for any outside group to set up separate organizations from existing tribal governments, as has been suggested in the Plaintiff's disposition, means a return to oppressive policies of this nation's past of determining what is best for Indian communities. It is rather the Indian communities' responsibility to determine their futures, their priorities, and their steps to accomplish their goals. If tribal members do not support their tribal government, they have the same avenues of change that any American citizen does of recall and submission of their own candidates. It has always been the case that in attempting to meet the needs of the largest number within a community that a minority is alienated.

The very existence of the ALC is predicated on the fact that Christianity is great enough not to be contained in only one set of doctrines and practices. In the same manner, while any of us may not agree with everything that is done by a specific tribal government, that tribal government is "the only game in town." For better or worse, it is the federally recognized body that handles affairs of tribal members. Any change of government must come from the grass-roots level, and not from outsiders, or else the comparison made between the ALC and American involvement in Iran will become a reality.

In closing, a quote from Ursula Le Guin is in order:

...an act is not, as young men think, like a rock that one picks up and throws, and it hits or misses, and that's the end of it. When that rock is- lifted, the earth is lighter; the hand that bears it heavier. When it is thrown, the circuits of the stars respond, and where it strikes or falls the universe is changed. On every act the balance of the whole depends. The winds and the seas, the power of water and earth and light, all that these do, and all that the beasts and green things do, is well done, and rightly done. All these act within the Equilibrium. From the hurricane and the great whale's sounding to the fall of a dry leaf and the gnat's flight, all they do is done within the balance of the whole. But we, insofar as we have power over the world and over one another, we must learn to do what the leaf and the whale and the wind do of their own nature. We must learn to keep the balance. Having intelligence we must not act in ignorance. Having choice, we must not act without responsibility. (4)

It is an old saying among the Pueblo people, that "if a man knows the right thing, he will do the right thing." Do not make your decisions lightly. Do not form your opinions without searching your own heart and seeking serenity through prayer, for these are not opinions to be formed in the storm of strong emotions.

NOTES

1. Deloria, Vine, Jr. God Is: Red, New York: Delta Books, 1973, p. 274.

2. McNickle, D'Arcy et al. "Captives Within a Free Society: Federal Policy and the American Indian" the First Chapter from the American Policy Review Commission Report, p. 9.

3. Ibid, p. 21.

4. Le Guin, Ursula, The Farthest Shore, New York: Atheneum Books, 1972, p. 74.

T H E L C A
and Ministry with Native Americans
Some Observations for Discussion

By the Rev. Robert L. Rains

Through the years I have had a great many conversations with a great many people, but one that stands out in my mind was with Merle Boos, Assistant Director for Church Extension of the Division for Mission in North America, (DMNA). The conversation was about the Lutheran Church in America's statement of "Goals and Plans for Minority Ministry 1978—1984"—and how that statement relates to the LCA's involvements with Native American peoples. That conversation has stimulated the writing of this paper.

It would seem to me, especially if one were to disregard the ministry at Rocky Boy's Indian Reservation in Montana, that Native Americans are being viewed as standing apart from the goals as a minority group worthy of consideration for LCA ministry. I know full well the LCA's involvement with the Native American Concerns coordinators in the Pacific Northwest and elsewhere, in the funding of the National Indian Lutheran Board through the Lutheran Council in the U.S.A. and in the funding activities of some "Indian Centers." But I submit that these activities have very little to do with the goals and plans on at least two very different counts. First, they relate almost completely to so—called "social ministry concerns" in contrast to the gospel (Word and Sacrament) ministry presumed to be paramount in the goals statement. Second, they do not relate because the involvement of the LCA is only vicarious or substitutional. The goals, as I read them, call for the church to be directly and actively involved in minority concerns and ministry.

As I have raised this matter with various individuals I could have received various responses that together could form a statement like this: "It is not the intent of the LCA to set ministry with Native Americans apart from the Goals. But the kind of results that we see from the ministry at Rocky Boy's Indian Reservation after more than fifty years of history, in terms of congregational membership, active communicants, self—support, and contribution to the church—at—large in stewardship and leadership, is not what LCA is looking for as we enter into other Native American ministries. In short, we do not know how to 'successfully' go about Native American ministry." Perhaps this statement is not deserved or accurate, but if it has any truth to it, this paper may be of some help.

In defense of the ministry at Rocky Boy's, I would submit that the ministry is far more successful than the statistics the church customarily looks for would indicate. The true test of the success of a congregation is not found in membership statistics, or the amount of benevolence provided, or the number of pastors produced, but in its impact in proclaiming the gospel of Jesus Christ. The thought suggests a question to be considered. "If the congregation ceased to exist, would anyone care—would its witness to the grace of God be missed?" By this test, the congregation and ministry at Rocky Boy's is highly successful. This would be amply witnessed to if one were to simply circulate in the reservation community asking what people think of the church.

I am not suggesting that the church cannot or should not look for the other measures of success from the congregation at Rocky Boy's now or in the future or from any other Native American ministries that the LCA should enter into. I am only suggesting that we keep our priorities in line with scripture and expect that congregations should first of all be faithful to the mandate of our Lord that the gospel be proclaimed at all times and in all places. The rest of our expectations can be adjusted to correspond with what we program our input for.

It is very much true that in terms of the membership, Our Saviour's of Rocky Boy's is small and financially dependent upon the resources of the LCA collectively, and members of the LCA individually, far out of proportion to the size of the membership itself. It is equally true that the congregation has not provided the resources of stewardship and leadership that would normally be expected of a ministry that has been in existence as long as this one has been. These two factors, to some degree, reflect the long—term individual and family poverty, poor health and housing, and high unemployment typical of Indian reservations. But alongside these truths, as I look at the history of the ministry here and look around myself now, I cannot help but feel that the church has achieved just exactly what the input was programmed for.

From the earliest days of the ministry here, pastoral leadership has either accidentally or deliberately discouraged lay or congregational responsibility except for a few key individuals. Pastors have either presented themselves, or have been presented by others, as being the "experts" in the ways of God. Pastors have not been able to, or have not been allowed to, take into account the theological understandings which have existed among the people since long before the church was encountered. It is a small wonder that there have been so few native leaders coming forward to assume leadership roles in the church, when the expertise bf the existing theologians was flatly denied without examination of what was being taught. It is extremely threatening to a person "new in faith" to think what will happen if he/she expresses himself/herself when an expert has just been denounced.

Again, from the earliest days of the ministry here, until only just recently, it would seem that the church viewed Native Americans as incapable of learning what the church was teaching or at least of learning sufficiently enough to share the information and experience of the gospel with others. In the past, whenever there were teaching tasks that could not be performed by the pastor and/or the parsonage family, additional staff people (missionaries) were secured, or groups from other congregations came in to "do for 'them' what they cannot do for themselves." Local people were used only to "assist" or to perform menial tasks. It would seem that the church has taught or at the least reinforced notions that Native Americans were only beneficiaries of, not participants in, "the white man's religion." This kind of teaching seems to me to be contrary to the gospel given to us.

It seems that financial dependence has been taught as well as theological and educational dependence. In many ways it probably started with a type of thinking that still seems to exist in the church today, that each congregation should have everything associated with a "typical" congregation: a full—time, fully paid Pastor; a worship center designed as a worship center; a parsonage, or provision for housing the pastor, complete with all the amenities; and a place for Christian education to take place. In the history of this congregation, whenever any of these things have been needed, including updates like central heating, electrification (before most of the homes in the area), or running water, the church has always been there to pick up the bills either through loans or grants or solicited gifts. Little to nothing has been expected of the people, and the response has matched the expectation. I am suggesting that the congregations and the pastors may not need so much. Local input should be sought as to what is needed, and local resources—especially of time, talent, and imagination—should be brought into play whenever possible.

Alongside these factors is another that has impeded the progress of this congregation in meeting standard expectations. This factor is that this congregation has never had the opportunity of being just another congregation. A great deal of congregational and staff time and energy that should be devoted to local ministry has been expended to maintain fund raising, public relations, and "show case ministry" activities—because of the ever pressing need for funding; because of our long—standing "mission status:" because we have been the only Indian congregation of the LCA (or ULCA); because of the need for Lutherans to be acquainted with at least the fact that "Indians" do exist; and because of the curiosity as well as well—meaningness of people.

I see no quick or easy answers for the ministry at Rocky Boy's to achieve "statistical success." I sometimes wish that we could go back to the first days and start all over again. But that cannot be done. There is too much history to ever have the opportunity to start over. Even if drastic measures were taken to try to change things constructively, there would still be much difficulty in working things out to achieve "success." We now have congregational leaders who are devoted to a theology of congregational responsibility in service to our Lord and Savior; and this is a solid first step in the right direction. But there is a lot of long, hard work and exhausting prayer that still lies ahead for us.

I am convinced that the LCA is truly concerned about becoming more inclusive and that intentionally Native Americans outside Rocky Boy's do fall within the scope of the goals and plans statement. I stated earlier my impression that the reason for holding back on aggressively working to meet the goals from a Native American standpoint seems to relate to a concern for a more "successful" ministry than has been seen from Rocky Boy's. I now suggest that more is known than what is being recognized.

Planning

While it is very likely true that no single person or office has any blueprint for a completely successful ministry, there is a pool of knowledge that can and should be utilized in advance planning. Each person who has been professionally involved with the Rocky Boy's ministry over any period of time—pastors, synod and DMNA staff—has learned something that will be of future value. The National Indian Lutheran Board staff and directors and the various Native American Concerns coordinators and contact people have insights that could prove essential as well.

And the people of Our Saviour's of Rocky Boy's have an understanding of problems that should not be overlooked.

I would plead, on behalf of Native Americans, that the pool of knowledge that is available be drawn together quickly so that affirmative action can take place. To begin this process, I would offer this paper to focus on issues and hopefully generate some creative conclusions for exciting, productive ministry in the future.

Making a Commitment

As we contemplate expanding Word and Sacrament ministry among Native Americans, it is essential that we secure in advance a firm commitment from DMNA to enter into at least one Native American ministry, expecting that it will be a long-term involvement embodying the concept of "total ministry" being called for by Native American people, and focusing on offering the most meaningful thing the church has to offer: the grace of God embodied in the person of the Savior—Redeemer of the world, Jesus the Christ.

This commitment should be firm and flexible enough so that a positive move to follow through on the commitment with exploratory activity could be made at "a moment's notice." While it might seem to some not involved with Native Americans that decisions are not always well thought through, I believe that I can testify that, especially when the decision is to seek or accept the services of any institution that is controlled by non—Indians, such is not the case.

In this day and age, if any community of Native Americans were to verbalize a decision to accept Lutheran presence and ministry in its midst, it would be far more than a test to determine our sincerity. The community would be prepared to accept us if we were to respond favorably, quickly. But if our response is "give us a chance to get our act together," the opportunity will be gone before we can deal with it creatively.

Identifying a Community

When this commitment to act is secured, then work to identify a Native American community, reservation or urban, which feels a need for the spiritual leadership, guidance, and ministry of the church can be begun. I have heard it said that "to be 'Indian' is to be religious." I have also heard complaints from many Native Americans, especially elders, that "Indians" are "dying off" from losing their spirituality. There are many reasons that are given for this including inattentiveness of youth to the ways that have been given to "the people," inability of the elders to share the continuity of the messages because of omissions through the centuries, modern mobility, infiltrations of "heresies" and greed, to name a few. (Perhaps this is part of the reason for "the resurgence of cultural programs" that has been seen in modern years.)

I believe that the church, in the gospel of Jesus Christ, has something to offer in answering this complaint. We can help people who know themselves to be children of God to retain or recapture their sense of being or identity as a people with a place in God's world and a destiny to be fulfilled in his creation and in is eavenly welling place. The task remains to identify a community that shares the conviction that the church, or more specifically, the Lutheran Church in America, can and will be truly of assistance to Native American peoples as a people. This task can easily be accomplished through listening to what is being said in "Indian country" and through collating expressed need to what the church has to offer.

Approaching the Work

Once a "target community" is identified, work must begin through a representative of the church who might eventually be the representative of the church for ministry. This person would secure an invitation to offer ministry in the identified community. Even with extensive consultation, the integrity and judgment of this representative will be a key ingredient in determining the viability of a potential ministry in a particular community.

The typical LCA approach of going into a community and surveying for "growth potential," the "number of identified Lutherans," or the number of unchurched that might endorse Lutheran confessions and practices simply will not work in Native American communities. Questionnaires and standard formats would have to be completely reworked to take into account the fact that there are simply not very many Lutheran Native Americans any place in the country, and not that many have even been exposed to Lutheran confessions and practices enough to respond meaningfully. "Growth potential" factors, whether on the reservation or in urban situations, can be thrown completely out of whack virtually overnight by any number of variables, including single acts of Congress. The more proper question for us is: "Are there people who do, or will come to, share the conviction that the LCA can and will be truly of assistance to the people?"

These viability factors are completely independent of another factor which would completely override them all. This factor is territorial respect. Reservations are legally sovereign though dependent nations within the bounds of the United States of America and thus are not "open territory" to church activity in the same sense that the rest of the nation is. It might be stretching a point legally to say that the church would be subject to trespass laws established by tribes if we were to send in representatives to "survey" or establish a congregation without permission or invitation; but morally I think this would be the case. Native Americans are proud of their sovereign status and their territory, and are protective of both. I believe that the church should respect and honor this status in every way possible.

While the situation would be somewhat different in urban situations, I believe that there is some carry over of territorial pride that should be honored in the same way as reservation territory. It is a simple thing to show respect for people, and if we can demonstrate it as a church towards Native Americans, permission for entry will be granted and invitations to establish meaningful ministries, even pleas, will be forthcoming from people and leaders both unofficially and officially.

Studying the Theology, Language and Culture

To my way of thinking, one of the greatest errors that has been committed against Native American people by well—meaning though misguided Christians of many denominations, including our own, is the categoric dismissal, rejection, and condemnation of their culture and spirituality as pagan or heathen. As I have listened to the stories of Native American elders, I have been pleasantly surprised to learn of striking parallels between the teachings of our Old Testament and the stories handed down through the generations of Native Americans about how God has been involved in the universe and the ways He has prescribed for His people. How much simpler the proclamation of Jesus Christ would be today if the earliest missionaries had been able to listen and understand that many of the tribes have these stories! They not only parallel the Old Testament but also prophesy the coming of the Son of God into the world to take care of His people. Instead, we have confusion, and to no small degree, rejection of the message of the church because we have insisted that truth is truth only if it comes through the Judeo—Christian heritage which belongs to those who brought the message of Jesus to this continent. I doubt that we will find any place on the North American continent that has been untouched by this conflict. But if we can begin ministry with understanding of where people are, theologically, then perhaps we can overcome some of the misconceptions of our faith, including our own, and truly minister with the spirit of Christ.

I would strongly urge that in—depth study of the theology and culture of the people to he ministered with be accomplished by the person responsible for the ministry before any activity of preaching, teaching, or evangelization is begun. I would also urge that this study should be "on site" and include language study because there are many Native Americans still more conversant in their tribal tongue than they are in English and, because language is definitely the medium of the transmission of theology and culture. Practically speaking, if this is not accomplished to a meaningful extent before active ministry is begun, it will not happen in any disciplined way. It could well take years for a given individual to put together piecemeal what could be learned in a few short weeks without the day to day pressures of involvement in ministry.

I am certain that with in—depth study of language, culture, and theology of Native Americans to be ministered with, common points of understanding will be discovered that will enable the person responsible for the ministry to build for faith and understanding, in much the same way as Paul ministered in Athens, in the seventeenth chapter of the book of Acts. Historically the church in ministering with Native Americans has wasted a great deal of time and energy tearing down or demeaning Native American understandings that would more appropriately be solid foundations for a dynamic faith in the Risen Christ. This could, incidentally, require some revision of the traditional language of proclamation.

Developing the Ministry

Once the LCA representative has reached the point of knowing how the truth of Jesus Christ might best be shared in that community, the active work can be begun. I would suggest that initially the activity would very closely resemble the work of "mission developers" speaking with people in their homes, at community gatherings, or wherever they might be found, letting it be known that the church is present and that God is actively involved in offering something that people need through his church.

As the "minister" becomes acquainted in the community and is identified as a person of a living faith, the process of assembly—baptism, study, worship, and finding ways to serve as a community of believers will come quite naturally. Perhaps there will be small groups or even just a few individuals at first, but the community assembled together will grow.

I do not see the location of the assembly as being of great importance as far as the LCA is concerned. It might be a fine church structure, a home, an available building used for other gatherings, an abandoned structure, a tent, or just a place with no protective cover whatsoever. It seems to me that site location or the lack of one should be left to the decision of the people and their resources, imagination and resourcefulness. Likewise regarding housing of the "minister." If it is determined that the best course of action is for him/her to be a resident in that community, as strange as it may sound coming from a full—time, fully paid pastor with a parsonage, this should be left to local option once active ministry is begun.

As the community of believers begins gathering, the sense of adequacy or security of the person responsible for representing the LCA in ministry will come into play. From the earliest moment, the "minister" should plan for and try to bring about a degree of lay involvement in the ministry of proclamation, education, and Christian service that will lead to the congregation being virtually independent of the "pastor" in continued growth in faith. The "pastor" should be involved in training liturgists, educators, administrators, preachers, evangelists, etc., from the very first moment of ministry. If need be the resources of Theological Education by Extension should be utilized to maximize the effort. The "pastor" should diligently refrain from yielding to the temptation to "take over" and accomplish tasks which should more appropriately and more beneficially be accomplished by the people. If this means that the role of the "pastor" should be reduced to that of providing training and administering the sacraments, even if that should reduce his role to only a relative few hours of ministry each week, then that adjustment should be made in our structure to guarantee that kind of role and no more.

It is highly likely that a community of Native Americans will find modes of worship and aids to worship that are in fact compatible with Lutheran theology and practice even though they are totally unfamiliar to those of us with European backgrounds. It is even possible that a community of Native Americans, allowed to develop its own free expression of faith, might come to a stage of development where it is recognizable as "Lutheran" only by what is distinctively and truly Lutheran, our faith in Jesus Christ and faithfulness in living out our calling as His people. We need to be free enough in our own understanding of our faith and the grace of Cod to not only let it happen but encourage it if desired by the people of the new community of faith.

I would expect that if a community of believers is enabled and encouraged to develop as I have outlined above, we will witness a remarkable program of witness and outreach in the neighborhood of the emerging community. I would expect that the community would grow naturally, and rapidly become strong as a community of believers. But there is and will continue to be a need to expand the efforts of the LCA into other communities. The strength of an emerging congregation can and should be a resource to meet those needs. We should be a part of asking each new congregation to share what is happening in its life outside its own framework, and if need be, to be a resource in helping it to happen again, and again.

WHITES
the Miracle of Wholeness

By James W. Mayer

Much of what I have to say is autobiographical. Yet I do not intend to deal in individualist categories. All of what I have to say you also already know. I won't apologize for that. Long after most of my friends had moved on to other issues (often for good reasons), I found myself "hung up" by the feeling that racism remained the major underlying explanation for most of the insanity going on all around—even if there are other valid explanations for it as well.

I am grateful that the issue of racism is brought back on center stage through these meetings, even though the institutional church often fails to acknowledge its own role in keeping racism a burning issue for millions of minority people in this country!

White Society Since the 60's, or: Where Has Whitey Gone?

What have whites been doing since the 60's regarding the transcendence or "inclusion" issue? In the '50's and '60's it looked as though a new, authentically plural society might one day be possible, even though its emergence would have to be fought for every inch of the way. Now, a decade or two later, we are not only farther from concerns for transcendence and inclusion than ever before, white society seems more contentedly and more sophisticatedly racist than ever before.

I will not make many works about a subject that you Afro—American, Native American, Hispanic and Oriental members of this society document with your lives every day. Since the heydays of civil rights we have jumped from one issue to another (Vietnam, feminism, gay liberation, world hunger, pollution, environmental concerns, nuclear energy and weaponry, human rights and natural foods). An evaluation of where this pathology of jumping from issue to unfinished issue leads might best be accomplished by taking a look at some indications of where white society—majority society—is today on the racism issue.

A few items by way of illustration should suffice for this:

• The Ku Klux Klan has renewed its activities and is reportedly growing faster than ever before. Ku Klux Klan growth and the lack of stir it seems to evoke in the society generally should instruct us.

• If KKK advances can be written off as a belated reaction to substantive progress in the South or to superficial dealing with racism in the North, how does one explain the growth of the American Nazi Party? Once they were easily dismissed as oddballs out of a different time and place. Today, American Nazi Party leaders are given time on major network talk shows (shouldn't all sides be heard?). One gets the eerie feeling when listening to the comments of those who call in that the callers object mostly to Nazi tactics, but have fewer fundamental objections to and offer few substantive rebuttals of Nazi presuppositions. It would be naive to conclude just from talk shows either that the country is on the way to fascism, or that the absence of good rebuttals is due solely to the fact that sane people don't bother to call in or have long since turned off their radios. The phenomenon, the existence and growth of the American Nazi Party, is itself an alarming indicator of where some people have their heads—be that in "reverse" or just "neutral."

• Once upon a time Whites blushed when caught in racist language or in acts of prejudice. No longer. White backlash against Native Americans prompted massive campaigns a few years ago through "sportsmen's associations," using high—sounding language to promote (of all things) "conservation." While white backlash continues also in that form, such covers are hardly needed any longer. The city employees of Sioux Falls, S.D., attending mandatory workshops on racism, let all of their hate and all of their fear hang out as they discuss how to circumvent affirmative action and open housing laws. Whether open reporting of hateful and prejudicial comments against minority people will help this community toward greater inclusiveness or will merely harden racist feeling remains to be seen.

• The Bakke case is clear warning at the judicial level that we may be back to square one. Public and private resentment of affirmative action among Whites who are or imagine themselves to be threatened with job loss suggests that we may have regressed behind square one.

 • The general silence about unemployment statistics in minority communities, and the amazing lack of organized minority "voice" regarding this desperate situation; the contradictory dynamics of excluding illegal immigrants while enjoying the benefits of their cheap labor; the unequal distribution of revenue—sharing funds; chronically unequal education, housing, job—opportunity—all of these point to a massive systemic sickness.

Because I am white, it scares me even more when I consider the items alluded to above together with what is happening on the international policy level. It is incredible that since about last October we have moved massively from peace—time to war—time rhetoric, spending and politics. The country seems to be "moving" again. There is new excitement in the air ——even with the prospect of recession on the stock exchanges. Carter was dubbed a blunderer six months ago. Now he seems about to become a national hero. Why? How is such a rapid massive shift possible with so little flack from so few people?

I fear that, internationally speaking, the answer is painfully clear throughout the Southern Hemisphere; domestically speaking, it is clear to everyone but Whites themselves; white is right—must be right. We're prepared to kill in order to prove it. Without even knowing it, the prospect of "showing the world" starts all our juices flowing again.

Blind Leaders of the Blind

"Would to God the grace he gives us to see ourselves as others see us."

How is it possible that a whole society can be sick and not know it? We who follow the God of our Lord Jesus Christ ought always to have known that we wrestle not merely with flesh and blood. Many societies are sick. As a missionary first in Asia and now to my own race in America, I'll try briefly to give my own explanation of the raison d'etre of our national sickness—racism:

a. In white society every person is trained, "programmed," to a most explicit superiority consciousness. We Whites are taught to be highly competitive, to hone aspects of discipline, shrewdness, assertiveness. So what? So are other societies. Except for us, this quest for excellence is always explained in terms of ascendance. To do well is always spelled out in a framework of comparison: to do better than, to outstrip others. You are somebody only insofar as you are better than, the biggest, the firstest, the mostest. Since God's gifts are profligate and diverse, to be the first and the best must often be achieved by downgrading others to second or last. Where "how well you do" is the chief measure of "what you are," doing better and being first become more than desirable goals; they become necessary elements of our identity.

For persons who live abroad for a long time, or who work in Third World communities right here in the U.S.A., it is both humorous and sad that everybody except white people themselves see us operating out of this superiority consciousness or syndrome. Many 'outsiders' love 'whitey' enough to point it out. But he/she rarely deals with it. The truth is that we whites can't afford to deal with it. Superiority consciousness, like its opposite dependency syndrome, is sick—unlike pride which need not be. Unfortunately, white society really doesn't have to deal with this sickness, domestically or internationally. When America has so much power and so much wealth, when the majority in society control what will be for the minority, who needs to listen to anyone else? Our power at home and abroad grants us the right to "name" the species—e.g. to decide that the minorities are the "problem" and not that society is sick with our sickness.

b. This is part of the explanation of how this sickness is perpetuated. The whole fabric of superiority myths surrounding white society, American society, is too patent to "Third World" or minority people to recount 'here. It is, however, important for our discussions here to note that these myths are inherently exclusivist. Nowadays many whites see through these myths, even smile at themselves and acknowledge that they are not the only or even the finest race that God created. But the medium is the message, and the programming goes on. Most of us Whites who have learned to acknowledge the "big lie" of racial superiority (or subsume it under American superiority) are still tongue—tied when asked to define ourselves in more realistic terms. We can usually only say, "I'm not something or other."

A word is in order about the special problem that all of this causes Christians. It is amazing how predominantly white churches have been able to remain part and parcel of the racist fabric of this country. The white church has often been kept from probing the radical depths of the mystery of God's grace and liberation because it generally insulates the full meaning of sin, the law, even the cross. Such concepts are in direct conflict to the superiority programming of the dominant society. They have, quite. understandably, been explained more in terms of individualist morality than in terms of corporate injustice and community brokenness. Theology done on the side of the dominant community by a revered elite of that community can hardly be expected to resonate more easily to a God who is a beggar and a reject than to a God who is a providential planner and a beneficent banker. Others, you, have to help us in our understanding of the suffering servant.

c. Even when, by God's grace, white consciences are pricked and white consciousness deals with the big lie of racial superiority, our long— term programming still enslaves us. Our knee—jerk reactions betray us. We must still always jump in and "do something." We are the intrepid planners, the chronic doers and problem-solvers. We hear throughout the world and often acknowledge that it is our planning and our solutions which are killing the "out" people of the world. But we still have no other response than to try harder and get busier on a better, less faulty or more noble solution "for all of the poor folks out there!" We can't seem to let go; we are trapped.

New Life from the "Other Side"

Thank God, not all is lost:

In the '5Os and '60s minority people in this country invested a great deal of time, energy and love on the education and the "humaniza-tion" of white folk. Many Whites benefited. About the same time, white females began organizing their resistance to sexist manifestations of the same supremacist sickness. To a lesser degree, white males on occasion came to resent their own enslavement to superiority mythology.

It is hardly curious to disciples of Jesus Christ that, although there was a lot of good honest confrontation in civil rights days, it was not confrontation that enabled a beginning process of liberation. New life is not generated out of guilt and self—hate, although to be crushed and broken by these must also preceded regeneration. New life begins when someone accepts us—when the white person feels the warmth of com-munity that says, "Hey, Honkie, you can stay—not because you're smart or well—intentioned—but because you're human—and we're going to dare you to be that!"

Thus begins the miracle of reciprocal process—the flow of normal contexts and their interactions is reversed. It is reversed in the sense that helping, loving, healing begin to flow opposite to the normal direction across a grid of power, legitimacy, status, self—perception and commu-nity solidarity. Those heretofore presumed to be patients ("the prob-lem") become the doctors.

True partnership (authentic peer interactions) can only begin to take place from the side of the "out people," that is, from the side of powerlessness and acknowledged brokenness. This miracle of partner-ship is transcendent. It is neither black, brown, red, yellow or white. It is the miracle of Jesus Christ and His cross, which is the powerful model of partnership that brings us together today. Only those who have no superiority left to stand on can begin to see with different eyes and be freed to reach out in a totally new way. And that is a problem as well as a call to mission. A problem because getting off one's high horse is painful and difficult. A call to mission because we believe that God's reconciliation is inclusive. It is Good News to the poor and a call to repentance (in the interest of Good News) for the supposed superior!

The possibility of the white person accepting new struggles comes always from the "other side"—the side of color (or sex)—the distaff side of power and control. Touched by undeserved acceptance, by the witness to a greater vision of wholeness, we are given at least the potential of embarking on a new quest: not for some new hegemony this time, but for truth, for our own humanity, for justice and for liberation.

All of this I say out of a deep faith in God, creator, redeemer and vivifier. All of this has to be set into the framework of a dynamic eschatology, as we struggle with something that "out people" have always known: "You ain't got nothing to live for if you ain't got nothing to die for."

Excursus

The pitfalls for those whites who accept the call to be free are many and worth documenting:

a. The white person will quickly find that even the slightest change is costly. The "woodwork"—the white system and community—will obfuscate, confuse and actively resist his/her efforts to discover who or why he/she really is. It is, after all, "treason" to refuse to be and act like you are "supposed" to be and act. Feelings of alienation and loneliness follow.

b. Alone and hurting, whitey gravitates more and more to the association of "out people." While he/she feels safer there, that often hurts even worse, because when the chips are down he/she expects still arrogantly to be accepted on his or her own terms. Even when accepted on the minority community's terms, whites cannot understand what the community intuitively understands: that even "new" white folk are to be trusted only up to certain limits. The minority community knows better than the white person how strong the temptations are to "take charge and do something." White persons must constantly work at enhancing their understanding of new equations. Sharing and vulnerability are graces that grow only as they are witnessed to, acted out and struggled with, much like St. Paul's war between the flesh and the spirit.

c. That is only to say that the long list of hang—ups and programmed responses, fears, expectations—the white person's own ego needs—have to be dealt with one by one. Long before substantive progress is made, loving friends and that person's own patience may well be exhausted.

d. Even as the white person makes progress, the constant need to hone or increase his/her sensitivity, patience and capacity for "hearing" the beat of another drum, remains.

e. As the "new" white passes across frontiers of race, culture arid related issues, the going gets trickier and often less productive of progress. One big disillusionment keeps throwing her/him back: The discovery of the extent to which white society and its values have bent "out people" out of shape, too. The temptation is constant either to excuse minority sisters' and brothers who are less than faithful with "That's what the System does," or to ease his/her own culpability with the lack of his minority sister's or brother's accountability.

f. Because de—programming and the way to liberation are fraught with so many obstacles, "burn out" is a constant danger.

"Cooptation" being the normal strategy of injustice these days, the "new" white person will again and again be placed in circumstances where he/she is tempted to "go along" with the crowd silently, or preen him/herself on newly found awarenesses.

A New Vision for Tomorrow

Whenever I say these things in white circles, as softly and as lovingly as I possibly can, I am heard as a prophet of doom, a peddler of negative and overstated lies. I don't feel at all a prophet of doom when I talk about "white sickness." The gospel of God calls us to a blessed undertaking: to acknowledge the poverty of our presumed superiority and find riches, wholeness, acceptance on the side of the poor, the broken and rejected. That's no cute conundrum. It is the mystery and the miracle of the gospel and of wholeness—"the aroma of Christ to God among those who are being saved and among those who are perishing, to one a fragrance from death to death, to the Other a fragrance from life to life. Who is sufficient for these things?" (II Cor. 3:15, 16)

If, by God's grace, the struggle for liberation of the oppressor is accepted by us who are white, and faithfully, prayerfully, humbly pursued, God can bring us to a new maturity, even in these latter days:

a. The white person so touched can know and live with the truth that analysis is no longer simple (Who's the real enemy? What can be done about it? etc.) She/he lives in a new hope, trusting only the promise, which is now no longer an individualist but a transcendent, global, inclusive promise. By God's grace we are kept from despair; by God's grace able to celebrate the vast and rich diversity of His creation; by God's grace less tempted to hedge bets, look back, or connive at having our cake and eating it, too.

b. To be free of the illusion that something can be done (in traditional triumphalist terms) frees one to discover that the most hopeless situation is precisely where truth can be most powerful; power most vulnerable; and eternity most contemporary. In short, white people, too, can now perceive that a little "nothing" can be everything, and can shake everything to its very foundations.

Example: Andy Young says there are political prisoners in the U.S.! Or, he has a chat with the PLO, whom we've decided don't exist, and 10,000 newspapers carry it in their headlines the next day!

Now, perhaps, in concert with others, and without illusions, whites can begin to strategize. Among all the agendas in which he/she participates, two will now stand out, even though he/she no longer sets the agendas:

a. The "new" white person can discipline, and force others in his/her community to discipline their compulsiveness, as she/he struggles to create, protect and nurture a little space for him or herself. Another way to say this is to say that the "new" white person can hang on to and renew her/his humanity.

b. The "new" white person can, in plural concert with others, participate in creating or preserving a little space for others. This will probably take the form of confronting his or her own kind. Again, I say "probably" because neither he/she or his or her white peers should be the ones to decide where and when, without plugging into the transcendent community—that is, with people on the distaff side of power who are aware of the problems we've been talking about.

Conclusion

I was a missionary. I am a missionary. I believe in the miracle of reciprocity, which is the miracle of self—transcendence and wholeness. I see no success scenarios for an inclusive, plural society in which "out people" get a better shake and the excesses of "in people" are drastically modified. But I see hope in the very fact that things are that bad: I say "stop concentrating solely on strategies of cure and the eradication of disease." We need strategies of spreading and infecting hurting oppressors, wherever and whoever they are, with wholeness.

It should be clear that only "out people," or those prepared to be in solidarity with "out people," can do that. Their understanding of the kingdom of God accords most with the biblical context in which witness to the kingdom was given and with the kingdom dynamics of how it works: Only those who realize they are lost can possibly be found.

"I am not ashamed of the gospel of Christ. It is the power of God unto salvation for everyone who believes:" That's all one should have to say to this audience. But predominantly white church institutions need your straightforward declaration of this profound truth, lest they sleep the sleep of death through long explanations about that which demands obedience and allegiance, not explanation.

WHITE LUTHERANS
Who We Are, What We Bring, What We Need

By James W. Mayer

In planning this conference, the Steering Committee determined that there should be a background paper for each of five ethnic groups participating: Afro—American, Hispanic, Asian, Native American and Euro—American or white. The committee further proposed an outline for these papers which would enable the various groups to express what was important to them regarding their roots, development and present expectations. The preparers were asked to adhere to the following format: I) who we are; II) what we bring to the Lutheran church and to the issue of inclusion; and III) our needs and what we expect from the Lutheran church through honest address of this issue.

Who We Are

A. White Lutherans have their roots in western civilization, particularly the European expression and development of that civilization. As a people we have thus consistently enjoyed a place in majority society —— racially, culturally and religiously. The fact that we have been able, for the most part, to take for granted our membership in majority society and its institutions all the way back to our earliest roots has affected our racial as well as our religious self—consciousness. Christianity enjoyed majority status in Europe for centuries, and a massive religious establishment impacted the consciousness and mores of most nations on the continent. Conversely, the vicissitudes of national and political developments impacted religious formation as church and state vied for hegemony.

Within the broad definition of white North American Lutherans as western and European, it is even more significant for understanding who we are to remember that Lutherans in this country stem largely from the North European block, specifically the Scandinavian countries and Germany. This fact further enforces the generalization that as a people, our cultural mores, religious sensibilities and theological thought have all been developed more in the context of the socio—political mainstream than in the context of disenfranchisement, repression or persecution. The extent to which the Lutheran Reformation is an exception to that may be worth further examination.

Viewed from a worldwide perspective, the development and the dominant role played by Europeans in recent centuries certainly has direct implications for understanding who we are.

As a people we are cognitive, industrious, acquisitive, competitive, disciplined, resourceful and expansionist. We have become masters of concentrating in a linear way on causes and their effects. We have tended to understand progress much more in terms of expansion and increased control over the physical world and its resources than in terms of any adequate integration of human existence with nature.

In that quest for ascendancy and control over our own (and often others') destiny, we have prided ourselves in our disciplined ability to say "No" to our emotions and our spirits in the pursuit of more "rational" ends, assuming the prerogative of defining what is rational for us as universal and applicable to everyone.

If will plus power (or will plus wealth) usually sets the stage for exploitation, then we white Lutherans should not be surprised when others consider us a relatively violent people. From our roots up until the present our racial history provides many examples of controlling and exploitative behavior, not only with respect to our treatment of peoples and nations with less power than our own, but often with respect to how we treat each other.

B. As Lutherans we are the proud inheritors, and like to think of ourselves as the chief proponents of the Protestant Reformation. We rather consistently stress the importance of or find our way back to a strong faith—base that takes its stand on the objective action of God (Incarnate) in human history. In a bold declaration of faith that God's grace alone is sufficient for life and the highest treasure of life, it was possible to take a stand against the 16th Century religious establishment and risk disenfranchisement. The strength and vitality thereby generated has informed Lutheranism in one context or another down to the present day.

It is probably no accident that Luther, a German, should have had so little confidence in the subjective side of religion. Lutherans place a high premium on concern for a right relationship between God and human individuals. Lutherans can be relatively casual (or become frustratingly complex and theoretic) when it comes to spelling out the implications of such a right relationship for human behavior or a social ethic. (1)

Our tendency to center theological thinking always on God's action rather than on ours is a contribution we bring to Christian understanding in a country of many sects. But the struggle to discern and consistently act out the implications of God's actions for our action is one that could profit from the input of other racial sensibilities and denominational traditions.

It should be noted that the break with Rome did not for long divest Lutherans of power or majority status in their own homelands. Indeed, it may have enabled them to operate on the side of ascendancy even more exclusively than before the Reformation. Lutheranism became the state religion of Lutheran states in Germany. All of the Scandinavian countries became officially Lutheran.

C. Lutheran emigrations in the early and middle nineteenth century brought hundreds of thousands of Lutherans to the U.S. from Germany and the Nordic countries. Emigrations from Europe were a) bold flights from interference in matters of religion; b) a quest for new wealth and a better life on the new continent; c) a sincere effort to send colonists who would evangelize Native Americans. (These latter, as it turned out, though motivated with lofty ideals, had underestimated the Native American tolerance for German chorales and resentment of the North European genius for occupying the best arable land wherever they went.)

Often, though not always, immigration cast Scandinavian and German Lutherans in a minority role in this country. Many of them had to start all over at the bottom rung of the socio—economic ladder. Their development followed the standard pattern for most immigrants described by Will Herberg (Protestant, Catholic, Jew): A strong determination in the first generation to remain (for example) Swedish and retain Swedish ways; followed in the second generation by a conscious determination to retain Lutheran identity as they sought authentic American identity; and finally, once they became in the third generation possessors of an unquestioned American identity, a touting of their ethnic roots and customs, e.g.: Strassenfest, Smorgasbord, Wienerschnitzel, etc.

A strong ethnic pride and a strong, well—articulated common theological heritage helped Lutherans make it in this country. They made it superbly, but as a relatively "closed" elite group, at least until World War

I. Following WW II, renewed mission awareness and marriage opened most Lutheran churches to whites of other ethnic origins. There was, in practice, virtually no openness to people of color except as "objects for conversion."

In spite of greater variety of ethnic means on church rolls everywhere, Lutherans continued to show their preference for exclusiveness by continuing in separate, sometime sparring church bodies comprised of the various ethnic streams of traditional Lutherans: Norwegian, Danish, Swedish, Finnish, German, Slovak. Neither the tendency in some cases to sanctify such separateness on the basis of doctrinal rather than ethnic grounds, nor the various church mergers of more recent times really alter the fact that Lutherans have had and still have tendencies to separatism and elitism.

In other matters also, white Lutherans bear many of the racial and cultural traits of their ancestors, even though these have been modified, adapted or added to through several generations on the North American continent. A rather patriarchal family tradition is one that is worth of note. Only in recent times have patterns of male dominance begun to be called into question—and that largely from socio—cultural pressures in American culture, not from some impetus within our particular ethnic or religious traditions.

In terms of the issue of inclusion or transcendence, it would appear on the surface that Lutheranism is more distinguished by its parochialness and the unbroken continuity of its tradition than by its capacity to open itself up to other traditions or to radical innovation.

Yet, we can affirm that the white Lutheran expression of culture and religion in North America has 'many gifts' also—a rich treasure of the past coupled with great racial, cultural and religious resources at least potentially releasable in the present and the future. In the following section, we shall try to point to some of these.

What White Lutherans Bring to Lutheranism and to the Issue of Inclusion

A. White Lutherans share with Lutherans in Asia, Africa and elsewhere a strong catholic tradition. By God's grace this avoidance of sectarian tendencies and this determination to remain within the catholic tradition have come to surface more emphatically than ever in recent years. As dialogue with other denominations continues, it is reasonable to assume that the practice of emphasizing the continuity and the commonality of a catholic tradition over points of difference or departures from that tradition will continue.

B. A strong, explicit—though not always unanimous—confessional base unites white Lutherans with, all other Lutherans. If the current period in world history is generating 'massive changes in our presuppositions, relationships and behavior—changes equal to or greater than the changes accompanying the Reformation and the Industrial Revolution—then the gift of a solid base and clear historic continuity are uniquely important. Both provide ingredients of a place to stand and a base from which to innovate. That is not less true because of white Lutherans' predilection to polish rather than translate or apply their tradition to present and emerging global realities.

C. All Lutheran bodies in North America are essentially conservative, in the good sense of that term. They value the tradition from which they must enter the future. Once convinced that a course of action is God's will, usually a conviction achieved through a tortuous process of squaring proposed action with the tradition, white Lutherans can be as stubborn about new commitments as anyone, and follow through on them.

That is an asset—even if in recent history the potential has not been distinguished by consistent fulfillment. The Lutheran church bodies in North America have not always been able to break free from conservatism of a very rigid kind, highly resistant to change on any front; nor have they escaped the trap on the other side of a too—easy liberalism. Consequently, revolution or revolutionary movements are highly suspect in white Lutheran circles, and even the slogan: "The church being ever reformed" (ecclesia semper reformanda) has been more prominent among other protestants than in Lutheran consciousness.

D. Lutherans have a healthy respect for rationality, order and authority, and have a tendency to equate the first with the latter two. Though congregational in polity in this country, we retain in our structures and our orders many of the values of the more hierarchical traditions of Europe. If we live in an age when such qualities are branded as "hang ups" which inhibit progress and liberation—and they certainly can be that—order and discipline are helpful ingredients for constructive change and long—term effectiveness in mission precisely because we are in a period of cataclysmic changes everywhere.

E. Potentially the strongest element that white Lutherans bring to an inclusive Lutheran church is a certain schizophrenia. One of the strengths and constant problems in Lutheran theology is the Lutheran refusal to resolve paradoxes. Lutherans are invited, indeed, expected to live schizophrenically in the tension between paradox, e.g., simul justus et peccator. For a people of North European roots that is something that goes so strongly "against the grain" that it can immobilize. Yet, that very tension can be creative and dynamic. It can, and often does motivate otherwise traditionalist white Lutherans to "bite some bullets" when they have to. To a frightening extent, it has also tempted successful white Lutherans to run away from the tension or dilute it by imbibing large doses of the triumphalism of American religion in general.

White Lutherans often show an extraordinary capacity to dare to believe and act transcendentally and catholicly, while at the same time having both the need and amazing ability to square such belief and action with their own brand of logic and Lutheran parochiality! They have an ability to understand in the boldest of terms what is implied in "The kingdom of God is at hand," but react against and resist strongly ever declaring the kingdom of God "in hand." They can affirm more convincingly than any that "God sets the agenda," but they recoil in horror at the thought that we can easily determine what God is doing in our town this week.

Another example of white Lutheran schizophrenia derives from white Lutherans strong racial need for structure and authority versus a spirit of independence that refuses to let any structure prescribe for it. That frequently contradictory spirit can be illustrated across the centuries by contrasting the picture of Luther at Worms thumbing his nose at Rome, with the often passive reverence of white Lutherans for their respective church bodies and leaders, or the widespread acceptance of "Herr Pastor" clerical styles—where the parish priest thinks, decides and does for the laity.

F. White Lutherans bring to the Lutheran church in this continent a specific kind of resourcefulness. In keeping with their history, it is a resourcefulness in improving and expanding what one has, not the kind of resourcefulness fashioned in the fires of slavery or developed through protracted struggles for sheer survival.

The point is made here because just as white Lutherans have proved resourceful in matters of capital and institutional development (properly understood: in their own self-interest), that very development could be an obstacle to inclusion unless informed by the resourcefulness of those for whom survival amid suffering has been the more normal context. We are talking about the difference between self-interest and enlightened self-interest. It is in the interest of white and all other Lutherans to combine their resourcefulness to discover new ways of vulnerable partnership—new creative ways of getting through giving and giving through getting! This point will become clearer in section III.

G. The Lutheran churches in North America bring to Lutheranism and the issue of inclusion vast financial, capital and institutional resources together with more than enough talent to manage them well. The combined assets of local parishes, synods or districts, national headquarters, church extension and pension funds, publishing houses, hospitals, colleges, schools, retirement homes, summer camps, social work and welfare agencies, etc. is simply phenomenal. Add to that the fact that hundreds of millions of dollars are generated annually through member contributions for all church and church related programs—and one can only wonder at the wealth of white Lutherans in this continent. With respect to the issue of inclusion, such blessings make it incumbent on us to wonder also about which programs are supported. What percentage of our resources are spent on ourselves and our institutions, and what percentage for change and/or ministry that affects others?

H. We must not close this section without noting that as a people, white Lutherans are a fairly well indoctrinated and committed constituency who genuinely seek to serve their Lord. They see themselves as a people concerned with faithful discipleship and with trying to square life in these affluent United States with it. White Lutherans often exercise a brand of piety that is pious without being merely pietistic; formal (and often stiff) but not devoid of deep feeling; biblical without becoming biblicistic; strongly individualist, yet capable of amazing "pastoral" concern and elitist, yet moderately responsive to mission.

What Do White Lutherans Need from the Goal of an Inclusive Church?

In the body of Christ, the gifts and the strengths God gives any particular people are gifts and strengths given to the whole church for his mission to the world. These gifts become actualized as blessing only as they are released, shared and risked in the church and the world!

Considering the many gifts and strengths of white Lutherans, their exclusiveness is a serious problem, a deep—seated cancer in U.S. Lutheranism. As documented some years ago by the "Study of Generations," Lutheran churches in North America are 98% white and decidedly middle class. Lutheran churches also appear to be 99.9% white run, and—in spite of over 200 women clergy, increased numbers of women on boards and commissions, and elders in local parishes—essentially male dominated.

In spite of these statistics, most Lutherans would be offended to hear themselves spoken of as exclusivist. Through protracted, serious and authentic address to the problem of exclusion, we white Lutherans need to recover sight—a cure for racial blindness apparent to the world of color, but hidden from ourselves. We need inner courage and outside pressure to deal with that blindness—in our own self—interest as well as in the interest of other Lutherans and the mission of the church.

A. We need to see how and to what extent we are victims.

1. We are victims of our own status and role as members of the white majority establishment. Racism, sexism and elitism are systemic diseases. We may with varying degrees of validity excuse ourselves, or with varying degrees of success extricate ourselves from personal prejudices. We can even, on the personal level, resolve to be non—racist and non—sexist. That does not, however, free us from our entrapment within a racist, sexist or elitist society. For we continue to participate willingly and to benefit substantially from racist and sexist structures. Or, more pointedly, we benefit from not confronting these structures. (2)

As white Lutherans we see ourselves and are seen by others in majority society as "in" people. Enjoying the fruits of double—standards that give white males and to some extent white females preference, while simultaneously excluding others, we are prone to respond:

• by constructing sophisticated rationalizations, or

• emphatically denying, or

• pleading ignorance, or

• experiencing deep qualms and guilt, or

• blaming the victims, or

• openly and honestly deploring discrimination.

We do any or all of the above depending on where and how we are "called to give an account." But we continue to go along! We won't rise up and say, "No," and begin to change the arrangement. We know all too well that for us to espouse and systematically pursue inclusion by becoming openly and consistently anti—racist, anti—sexist and anti—elitist would be costly. We sense the hostility and the loss we would swiftly bring on ourselves in both church and society arenas. So we settle for strategies which avoid incurring such risks and fall far short of authentic dealing with structures we ourselves claim to deplore. We need to see how our "preferred" status works against us so that we are freed to deal in an authentic manner with inclusion. How we are victimized by exclusivist structures will become clearer in the sections that   follow.

2. If our place and role in majority society in North America traps us structurally, some elements in our racial programming make getting out of the trap doubly difficult. We have a long history of being a viable, successful people. We also have strongly developed needs to be superior—the first and the best in any arena. From a very young age we are taught to compete to the utmost—to be strong and' refuse to let limitations stop us ("There ain't no such word as can't"!). While such values are in themselves not limited to whites nor necessarily destructive, they can be developed at the expense of other equally important values only where "success" is more consistently a possibility than "failure."

A dominant majority usually also develops positive evaluations of itself at the expense of truth and of other people. Even for white Lutherans, "being on top" is not a consistent reality. When we fall short of the expectations of our own programming, the temptation looms large for us to gain feelings of superiority by contemplating the "inferiority" of others.

The extent to which Whites believe positive myths about them selves and less favorable myths about others is read as a blind "superiority consciousness" by people of color throughout the world. It is not our achievements or our capacity to plan and to act that is resented nearly so much as our ill—controlled need to be planners, doers and problem solvers for everyone. We are victims of our own compulsions—a people who can master most everything except our inability to say, "I can't," (and mean it) to people of color! We are sometimes a people so committed to being strong that we fail to perceive how dependent we are on the toil of other people.

"Superiority consciousness" often expresses itself in two kinds of behavior which are uniquely critical to the issue of inclusion: a) Eagerness to "own" or be the chief sponsors of a programmed solution; and b)Moves that ensure that the prerogative to define people (and establish criteria for people evaluation) will remain in the hands of the majority institution.(3)

We need help in seeing that such institutional arrangements serve our need to be neatly on top of things much more than they serve the effectiveness of the church in mission. Though organizationally "logical" they prevent us from seeing ourselves and others' in more realistic terms.

B. We need to see how and to what extent we have paid (and continue to pay) too high a price for the gratification of the need to be "on top" and the need to stay in control.

1. Coming as we do out of a very strong and vital Christian tradition, it is very costly for us as persons and as a community to have to maintain racial and ethnic myths about ourselves and others in order to feel good about ourselves. Taught from a very young age both about brokenness in the doctrine of original sin and about free and full forgiveness purchased and won for all alike in Jesus Christ, we cannot go on living by superiority myths without inviting deep—seated neuroses, or without calling into question our authenticity as faithful Lutheran Christians.

As Lutherans we affirm our solidarity with all human kind as creatures of one Lord and, since the Fall, as creatures with a common need for the salvation God offers broken, alienated and inherently selfish human beings. Such affirmations imply inclusivist attitudes and practices on the personal as well as the institutional level. To the extent, therefore, that our dealings with each other and the world are racist, sexist or elitist, we have to fill or hide the gap between what we say and what we do with all kinds of inauthentic behavior. Who we are is thus something other than we purport to be. This results not only in a loss of authenticity and the freedom that goes with it, but encumbers us with tons of "baggage" that inhibits forceful action in the world.

2. Loss of authenticity invariably leads to a distorted sense of purpose—of mission. This is true both individually and corporately, but more readily observable in the church as church bodies grow into large corporate structures. We are committed to live as self—less ambassadors of reconciliation in the world (individually and corporately). We affirm that as our first agenda. Our second agenda is to retain enough institutional viability to do the first agenda faithfully and effectively.

It is perhaps in the nature of all institutions, even hurchly institutions, to become ends in themselves —to make agenda two the main agenda, and to tackle the first agenda if and when it is convenient and safe to do so. But to make the maintenance and growth of our own institutions (agenda two) our first priority in the name of mission (agenda one) requires bigger and bigger rationalizations as our institutions grow in size.

We pay an incalculably high price for this distortion of purpose. Institutionally that may not always be apparent. Yet in this day and age, when pain, violence, hunger and tragedy are so massive and so common as to immobilize a whole nation, we often find ourselves fighting with words instead of action or with resolutions instead of the considerable weight of our corporate and personal assets. Or we switch to matters of technique and strategy because we can't recover a clear, authentic sense of our purpose.

How else can we explain why, as we move close to the twenty-first century, most Lutherans still think of mission as "world mission" and world mission as overseas, despite plenty of official pronouncements to the contrary? How else can we explain new drives by all Lutheran church bodies for new congregational starts in predominantly white and middle class neighborhoods at the very time when urban decay takes a higher toll in human life and dignity than ever before in the history of this country? How else can we explain that after a hundred years of sometimes self—sacrificing effort, mission in this' country has not resulted in a "rainbow" church, but has only enlarged the size of 92% white churches?

3. Just as a loss of authenticity leads to a distortion of our sense of purpose, so it dulls our sensitivity to people and the cause and effect relationship between how we live and how they must live. This is due in part to our need always to defend ourselves before the less fortunate of the world and each other. For example, many people will resent the questions raised in the previous paragraph or the context in which they are raised. Some will point out, correctly, that hundreds, maybe thousands within the institutional church, structures are trying to make those structures better servants of authentic mission purposes. Still others will see in much of this analysis a confusion of "kingdoms" that makes helpful solutions downright impossible.

Precisely! The point is that we have a need to explain—to show reasons why the pain persists or why it is not appropriately our business. We white Lutherans are not without sensitivity to people and their needs. Rather, our sensitivity shifts quickly to a concentration on our response to such need. We want to respond as helpers, and do—in ways that inevitably cast others in the role of "helpee."

We have difficulty understanding either how our offer of help can sometimes be the last and worst of all insults, or why, in the absence of anything useful to do, just standing by in solidarity with those who suffer can be the most useful of all. Said differently, our sensitivity to what other people are going through is often dulled by our compulsion to get on with business as usual. And in our eagerness' to do that we often treat even each other in ways that are insensitive and sometimes violent.

C. We need new courage and faith—an increase in our capacity to be vulnerable.

All of this section has dealt with the same problem: our resistance, indeed, our incapacity as white Lutherans to be vulnerable. Gifted with many strengths refined through a positive interpretation of our history, vulnerability comes hard to us. To consider vulnerability as an asset makes no sense at all in the present—day majority society in which we are such respected members. So it is here, more than at any other point, that white Lutherans need the help of Lutheran sisters and brothers who have different racial and cultural histories. For- tunately, as Lutherans, we still affirm that resurrection comes only after suffering and death. Even though the empty tomb, Christ's victory over death, may seem to fit the sensibilities of majority society better than the cross, for Lutherans they are always together. None know that better than those who've borne crosses for long periods in their racial or their personal history. Be they numbered with the majority or the minority, those people understand that true strength and liberation are ultimately measured by a capacity for vulnerability, not by invincibility or by independence.

Inclusion means simply that we learn to bear one another's bur- dens across all fences of the mind—that we remain vulnerable to each, other. An inclusive church., by that definition, becomes more than an ideal that white Lutherans ought to uphold and -more than a command demanding their obedience.

It becomes a necessity, a gift of God we can no longer pretend we don't need.[4]

NOTES

1. Relative to this and following paragraphs it may be worth noting:

a. That the comparatively passive socio—political posture Max Weber (The Spirit of Capitalism and the Protestant Ethic) attributed to Lutherans in Europe, seems applicable to Lutherans in this country at least up to relatively recent times.

b. That Lutherans distinguished themselves in ethical response through hospitals, old folks homes, orphanages, schools and colleges—all, however, primarily for Lutherans! Early missions were established to find and minister to immigrants from the Lutheran countries; seamen's missions were established for ministry to Lutheran seamen.

c. That the annals of one of the larger Lutheran bodies in North America are full of mission board statements which refer to both Native Americans and Blacks in the South as "pagan" and "heathen."

2. The arguments in this and subsequent paragraphs are spelled out in a more complete and competent way by the Rev. Joseph Barndt (LCA pastor) in Liberating Our White Ghetto. Augsburg, Minneapolis, 1972.

3. Someone has said, "The law of the jungle is: 'Kill or be killed.' But humans translate that in seemingly less violent terms, 'Define or be defined." The Cornwall Collective provides an excellent discussion of who defines whom, and how in certain institutions of the church, women have simply been defined "out of existence." Your Daughters Shall Prophesy (Feminist Alternatives in Theological Education) by the Cornwall Collection. The Pilgrim Press, New York, 1980. The fifth chapter of the same book, "Power and Institutional Change," is also helpful material for our discussion.

4. A resource deserving of careful study in connection with all of Section III, but particularly this last section is Douglas John Hall's book, Lighten Our Darkness—Toward an Indigenous Theology of the Cross, The Westminster Press, Philadelphia, 1976.

TOWARD A
NEW COMMUNITY

Prepared by:
The Rev. James Bergquist
Mr. Elwyn Ewald
The Rev. Dr. Kenneth Senft
The Rev. Dr. Donald Larsen

In 1977 a group of black Lutherans approached the North American mission executives of the American Lutheran Church, the Association of Evangelical Lutheran Churches, the Lutheran Church in America and the Lutheran Church Missouri Synod with the request that the divisions of ministry represented by those men convene a series of meetings—a process—to discuss what was then called "transcendency" within the life of the churches. How could we as Lutherans stand above the historical divisions of race and culture and learn from each other what it means to be Lutheran in each culture? How could we then create a new community of believers, one that would respect each culture and become more whole because of the incorporation of all races and cultures into the mixture of its life?

To clarify why such as series of meetings or such a process was necessary, and to plan how it might be done most effectively, a Steering Committee was appointed which consisted of members of each of the five racial constituencies (Afro-Americans, Anglo-Americans, Latino-Americans, Native Americans, Asian Americans) in each of the three participating church bodies (the LCMS dropped out of the process). The mission executives of the each of the three church bodies also continued to discuss recommendations from the committee of what, by this time, had come to be known as the Transcultural Seminar.

Working on plans for this process over a period of several years, the committee identified specific goals and proposed specific formats for two major conferences: a mini—conference (held in Cincinnati in May and a maxi—conference (to be held in Chicago in October, 1981).

Both of these conferences introduce an all—important new concept regarding the basis upon which participation is determined. It was decided that each of the racial or cultural groups in our Lutheran family should be represented equally with every other group. The demographics of the Lutheran church in the U.S.A. (predominantly white) makes this shift away from the usual proportional representation a matter of critical importance for the work of these conferences and the future of Lutherans in the U.S.A. This intentionally scaled down white participation makes possible equal ownership of the processes by all the groups involved.

The first session of this process is now history. It is not the purpose of this paper to report on that session. Others have been given that responsibility. The goal of this paper is to share with you the dreams that the mission executives of the three participating church bodies had for this process.

Since the formation of the three church bodies (ALC in 1960, LCA in 1962 and the AELC in 1976), each of them has had a strong commitment to including peoples of color and cultural difference in the life of the church body. Many resolutions have been adopted by each church body espousing civil rights for all races. Each church body has established goals for including ethnic minorities in the mission of the church —hoping they might become members of the church, and, through their participation, move the churches toward a fuller, richer community.

Some growth of participation of other than white persons in the life of the Lutheran church bodies has taken place as a result of these goals and these commitments. But, much more needs to be done. The Lutheran churches we represent continue to be predominantly white and Western European in both membership statistics and style – i.e. worship, confessional statements, organizational designs, etc. James Mayer's paper prepared for the first session of this process addresses this reality in more detail than we intend to do in this paper. However, this brief statement serves to introduce us to the actual goals of this process as the executives have perceived them.

We hope that this process can lead to a more "inclusive" church among Lutherans in the U.S.A. and that it may also lead to the development of a model of life within a church body that may be emulated by others. To accomplish that goal, we must begin with the question, "What do we mean by 'inclusive'?"

Are we talking about "assimilation" of peoples of color and cultural difference into the predominately white Lutheran church in the U.S.A.? Are we talking about the "integration" of racial/cultural constituencies of the Lutheran church in the U.S.A.? Are we talking about something much more complete than either assimilation or integration? How do we perceive of that "new community" of the New Testament where there is neither "Jew nor Greek, slave nor free, male nor female, for we are all one in Christ," but where the "isness" of each is still "chosen, holy, beloved" in one body?

At the risk of having too much time spent on discussing the quality of a diagram, we are going to use three of them in hopes that they will clarify words used to explore ideas.

Our first diagram represents what many Whites and non-whites (Sic!) perceive to be the goal; assimilation of non-whites into the white world.

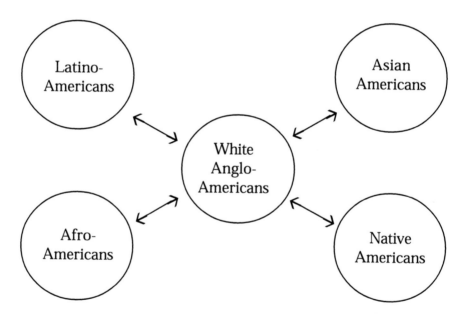

In this design the center of the universe is the white, Western European culture and religion. The goal, stated as simply and clearly as possible, is a white goal. It intends to include non—whites or non—Western Europeans when they have assumed the forms of life and the manner that the Whites have determined to be best for themselves and for all others.

Conversations are always directed to Whites or from Whites. Discussion between the other ethnic groups is discouraged and takes place infrequently. Operating within this model requires that forms of education be those suited to supporting and re—enforcing the traditional white, European style of life and world view; it requires that the theology be based on white, European perceptions of God and the universe that he has created; it means that family Life and styles be altered to fit the white, European model. In this model, control is in the hands of Whites, with non—whites who have learned the white style well being given token jobs of token importance within the structures of the white world.

We hope that the church has moved beyond this model, but we recognize that it does continue to influence many Lutherans as we try to change our style and our perceptions of the world around us. We also recognize, that like it or not, many of the minority persons in this country and in our churches operate within this model because they see no other way to get along with the Whites in this land and to "move up in the world."

There is another picture of the world that we see used in many places today:

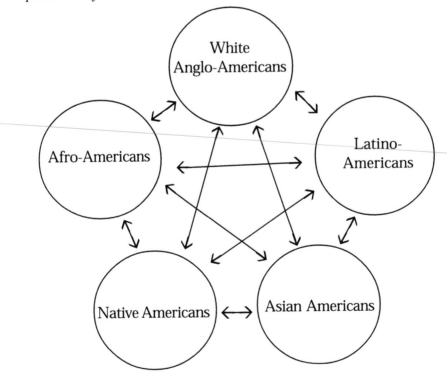

This diagram tries to recognize and appreciate the unique ness of each culture and race in this world and to maximize communication between each of these unique communities. Communications **around** and **between** the spectrum of cultures and races are seen as legitimate, but the diagram views the world as locked-in cultures (closed circles representing closed communities). Persons are free to step out of their own circle to communicate or negotiate what they want from another culture or community, but it is expected that they will go back into their own community and remain separate from and have no responsibility for the other communities.

In this model, change takes place in each community as contact with other communities, cultures and races is increased. The change is always **within** the closed circle. This model does not easily lend itself to the emergence of new configurations of circles or new communities of people of a variety of racial and cultural perspectives.

This model expresses itself in all the old "separate but equal" doctrines: separate but equal education; segregated but equal housing; and the development of communities where all the races and cultures share service arenas. However, the different races and cultures are expected to live in separate communities after the day of work and recreation is completed.

This model lends itself to racial and cultural competition for power and money as much as any model of the past. It continues to support the idea of separateness in the interest of the domination of the majority over the minority. It adds little to the concept of "inclusiveness" or the idea of the new community of the New Testament.

We, as members of the one church serving the one God who has created and redeemed us all, have got to work to find a more complete expression of that new community we have in Christ. Maybe the world will have to be satisfied with the model above. But surely we as members together of God's community of believers where in one body each member is essential to (and actually contributes to) defining the whole, and where the whole is seen as authentically present in every part— surely we have to struggle together to become (and express) more than separate but equal.

As an example we would suggest that the following diagram may lead us to discuss what an authentically inclusive community could be within the church, if not within society at large (See next page):

This design suggests that the church is indeed a "new community" made up of all of God's people with their peculiarities of race, culture and history. It also suggests that in the church these peculiarities are not

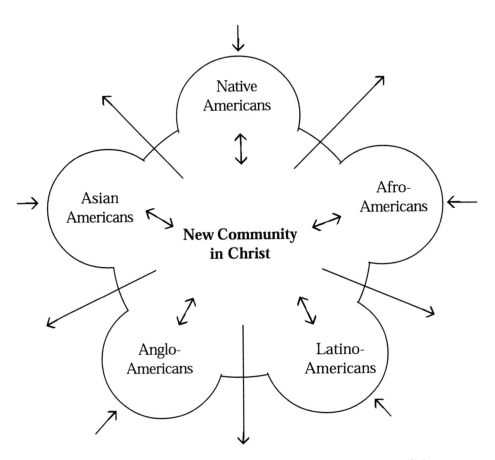

seen as divisive or separating. On the contrary, they are part of the important mix of God's creation that when brought together help to create a new, more whole community than was present before each came in contact with the other.

This model suggests an ideal where no one of the peoples that are part of God's church are less than another. No one of them has a more complete picture of God's world and his intended purpose for it than another. No one history is preferred to another and no one culture is considered superior to another. It suggest that as the church views the world and the changing situation for ministry to and in that world, it ought to do it through a multifocal lens of all the differences (race, sex, class, age) of its fellowship—brought into one focus, the focus of all touched by the light of the King's Son.

It also suggests that the various identifiable groups no longer can think of themselves in isolation from others in this new community.

When changes are contemplated, when educational programs are planned, when housing patterns are advocated, when financial considerations are determined, decisions are made with all of these people and their perceptions of their needs in mind as we together shape the compromises we must follow in this world.

All of the above suggests that the church as an organization has to create forums for this truly inclusive communication, sharing and creation to take place. It suggests that we have to make real efforts to quit thinking about "us" and "them." We have to perceive and challenge each other constantly to perceive of ourselves as "we."

All of the above suggests some really revolutionary challenges to the world in which we live and to ourselves as we live in that world. This kind of perspective of who we are will fundamentally and radically affect what we as church say and do: how we pattern participation on committees; how we structure liturgies for our worship; and what we advocate in terms of school desegregation, war or peace, nuclear proliferation, and so forth.

This vision of an inclusive community no longer allows one culture or people to make selfish decisions in any of these areas. The church is not the property more of one than another, nor is the universe the property of one more than another.

The intention of this paper is not to answer questions or to advocate one particular model for an inclusive church over another. Rather, it is an effort to focus our discussion and to raise some of the right questions that we hope this group will work toward resolving. As we see it, the questions before this group are at least the following:

1. What do we mean by transcultural "inclusion"?

2. How can we visualize this concept so that others can comprehend what it is we are saying?

3. What are some of the practical implications of this vision for the church in terms of its:

    a.   functions—i.e. worship, witness, fellowship, nurture, service?

    b.   organizational style and design?

4. What kind of commitment to become inclusive and to work to resolve the brokenness among us (racism, classism sexism, ageism) do we expect from ourselves, our churches, our society? What are the ways that we agree we could continually monitor and measure implementation of that commitment?

As this process moves toward a careful study of these questions, we feel it will be well worthwhile and will have a positive affect on how we as church live and work in a broken world.

PART THREE

How to Place the Star in Our Pockets
(Synthesis)

CROSS-CULTURAL GROUPS

The task of the cross-cultural groups was to identify the character and dynamics of an authentic community. In this assignment, participants were to act and react on the assigned topic in a cross-cultural setting, to build a theological and structural frame for an authentic community within the emerging new church.

The following is our attempt to sum up the essence of each group's discussion. Therefore, should misrepresentation occur, the editors assume full responsibility.

GROUP I: A Theological and Global Foundation

This group highlighted a theological base and a global perspective as the foundation of an authentic community – baptism as a common base and the world as the individual's family. However, as soon as this basic foundation was suggested, a question arose: can an honest bigot be part of this family?

To counter this question, the group pointed out that so long as reconciliation and forgiveness are operative in the community, the honest bigot might become a member. Also, for the community to function effectively, it must operate with honesty, integrity, and vision as well as know who/what/where is the control. Moreover, members must understand ownership and listen to "out" people of [their] own ethnic group, and attempt to "get through" to each other.

But the difficulty in transcending the boundaries was also acknowledged. How can transcendence be achieved? It can be achieved through a theological education process. If the people are committed to using a Transcultural Seminar style to develop changes in the theological process, then transcendence will occur.

GROUP II: Sharing of Power and Styles

The dynamics of an authentic community are viewed in terms of: 1) sharing of power and 2) style. The sharing of power, on the one hand, was defined as total surrender of the resources of the Christian church for the sake of the whole world. Closely connected with this was a call to address the impact of the current (Reagan) economic policies. On the other hand, the sharing of power also involved a commitment to ministry and outreach to others. Through economic equalization and commitment to ministry, a new community can be formed in which the people of God will have shared rituals, heroes, faith and stories.

The true operational styles of this new community involve commitment, equality and vision. Although the last two are left undefined, the first, concretely spelled out, includes commitment to:

- the poorest of the poor
- those who have limited opportunities
- the diversity of humankind
- a multilingual church
- the creation of a new ecclesiastical structure
- multicultural seminary education
- simplicity and humanity in property acquisition, i.e., tent making ministry
- diversified styles in worship
- a true lay/clergy partnership.

GROUP III: Affirmation of all Members

The dynamics of an authentic community include intentionality. This means deliberately focusing on common goals and vision, listening, sharing, freeing (free to be oneself), forgiving, being interdependent, congruent, accepting (oneself and others), and having a sense or clarity, balance and creative tension. The theological and historical foundations for such a community are the word and sacraments and the community's remembering its ultimate roots, suggesting a concept of unity in its diversity. As such, the community is always in a dynamic process of becoming.

The group, as its goal, envisioned in the new church an inclusive community which affirms in all its diversity.

GROUP IV: Freedom, Acceptance and Calling

Authenticity was equated with freedom of expression. Community was inseparably linked with people who are different and yet able to accept differences as the glue that holds together the community.

This community also shares the following commonalities: Christian, Lutheran, U.S. residents, shared history, mobile people and a love for one another.

However, in order for this community to become real, individuals need a strong affirmation of self, and must recognize that Jesus calls them out of their most favorite community into a larger community.

GROUP V: A Common Faith and Identity

This group defined the dynamics of a Christian authentic community in theological and cultural terms. For the community to be authentic, it must share a common faith and identity in Jesus Christ. There must be a common shared vision to a new identity, defined as countercultural. Within this new identity, there is a dynamic tension between that which is non—negotiable and that which must be modified for an authentic larger community and a new order. This group did not define what is non—negotiable, nor did it identify what can be modified.

The group then listed seven goals which, if implemented, would actualize an authentic community:

1.   Actualize our faith in ways that are authentic so that we may attest/witness to it back in our respective communities.

2.   Inform the leadership of the church that what we are doing here is beyond Eurocentric theology.

3.   Bring in a global perspective throughout the church.

4.   Help people to understand that the essence of the church is mission and not maintenance.

5.   Help local congregations recognize that we are transcultural.

6.   Eliminate any perception of anyone as a "second class Christian."

7.   Return to the cities.

Summary

We conclude this section by highlighting the universals the groups seemed to have in common. A model for an authentic community embodies both theological and cultural characters and dynamics. The common theological foundation for such a community includes baptism, forgiveness, and reconciliation, while affirming cultural diversity and freedom of expression.

Within this theo-cultural frame of reference, the members must share a commitment to faith and ministry, as well as to the sharing of power.

OUR WORD
To Our Church for Our Church

We, the undersigned, part of the family of God, see ourselves engaged in the creation of the new church as our reasonable participation under the gospel, or we must proclaim God's law to a disobedient church.

Through the Transcultural Seminar Coalition we affirm our God—created and God-redeemed cultures as the expression and representation of our cultures in the Oneness of our Spirit.

We propose to meet the needs of inclusion; vis-a-vis identity, relationships, and mission as follows:

a. Establish a church which represents its people at all levels of ecclesiastical polity, theology, mission, and education. We acknowledge that this representation will require the cooperation of the dominating white culture in intentionally releasing its control of our church in favor of giving equal voice (in terms of numbers and power) to Lutheran peoples of color.

b. In order that our Word be implemented we request each ethnic community here assembled to provide one representative, respectively, to establish the framework and plans for our involvement with Our Word.

c. This word and, the future plans should be communicated by the Rev. Will Herzfeld, a member of the Commission on Lutheran Unity and a member of the Transcultural Seminar Coalition.

Editor's Note: The original manuscript includes the signatures of participants in the 1981 Transcultural Seminar.

LUTHERAN DIVERSITY
And Cosmic Harmony:
Proposed Models

During the Transcultural Seminar in Chicago, our unity in diversity was displayed over and over again. The transcultural group conversations recorded here are one example of this unity. Videotapes also give a very graphic display of the synthesis that occurred. We would like to emphasize here a few models of particular importance.

Multicultural Worship

In the worship and music experienced in the conference, we understood fully the meaning of Pentecost. In planning worship, the traditional Lutheran liturgy was used only once, in the celebration of communion at the end of the conference. The other worship experiences centered on the participation of all the cultures in their unique way.

The first worship was dedicated to the expression of each culture's identity: each culture expressed itself in word and song, addressing itself to the university of God. The second worship focused on the relationships that we have in Christ and was epitomized by leadership from lay women, one from each culture. In the final worship experience, all five cultures participated fully in, as we stated earlier, a traditional Lutheran liturgy.

The crucial emphasis in all the worship experiences was not that each culture was represented, nor was it which culture did what when. On the contrary, the emphasis was that each culture express freely their experience of God—hearing God's word in their own language; feeling the movement of the Holy Spirit; knowing, through worshiping and glorifying God, their rootedness and oneness in Christ; and recognizing and acknowledging their brothers and sisters in the faith. The joy which this freedom unleashed cannot be described. We attempted to capture some of it on videotape for all who are curious enough to pursue it. The worship bulletin is included for your information.

Evangelism in Pluralistic Communities

To come to terms with evangelism in pluralistic communities, one has to explode the presupposition held by many Christians that evangelism has to do with heaven, the promise yet to be fully revealed. This assumption focuses on salvation of unsaved, heathen, pagan, lost, and un—Christian souls. Pastors, consequently, need not concern themselves with this life and the socioeconomic conditions in which the people find themselves.

The task of the institutional church is derived from the Great Commission (Matthew 28: 16—20). Based upon this biblical mandate, European Christians have invaded Africa, the Americas, Asia, Australia, and scattered island nations around the globe colonizing and enslaving 'the heathen." They have assumed that "the heathen" were not created by God and, therefore, needed to be Christianized. This same motive has given rise to contemporary evangelistic movements in our society and world.

Third World Christians, however,, are seriously questioning this type of evangelism. They have begun to think about the gospel in the historical context of their struggle for freedom from this kind of domination. The following question is appropriate: What does it mean to preach the gospel in the context of poverty, exploitation, and oppression? Naturally, then, the issue becomes how to relate evangelism to both the horizontal and the vertical aspects of life, both in our relationship with God and with other human beings created by God.

Based on the above theological and ethical formulations, Third World Christians are suggesting alternative evangelism methods and processes which have emerged in their particular contexts and cultures. The correlation of the scriptural and confessional principles with the immediate context, the existential situation, will produce a different methodology with the same theological substance. These methodologies are presently being developed and, of necessity, will be incorporated in a new Lutheran church body.

Implications

The implications of this work are vast and formidable. The reader cannot expect that all of the implications could or should be covered. However, this study is designed to create dialogue and stimulate thinking for future research. The following represents a general perspective on implications:

The incarnation or actualization of a culturally inclusive or universal church has always been a troublesome, conflict laden reality of the church. The universal church equals the universal Christian identity. But identity has always been considered as specific relative to one's cultural context and therein lies the problem which we have struggled with over the years. The problem certainly reared its head often within the transcultural group of five cultures.

On the one hand, culture, class, and sexual identity bring with them the complex problem of determining how the gospel or the fruits of the Spirit are embodied in their particular context. It is always ambiguous whether the gospel is faithfully embodied in any specific form. On the other hand, our experiences are that these kinds of identities are an open invitation to ethnocentrism, racism, classism and sexism. This is what we have defined as putting ourselves on a collision course with one another and with God.

But, precisely because we as human beings must particularize indigenous identities, which have been permeated by the Gospel, they are precious to us. Therefore, we do not want our contexualization or indigenity to be universalized. The character of our contexts as vehicles of God's grace and meaning of the faith is a legitimate form. However, when this is transformed into negative ethnocentrism along with the other "isms," it becomes demonic. What was unspoken with the group, but which I experienced as traumatic for us nonetheless, was to acknowledge that our Godly identity which we held as Christians was larger than our context.

Since Lutherans are by tradition German, Scandinavian, Swedish, and so forth without the other ethnic groups of color, they would probably tend to equate the gospel with their particular ethnic forms, thus rendering it difficult to transcend to other forms.

From my perspective, since one of God's gifts to Lutheranism is its dogmatic theological in—depth—ness, they tend to be particularly meticulous and "picky" about other formulations of the faith. Dialogue about this book may assist in a more liberated, open approach.

In designing a culturally inclusive church, it does not help that some Lutherans equate Lutheranism with certain doctrinal formulations that are culture—bound and time—bound (16th and 17th century German and Aristotelian). We have suggested other views on the essence of Lutheranism which must be implemented if a truly culturally inclusive church is to prevail.

Cultural dialogue and transformation, then, are chief places where Asian, African, Hispanic, and Native American identities challenge

Lutheran heritage. How does a Lutheran accept the gifts of specific cultures other than German, Scandinavian, and Swedish? How does "self—transcendence" take place and give rise to the new community (church) in Christ? The implications of these questions could and should cover the gamut of theology and ecclesiology.

Finally, the church's creeds and rhetoric will always be more grandiose than its practice. Indeed, this area is where the people of color have critiqued the church the most. We should recognize this, and never tire in pressing the church to live up to its creeds and rhetoric. We should not press the church to give them up, even though they leave much to be desired in actions; for they are not hypocrisy. Their formulation of universal grace and universal brothers and sisters together in Christ is precious. But, the actions and practice of the church are lamentable and must always be critiqued.

Lutheran theology can and should facilitate a culturally inclusive church, because Lutherans have always emphasized that God's grace relativizes human achievement, and that forms are a diaspora.

A church struggling for cultural inclusiveness must remember that in theory, there is no theology that is less addicted to ethnocentrism, classism, racism, and sexism. In practice, we are all addicted to cultural narrowness or monoculturalism. We are challenged to transcend this narrowness to become a church willing to affirm and celebrate more than one cultural tradition in its midst while moving toward the oneness which is ours in Christ.

America and its institutions, including the Christian church, is facing the effects of some 350 years of exclusionary and oppressive policies of racism, classism, and sexism. Thus, America has a tremendous collective responsibility for redressing the effects of these past injustices.

The rising numbers of people of color will share much of the ethos of their white counterparts. The Lutheran church will have much to offer and I would suspect that the continued growth of Lutheranism among the Third World people both here in the U.S. and across the world will push not the dramatic but rather the solid theology of Lutheranism toward a more holistic witness of its confessional heritage. With heavy need for other ethnic pastors, teachers, and staff of color, it is an interesting question whether places will be provided in "white" churches for Asian, African, Hispanic and Native American pastors, should they seek them.

The story of Lutheranism in North America has been largely a story of Germanic roots. Lutherans have been an immigrant church transplanted from Europe to American soil. For this reason, the church has suffered from dialogue between the gospel and other cultures within a pluralistic American context. As Lutheranism journeys into the future, its story will change from European, rural roots into the pluralistic urban life of North America.

This journey toward the vision of Paul will carry it out of its isolated ethnic ghetto into a multicultural stream of God's creation. This implies a journey into new languages, new styles of worship, witness, support, service learning, church polity, pastoral care, and more.

It involves, for example, a liturgical journey from Beethoven to Latin folk music to African dance, to Native American life in harmony with nature, and so forth. It implies a beginning transformation that will change the color and character of our bishops, pastors, professors, and staff. It implies a major metamorphosis in theological education: a unified approach with explicit, comprehensive goals relative to the "self—transcendent document," which affirms the universal within the indigenous.

Finally, this journey implies that there is a "courage to be" in the face of threat to self and culture. Again, the implications are vast and formidable, but once you have caught the vision, the courage and the will to lead the way into the implications will roll down like water and righteousness like a mighty stream.

Conclusion

The major task of this work was to lay out a theological principle for a culturally inclusive church, This task was attempted in the document on self—transcendence. The scope of this work was represented in the outline of the book itself as synthesizing the indigenous ethos with denominational heritage. This is of utmost importance in developing an authentic multicultural church. We have offered it as a major principle to be used in every aspect of theology and eccesiology.

Moreover, with the majority of white institutional churches, denomination and the white ethos generally converge. Even among those without the denomination's background, white middle—class cultural background helps to bridge the gap.

Among other cultures (Asian, black, Hispanic, Native American) the gap is serious and impedes both unity and the mission of the church. It is important for the mission of the church that the people of color speak, act and participate in the continuing witness of a united church as the reciprocity document advances.

The material alludes to the fact that there should be an intentional effort to synthesize one's cultural ethos with one's denominational heritage. For example, the Lutheran heritage is especially founded in an experiential matrix which gives it a common ground with many other Third World cultures.

Moreover, a close reading of the cultural roots and histories modeled in the black culture in this work argues that no evangelical program of a people can be adequate for membership, citizenship and harmonious development. Also needed are ingredients that enhance proud identification with a past, a heritage, a culture and an assurance that one will be able to contribute to the future of the church's mission.

The failure of the established church to recognize minority people as historical figures has left a significant portion of them with an identity crisis; a serious lack of inspirational figures; and a lack of skills to deal with the political, economic, and theological problems which have made them second—class persons in church and society.

Clearly, then, all Christians need to know the facts of history, culture, religion and their relevance in a multicultural church. It is an open question as to which of these Christians has the greater need and will benefit more from such a self—transcendence synthesis. Whatever occurs, we may help to reverse the ominous trend of cultural decay simply by analyzing and synthesizing the two components. At least, we will know why we agree to disagree.

We are in a perennial process of articulating just what we are about as created and redeemed people of God in our different cultures, and most of all, how what we do expresses what we are and believe. It seems to me that we are attempting to tell ourselves and the world how we see ourselves together in a culturally inclusive church, and how our being together shapes progress toward our inclusive vision.

This book shows that we have made some progress which, obviously, should be continued in some form. This opinion is reinforced by the effect we have already had upon Lutheranism up to this point. Nevertheless, the progress seems to have been uneven among the participating cultures and there seem to be certain problem areas that need further thought if we are to make even more headway in the future. Many of the pressures of indigenous theology and cultural inclusiveness come from our inability to transcend our culture and enter the new community in Christ.

Within the family of Christians, we have been pressed to demonstrate the truth of our theology by showing that it is more faithful to the tradition of the gospel. Outside the family we are pressed to show that what we say is credible to what we do. That is to say, are our actions life—giving or life—destroying? Within our pluralism, we have tried to present a coherent and confessional document of self-transcendence in an attempt to be constructive and provocative for future dialogue and growth.

It is our confession of faith that the Christian theological system is a system which gives all cultures of people meaning in life. This means that each culture attempts to make sense out of life in the light of the revelation in Jesus Christ. This meaning must be related to their world of nature, history and experience. This struggle is represented in the indigenous cultural section of the book. The Christian's understanding of the world can also be articulate: that is, "to be me is to become you" in Christ. This is universally Christian and hence Lutheran.

Throughout these seven years of reflection and practice in coming to grips with what it means to be a culturally inclusive church, we have tried to understand the situation in which the people of color found themselves. We tried to find our way out of a world of illusion into a world of reality, in order to recapture the reality of God's act in Jesus Christ.

There is no better way for me to summarize this segment of our research findings than to have you look once again at a man whose vision of reality placed upon him the burden of obedience in Acts 26: 19. "And so, King Agrippa, I did not disobey the heavenly vision."

Properly understood, it was Paul's obedience to the vision which was and is largely responsible for the five representative ethnic groups coming together, fighting, playing, fellowshipping and ultimately agreeing to witness to others their findings; namely, knowing ourselves to be one with all of every race, color, class, sex, denomination and nationality who proclaim and live out Jesus as Lord and Savior.

It would be a mistake for the reader to think that Paul's obedience and our obedience to the heavenly vision on the roads of Damascus, New York, Chicago, Kansas City, and so forth, was easy. He was a true believer as we are; a member of the establishment as we are; he had committed himself to the task of exposing the heresy that had been planted in the established religion as we are to exposing racism, sexism and classism. So in a peculiar sense those responsible for this book (and I am sure many others) have all taken that Damascus road over the years.

Whether the black paradigm used in the book reflected it or not, I can bear witness to the fact that as we watched with awe how demonically clever people can be in taking the gifts of God to use them against him. We have also seen much more clearly what the gospel is all about— what "earthly treasures" men and women in high and low places are willing to throw away for he precious treasure of the gospel.

As you can recall in Acts 26, Paul spoke about his vision as he was near he end of his road. Most of the oppressive and exploitative acts of hatred, abuse, hardships, imprisonments and disappointments were behind him. He then stood before the political power of his time, Agrippa, to tell the story once again.

In another peculiar sense, just as the Lord appeared to Paul, so the Lord appeared to some 125 people of the Transcultural Conference. We could only really hear and understand one another when the pins of culture, sex, nationality and class had been knocked out from under us, when the carefully constructed plans for our lives were so disrupted that we had to cry out with Paul: "Lord, what do you want me to do?" This is where we are as church as we approach the formation of a "new church."

The key to Paul's obedience and ours is commitment not to the gifts of God, but to the God of the gifts—the Lordship of Christ in all of our lives. After our vision there was no way for us to turn back any more than here was a way for Paul, In addition, Paul knew that he was not perfect. He ailed himself the chief of sinners, the least of the apostles. Likewise, his research is not perfect, the cure—all, or the last word.

But the other side is there also—what communities, cultures, classes, sexes, and persons can be and do when caught up in the vision of a moral corridor; of what life can be when it is totally committed to the Lordship of Christ.

There may be many who have different perspectives on what has happened to us. Indeed, it would be strange if that were not the case. But the vision we have received of a living Lord who has given us our identity and behavior and by whom everything in heaven and earth was created, in whom all things are held together, cannot be taken away from us or taken lightly. Nor can we allow anyone to substitute ecclesiastical constitutions, by—laws, or resolutions of conventions for the transcendent Lordship of Christ who is de facto, the head of His body and church.

Paul's obedience to the heavenly vision by the power and conviction of the Holy Spirit, was a conversion to Christ. But it was also a conversion to the world as he saw it in an entirely new light—a world of God's creative activity. Paul's concern and ours is the overwhelming fact that we all belong to God and that Christ is Lord of all. When that is actualized, it becomes a radical new behavior for a new church.

The new learnings which God has taught us these seven years are many. I shall attempt to glean a few from this research:

For some of us in the Transcultural group, our particular judicatory or institutions affiliation became relatively unimportant. Based upon our identity in Christ, we gained a deeper understanding of what it means to be a church as we responded to the call to become the other person through mission and ministry in and to God's world.

We confessed that for too many years we had been guilty of participating in instead of resisting our own oppression, by confusing religious institutions which act demonically with the Body of Christ. I cannot imagine after seeing the "heavenly vision" that there will ever be a day when our salvation, liberation or destiny will be determined by whether we belonged to a given denomination, class, race, or sex or even obeyed its resolutions, values or ideologies.

We can, however, visualize a scene as the one pictured by Matthew 25 where the hungry, thirsty, naked, lonely, sick and imprisoned can be a witness to whether any of us as people of God obeyed God's heavenly vision—or rather the church and societal resolutions and by—laws that had nothing to do with the heavenly vision.

Many of us know what God the Holy Spirit has empowered us to do—to give up the idolatry of our worship and commitment of self, race, class, sex. By doing so, we are free to move into God's future with a radical new kind of obedience and commitment which marked the life of Paul, King, Bonhoeffer, Gandhi, Sojourner Truth and finally us.

The heavenly vision which called us to the task reflected in this book calls all of us to that kind of task and commitment, namely, to become one another as Christ became us.

Diverse, yet one in Christ, the people of God do not view the Christian community as one in which all ethnic cultic differences have been melted into one plastic American culture across the world. They are too busy discovering and celebrating that in Jesus Christ each is a gift to the other.

They are joyfully busy sharing and putting their respective talents to work to the glory of God and to the vision of the more abundant life God offers to people everywhere in Christ.

Dr. Albert 'Pete" Pero

READING LIST

ASIAN AMERICAN

Aye, Mario Paguia. Characteristics of Filipino Social Organizations in Los Angeles. San Francisco, 1974.

Barth, Gunther. Bitter Strength: A History of the Chinese in the United States, 1850-1870. Cambridge, 1964.

Bosworth, Allan R. America's Concentration Camps. Berkeley, 1956.

Bulosan, Carlos. America is in the Heart, a Personal History. Seattle, 1973.

Chen, Jack. The Chinese in America. San Francisco: Harper & r o w , 1980

Griffis, William B. "The First Koreans in America." Korea Review (4:3, 11 May 1922).

Herman, Masaka comp. The Japanese in America, 1843-1973: A Chronology and Fact Book. New York, 1974.

Hsu, Kai-yu and Helen Palubinskas eds. Asian American Authors. Boston: Houghton Mifflin Co., 1972.

Ichihashi, Y. Japanese in the United States. Stanford, 1932.

Kim, Hyung-Chan. "History and Role of the Church in the Korean American Community." Korean Journal (14:8, Aug., 1974), pp. 26-37.

_____ "Some Aspects of Social Demography of Korean Americans." International Migration Review (8:25, Spring, 1974).

_____ and Wayne Patterson comp. The Koreans in America 1882-1974: A Chronology and Fact Book. New York, 1974.

Kim, Warren. Koreans in America. Seoul, 1971.

Kitagawa, Daisuke. Issei and Nisei: The Internment Years. New York, 1974.

Kitano, Harry H. L. Japanese Americans: The Evolution of a Subculture. Englewood Cliffs, 1969.

Lyman, Stanford, M. Chinese Americans. New York, 1974.

Melendy, H. Brett. "Filipinos in the United States."

Counterpoint: Perspectives on Asian America, Emma Gee, ed. Los Angeles, 1976.

Morales, Royal F. Makibaka: The Philipino American Struggle. Los Angeles, 1974.

Patterson, Wayne. The Korean in America: 1882-1974. Dobbs Ferry: Oceana Publishers, Inc., 1974.

Quinsaat, Jesse ed. Letters in Exile: An Introductory Reader on the History of Pilipinos in America. Los Angeles, 1976.

Tachiki, Amy, Eddie-Wong, Franklin Odo & Buck Wong eds. Roots: An Asian American Reader. Los Angeles: Asian American Studies Center, 1971.

Tung,Wiliiam.L. comp. The Chinese in America, 1920-1973: A Chronology and Fact Book. New York, 1974.

Yun, Yo-Jun: "Early History of Korean Emigration to America (I) . " Korea Journal (14:6, June, 1974), pp. 21-26.

_____. "Early History of Korean Emigration to America (II)." Korea Journal (14:7, July, 1974). pp. 40-45.

BLACK AMERICAN:

Adam, William ed. Afro-American Authors. Boston: Houghton Mifflin Co., 1971.

Aptheker, Herbert. A Documentary History of the Negro People in the United States. New York: The Citadel Press, 1968.

Bennett, Lerone, Jr. Before the Mayflower: A History of the Negro in America, 1619-1964. Baltimore: Penguin Books, 1967.

Blaustein, Albert P. and Robert L. Zangrando. Civil Rights and the American Negro: A Documentary History. New York: Washington Square Press, 1968.

Broderick, Francis L. and Meier, August. Negro Protest in the 20th Century. Indianapolis: Bobbs-Merrill, 1965.

Butcher, Margaret Just. The Negro in American Culture. New York: Mentor Books, 1967.

Chametzky, Jules, comp. Black & White in American Culture: An Anthology from the Massachusetts Review. Amherst: University of Massachusetts Press, 1969.

Cone, James H. A Black Theology of Liberation. Lippincott, 1970.

Eckels, John. Pursuing. the Pursuit: The Black Plight in White America. Hicksville: Exposition Press, 1971.

Elkins, Stanley M. Slavery. New York: Grossett and Dunlap, 1963.

Franklin, John Hope and Isadore Staff. The Negro in Twentieth Century America: A Reader on the Struggle for Civil Rights. New York: Vintage Books, 1967.

Frazier, Edward Franklin. The Negro Church in America. New York: Schocken Books, 1974.

_____. The Negro Family in the U.S. Chicago: University of Chicago Press, 1966.

Greene, Lorenz. The Negro in Colonial New England, 1620-1776. New York: Atheneum, 1968.

Hill, Herbert. Anger, and Beyond: The Negro Writer in the United States. New York: Harper and Row, 1966.

Katz, William L. ed. The American Negro: History and Literature. New York: Arno Press, 1968.

Kelsey, George D. Racism and the Christian Understanding of M a n . New York: Charles Scribner's Sons, 1968. Charles Scribner's Sons, 1965.

King, Martin Luther, Jr. Why We Can't Wait. New York: Harper and Row, 1964.

Kochman, Thomas. Black and White Styles in Conflict. Chicago: University of Chicago Press, 1981.

McPherson, James M. The Struggle for Equality: Abolitionists and the Negro in the Civil War and Reconstruction. Princeton, N.J.: Princeton University Press, 1964.

Metcalf, George R. Black Profiles. New York: McGraw Hill, 1968.

Quarles, Benjamin. The Negro in the Making of America. New Y o r k : Collier Books, 1964.

Rainwater, Lee, The Moynihan Report and the Politics of Controversy, Including the Full text of "The Negro Family: The Case for National Action," by Daniel P. Moynihan. Cambridge, Mass.: MIT Press, 1967.

Roberts, J. Deotis. A Black Political Theology. Westminster, 1974.

Sally, Columbus and Behm, Ronald. "What Color is Your God? Downers.Grove: Inter-Varsity Press, 1981.

Scott, Benjamin. The Coming of the Black Man. Boston: Beacon Press, 1969.

Sloan, Irving J. Blacks in America: 1492-1970. Dobbs Ferry: Oceana Publishers, Inc. 1971.

Washington, Joseph R. Black Religion: The Negro and Christianity in theUnited States. Boston: BeaconPress, 1966.

HISPANIC AMERICAN

Auna, Rudy. A Mexican American Chronicle. American Book Company, 1967.

Alba, Victor. The Mexicans. Frederick A. Praeger, 1967.

Carter, Thomas P. Mexican Americans in School: A History of Education Neglect. Connecticut Printers, Inc. 1970.

Day, Mark. Forty Acres: Cesar Chavez and the Farm Workers. New York: Praeger Publishers, 1971.

Dunns, John G. Delano: The California Grape Strike. New York: Farrar, Straus and Giroux, 1973.

Duran, Livie Isauro comp. Introduction to Chicano Studies: A Reader. New York: Macmillian, 1973.

Galarza, Ernesto. Spiders in the House and Workers in the Field. London: University of Notre Dame Press, 1970.

_____. Merchants of Labor. Charlotte/Santa Barbara: McNolly and and Loftin Publishers, 1970.

Heller, Celia. Mexican American Youth: Forgotten Youth at the Crossroad. New York: Random House, 1966.

Hoffman, Abraham. Unwanted Mexican Americans in the Great Depression. Tucson University of Arizona Press, 1974

Kessell, John L. Friars, Soldiers, and Reformers: Hispanic Arizona and the Sonora Mission Frontier. Tucson University of Arizona Press, 1976.

Lamb, Ruth. Mexican Americans of the Southwest. Claremont, CA: Ocelest Press, 1970.

Ludwig and Santebanez. The Chicanos: Mexican-American Voices. Baltimore: Penguin Books, 1971.

Martinez, Joe L. Chicano Psychology. New York: Academic Press, 1977.

Meier, Matt S. The Chicanos: A History of Mexican Americans. New

York: Hill and Wang, 1972.

Mirande, Alfdredo. La Chicano: The Mexican-American woman. Chicago: Unisity of Chicago Press, 1979.

Moore, Joan W. Mexican Americans. N.J. Prentice-Hall, 1976.

Moquin, Wayne ed. Documentary History of: the Mexican—Americans. New York: Praeger Publishers, 1972.

Nava, Julian. Mexican Americans. New York.

Paredef, Ainerico, ed. Mexican-American Authors. Boston: Houghton-Mifflin,Co., 1972.

Rivera, Felicano. A Mexican American Source Book with Study Guideline. Menlo Park, California, 1970: Educational Consulting Associates.

Sanchez, I. George. Forgotten People: A Study of New Mexicans. Albuquerque Calvin Horn Publishers, Inc. 1970.

Shockley, John Staples. Chicano Revolt in a Texas Town. Notre Dame: University of Notre Dame Press, 1974.

Steiner, Stan. La Raza. New York: Harper and Row. 1970

Trejo, Arnulfo D. The Chicanos: As We See Ourselves.Tucson: University of Arizona Press, 1979.

Weber, David J., comp. Foreigners in their Native Land: Historical Roots of The Mexican Americans. Albuquerque University of New Mexico Press, 1973.

NATIVE AMERICAN

Allen, T.D. Arrows Four: Prose and Poetry by :Young American Indians New York: Washington Square Press, 1974.

Akesasne Notes. Trail of Broken Treaties: B. I. A. I'm Not Your Indian Anymore. Mohawk Nation: Akwesasne Notes   1974.

Bierhorst, John ed. The Red Swan Myths and Tales of the American Indian New York: Farrar, Straus and Giroux, 1976.

Brandon, William. The Last Americans: The Indian in American Culture. San Francisco: Mc Graw-Hill, 1974.

Brown, Joseph Epes. The Spiritual Legacy of the American Norman, Oklahoma: University of Oklahoma Press, 1954.

Brown, Vinson. Voices of the Earth and Sky: The Vision of Life of the Native Americans and their Culture Heroes. Harrisburg: Stackpole, 1974.

Cahn, Edgar S., ed. Our Brother's Keeper: The Indian in White America. New York New Community Press, 1970.

Collier, Peter. When Shall They Rest? The Cherokees' Long Struggle with America. New York, Dell, 1973.

Costo, Rupert. The American Indian Reader: History. Henry, Jeanette,ed. San Francisco: Indian Historian Press, 1974.

Dennis, Henry C. The American Indian, 1492-1970: A Chronology and Fact Book. New York: Oceana Publishers, 1971.

Fey, Harold E. Indians and Other Americans. New York: Perennial Library, 1970.

Garharino, Merwyn S. Native American Heritage. Boston: Little, Brown, 1976.

Heizer, Robert F. The California Indian: A Source Book. Berkeley: University of California, 1971.

Henry, Jeanette. The American Indian Reader: Literature. San Francisco: Indian Historian Press, 1973.

Hertzberg, Hazel W. The Search for an American Indian Identity: Modern Pan Indian Movements New York Syracuse University Press, 1971.

Highwater, Jamake. Ritual of the Wind: North American Indian Ceremonies Music and Dances. New York, 1977.

Hurdy, John Major, Amercan,Indian Religions. Los Angeles: Sherbourne, 1970.

Locke, Raymond Friday. The American Indian. Los Angeles: Mankind Publishing Company, 1970.

Lowenfels, Walter ed. From the Belly of the Shark: A New Anthology of Native American Literature. New York. Vintage Books, 1973.

Marx, Herbert L. ed. The American Indian A Rising Ethnic Force. New York: H W. Wilson, 1973.

Momaday, Natachee Scott American Indian Authors. Boston: Houghton Mifflin Co., 1971.

Rothenberg, Jerome ed. Shaking the Pumpkin: Traditional Poetry of the Indian North Americans. New York: Doubleday, 1972.

Schmeckebier Lawrence F. The Office of Indian Affairs: Its History, Activities and Organization. Baltimore: AMS Press, 1972.

Sorking, Alan L. American Indians and Federal Aid. Washington, D.C.: Brookings institute, 1971.

Trennert, Robert A. Alternative to Extinction Federal_Indian Policy and the Beginning of the Reservation System, 1846-51. Philadelphia: Temple University Press, 1975.

Waddel, Jack O. ed. The American Indian in Urban Society. Boston: Little, Brown, 1971.

Washburn, Wilcomb E. Red Man's Land, White Man's Law: A Study of the Past and Present Status of the American Indian. New York: Scribner's, 1971.

Young, Robert W. Historical Background for Modern Indian Law and Order. Washington, D.C.: GRIC, 1969.

LIBERATION THEOLOGY

Anderson, Gerald H. Asian Voices in Christian Theology. Maryknoll, N.Y.: Orbis Books, 1976.

Assmann, Hugo. Theology for a Nomad Church. Maryknoll, N.Y.: Orbis Books, 1975.

Cone, James H. A Black Theology of Liberation. Philadelphia: Lippincott, 1970.

Deloria, Vine. God is Red. New York: Dell Publishing Co., 1973.

Koyama, Kosuke. Waterbuffalo Theology. Maryknoll, N.Y.: Orbis Books, 1974.

Gibellini, Rosino. Frontiers of Theology in Latin America. Maryknoll, N.Y.: Orbis Books, 1979.

Lee, Jung Young. The Theology of Change: A Christian Concept of God in an Eastern Perspective. Maryknoll: N.Y.: Orbis Books, 1979.

Miquez Bonio, Jose. Doing Theology in a Revolutionary Situation. Philadelphia: Fortress Press, 1975.

Seguendo, Juan Luis. Liberation of Theology. Maryknoll, N.Y.: Orbis Books, 1976.

Sobrino, Jon. Christology at the Crossroads: A Latin American Approach. Maryknoll: N.Y.: Orbis Books, 1979.

Song, Choan-Seng. Third Eye Theology: Theology in Formation in Asian Settings. Maryknoll, N.Y.: Orbis Books, 1979.

Torres, Sergio and John Eagleson eds. Theology in the Americas. Maryknoll, N.Y.: Orbis Books, 1976.

Wennaappuwa, Sri Lanka. Asia's Struggle for Full Humanity: Towards a Relevant Theology. Maryknoll, N.Y.: Orbis Books, 1980.

Wilmore, Gayraud S. and James H. Cone. Black Theology: A Documentary History. Maryknoll, N.Y.: Orbis Books, 1979.

TRANSCULTURAL SEMINAR VIDEO PROGRAMS

Rethinking Lutheran Mission Transculturally is a two part series featuring clergy and lay perspectives on the Lutheran church fully becoming a "church for all people." Both videotapes show interviews and presentations that took place at the Transcultural Seminar at the Lutheran School of Theology at Chicago, October 1981.

"Considerations for Transcultural Outreach" (28 min.) offers congregations a close and personal look at some of the issues as seen by various conference participants.

"Transcultural Perspectives on Theological Education" (30 min.) focuses on specific needs in Lutheran theological training.

"RLMT: Outreach" and "RLMT: Theological Ed." are both available on 3/4" and 1/2" (VHS) video cassettes. Please specify which title and format is desired.

Transcultüral Task Force
c/o the Rev. Lee Wesley
Lutheran Community Services
33 Worth Street
New York, N.Y. 10013

ENDNOTES

[1] Jopward Thurman, <u>Deep River and the Negro Spiritual Speaks of Life an Death</u> (Richmond, Ind: Friends United Service Press, 1975), 70.

[2] Jaroslav Pelikan, a Lutheran, uses this phrase to describe Martin Luther. See his book <u>Obedient Rebels: Catholic Substance and Protestant Principle in Luther's Reformation</u> (New York: Harper & Row, Publishers, 1964), and "Obedient Rebel," *Time*, March 24, 1967, 70-75.

[3] W. E. B. Du Bois, <u>Darkwater: Voices from within the Veil</u> (Mineola: Dover Publications, Inc., 1999 [1920]), 17.

[4] The phrase "people of color" is meant to include the following communities: African/African American/Black, American Indian and Alaska Native, Arab and Middle-Eastern, Asian and Pacific Islander, Latino/Latina, and White communities. This is the current uisage adopted by the Commission for Multicultural Ministries of the Evangelical Lutheran Church in America.

[5] Thurman, 71.

[6] See Bernard Lonergan's material on "insight."

[7] E. Franklin Frazier, <u>The Negro Church in America</u> (N.Y., 1962), pp. 8-9.

[8] E. Franklin Frazier, <u>The Negro in the United States</u> (N. Y., 1957), p. 665.

[9] Ralph Ellison, <u>Invisible Man</u> (N. Y.: Signet Books, 1952), p. 7.

[10] Richard Wright, <u>Black Boy</u> (New York, 1945), pp. 203-04.

[11] Many black history books give us much empirical documentation concerning illustrations and examples of black women engaged in self-transcendence which I am reserving for a book on this subject.

[12] <u>Chicago Defender</u>, Saturday, February 16, 1980 (Robert S. Abbott Publishing Co. newspaper), Vol. LXXV, No. 200, p. 11. Crossover roles are roles which can be played convincingly by persons from any ethnic background. Black star Ron O'Neal plays a white detective sergeant.

[13] Reuel L. Howe, <u>The Miracle of Dialogue</u> (N.Y.: The Seabury Press, 1964), p. 20ff.

[14] Edward T. Hall, Beyond Culture (New York: Anchor Books), p. 44.

[15] Ibid., p. 29. See Hall, Chapter II for a full treatment of Extension Transference (ET).

[16] 1. Intellectual. He sought here to reconcile the separation between God and the person. 2. Moral. He sought to reconcile the separation between the violent advocacy of change and the non-violent acceptance of the status quo. 3. Political. His goal was to reconcile a faulty political present with an ideal future. For explicit theological positions see King's The Measure of a Man, Strength to Love, and his dissertation, "A comparison of the Conceptions of God in the Thinking of Tillich and Wiemann."

[17] M. L. King, "A Comparison of the Conceptions of God in the Thinking of Paul Tillich and Henry Nelson Wiemann," p. 22.

[18] King, Strength to Love, p. 107.

[19] C. Westermann, Creation, trans. By J.J. Scullion, S.J. (Philadelphia: Fortress Press, 1974), pp. 32-65 & es. p. 49f., 55-60. The most acceptable view of the "Imago Dei."

[20] See unpublished document by Cheryl Steward, DMNA, 231 Madison Ave., New York, N.Y. 10016.

[21] World Council of Churches, Guidelines on Dialogue with People of Living Faiths and Ideologies (Geneva: WCC, 1979).

[22] Franklin Frazier, The Negro Church in America (New York: Schocken Books, 1974), p. 16. Because of this many of them were suspect and were allowed to hold services only under the watchful eye of the slaveowners.

This was the period too when laws regulated church gatherings and prohibited black preachers along with slaves or free men from acquiring literacy. All of this combined, with few exceptions, to restrict the development of the black church.

Though white men suppressed every attempt on the part of black people to be free, they failed to listen to the slaves' songs or to their philosophy wrapped up in those songs. Black people not only sang to make their 15-16 hour work days easier, they sang with hope about their miseries, and gained existential, metaphysical and eschatological insights which were impossible for most white men to ascertain at that time. Examine if you will, the following Black songs:

Didn't my Lord deliver Daniel
And why not every man?
He deliver's Daniel from the Lion's den,
Jonah from the belly of the whale,
And the Hebrew children from the fiery furnace,
And why not every man?

Nobody knows the trouble I've seen,
Nobody knows but Jesus.
Swing Low, Sweet chariot,
Coming for to carry me home.

Go down Moses
Way down in Egyptland,
Tell old Pharaoh
To let my people go.

These few excerpts from black spirituals historically typify what the Christian religion has meant to the black experience.

[23] Frazier, p. 44. There are those with whom I have been in extensive dialogue who say that, without music, it is doubtful whether the black person would have survived. It serves as a cleansing agent in eradicating present difficulty through emotional expression; it lifted up a future with better possibilities than the present; and, it brought the celestial down to earth. Troubles, joys, trials, tribulations, power, and heaven are basic themes in most of the the Negro spirituals. Shouting and great exultation were still basic characteristics of the black church of this period. The slave Christian was ingenious; by singing and shouting, strength to endure physical and mental suffering was received that few others could endure.

[24] John Howard Griffin, Black Like Me (New York: New American Library, 1961). This book has been made into a movie.

[25] E. Franklin Frazier, The Negro in the United States (New York: Macmillan Co., 1957), p. 665. To see the effects of segregation on the black community in America, we recommend Part V of the book entitled "The Negro in the United States" by Franklin Frazier. The chapters deal with the problem of health and survival, of unemployment and poverty, of family disorganization, of crime and delinquency, of mental deficiency and insanity. Of particular importance is Chapter XXVII which deals with the nature of race prejudice and its effect on the Negro. In short, the white majority has built up a whole set of groundless ideas and behavior patterns concerning the black race. Black persons then suffer the consequences of this falsely based behavior.

[26] Ralph Ellison, Invisible Man (New York: Signet Books, 1952), p. 7.

[27] Richard Wright, Black Boy (New York: Harper & Bros., 1945), pp. 203-204.

[28] Alvin F. Poussaint, Why Blacks Kill Blacks (New York: Emerson Hall Publishers, Inc., 1972), p. 49.

[29] Ibid.

[30] Ibid., p. 50.

[31] Ibid., p. 52.

[32] Ibid., p. 53.

[33] Ibid., p. 70.

[34] Ibid. Langdon Gilkey would probably call such a move consistent with finding alternatives for salvation within one's nomological existence, but far from the theological redemptive alternative.

[35] Ibid.

[36] Ibid.

[37] bid.

[38] Ibid., p. 72. Few people are as qualified as Alvin F. Poussaint to write about the psychological experiences of Blacks in America. His psychiatric analysis is indispensable to the theologian attempting to correlate the Kerygma to the black situation.

[39] William E. Cross, Jr., "The Negro-to-Black Conversion Experience: Toward A Psychology of Black Liberation," Black World (July 1971), pp. 13-27. The model depicts an illustration of an indigenous resource attempting to solve a problem within our nomological existence. The theologian should indeed accept the model as a resource to analyzing the indigenous situation with the proper correlation of theology. For example, the model when correlated theologically with our previous law/gospel model has the sequence of struggle, resignation, insight and new interpretation.

[40] William H. Grier and Price M. Cobbs, Black Rage (New York: Basic Books, Inc., 1968), p. 8.

[41] Lerone Bennett, The Challenge of Blackness (Chicago: Johnson Publishing Company, Inc., 1972), p. 34.

[42] Leon W. Chestang, "Character Development in a Hostile Environment" Occasional Paper No. 3 (November 1972), School of Social Service Administration, n.p., p. 2.

[43] K. H. Fishel, Jr. and Benjamin Quarles, The Negro American (Glenview, Illinois: Scott, Foresmen and Company, 1967), pp. 204-205.

[44] August Meier and Elliott Rudwick, editors, Black Protest in the Sixties (Chicago: Chicago Quadrangle Books, Inc., 1967), p. 130.

[45] Negroes in Policy-Making Positions in Chicago: A Study in Black Powerlessness (Chicago: Chicago Urban League, 1968), p. 5 (mimeographed.

[46] James H. Cone, Black Theology and Black Power (New York: The Seabury Press, 1969), p. 8.

[47] W. R. Mueller and J. Jacobsen, "Samuel Beckett's Long Last Saturday: To Wait or not to Wait," in Nathan Scott, Jr., Man in Modern Theatre (Richmond, Virginia: John Knox Press, 1965), p. 77.

[48] Jean D. Grambs, "The Self-Concept: Basis for Reeducation of Negro Youth," Negro Self-Concept: Implications for School Citizenship (New York: McGraw-Hill Book Company, 1965), p. 41.

[49] Allport, The Nature of Prejudice, p. 142. This research is not specifically designed to analyze the problems of women, Spanish-speaking people or Indians. This writer believes that they are vital areas to be concerned about and gives encouragement to those who are working in these areas. This research is concerned about correlating the gospel to the black condition and if by solving the problem others who have had a similar experience take clues from it, well and good.

[50] See Melville J. Herskovits, The Myth of the Negro Past (Boston: Beacon Press, 1941), Chapter 4 and also W. E. B. Du Bois, The Souls of Black Folks (New York: Premier Books, 1952), Chapters 4 & 10.

[51] Grier and Cobbs, p. 86.

[52] Allison David and John Dolland, Children of Bondage (Washington, D.C.: American Council on Education, 1940), Chapter 10.

[53] Grier and Cobbs, p. 95.

[54] Andrew Billingsley, Black Families in White America (New York: Prentice Hall, Inc., 1968). See especially Chapter 4.

[55] Benjamin E. Mays, The Negro's God (New York: Atheneum, 1968).

[56] James H. Cone, "Black Consciousness and the Black Church," Christianity and Crisis, XXX (November 2 and 16, 1970), 247.

[57] Reuben A. Sheares, II, "Beyond White Theology," Christianity and Crisis, XXX (November 2 and 16, 1970), 229.

[58] Ibid., 229.

[59] Ibid., 230-231.

[60] Cone, "Black Consciousness," Christianity, XXX, 247.

[61] Ibid., 247.

[62] Ibid., 246.

[63] Ibid.

[64] Sheares, XXX, 233.

[65] Albert B. Cleage, Jr., The Black Messiah (New York: Sheed and Ward, Inc., 1968), p. 37.

[66] C. Eric Lincoln, "Who's Listening?, Christianity and Crisis XXX (November 2 & 16, 1970), 225-226.

[67] McClain, XXX, 250.

[68] Ibid., 252.

[69] Leon W. Watts, II, "The National Committee of Black Churchmen," Christianity and Crisis, XXX (November 2 & 16, 1970), 243.

[70] Sheares, XXX, 235.

[71] Dietrich Bonhoeffer, Letters and Papers from Prison (New York: n.p., 1967), p. 14.

[72] H. Richard Niebuhr, Christ and Culture (New York: Harper & Row, Publishers, 1951), p. 158.

[73] Henry H. Mitchell, Black Preaching (New York: J.B. Lippincott Co., 1970), p. 25.

[74] Sydney E. Ahlstrom, "Theology in America: A Historical Survey," The Shaping of American Religion, edited by James W. Smith and A. Leland Jamison, Vol. I of Religion in American Life (Princeton: Princeton University Press, 1961), p. 275. Ahlstrom notes here how the Lutheran Church held on to

the Reformations' biblical and doctrinal heritage. See also Sydney E. Ahlstrom, "The Lutheran Church and American Culture: A Tercentenary Retrospect," The Lutheran Quarterly, IX (November 1957), 326-327. Ahlstrom poses strong arguments that Lutheranism is best understood when it is seen not as a "melting pot" into American denominationalism but as in tension with America.

[75] See F. E. Mayer, "The Prior Distinction Between Law and Gospel and the Terminology 'Visible and Invisible Church'," Concordia Theological Monthly, XXV (March 1954), 177-198. Mayer also bears witness here to theologians obscuring the understanding of Luther and the confessors relative to an understanding of the church.

[76] See John M. Headley, Luther's View of Church History (New Haven, Conn.: Yale University Press, 1963). We suggest that this topic requires an in-depth consideration in separate research. Our point in raising the issue is to establish yet more proof of problems connected with the contemporary Lutheran correlating of the Kerygma to the black situation.

[77] Gerhard Ebeling, "The Significance of the Critical Historical Method for Church and Theology in Protestantism," Word and Faith, translated by James W. Leitch (Philadelphia: Fortress Press, 1963), pp. 17-61.

[78] See, for example, Martin H. Scharlemann, "God's Acts as Revelation," Concordia Theological Monthly, XXXII (April 1961), 214-215. This section is quite supportive to the importance of one's understanding of the situation. We might illumine the subject by saying that one who understands the historical critical method is one who has no problems in understanding the particularity or indigenization of theology out of which it is communicated.

[79] Ebeling, pp. 9 & 11.

[80] Deotis Roberts, Liberation and Reconciliation: A Black Theology (Philadelphia: The Westminster Press, 1971), pp. 18, 19.

[81] Richard H. Soulen, "Black Worship and Hermeneutics," The Christian Century, XXXVI (February 11, 1970), 171.

[82] Mitchell, p. 27.

[83] Niebuhr deals with this problem quite extensively in his book Christ and Culture, Chapter III, p. 115 and concludes that "It becomes more or less clear that it is not possible honestly to confess that Jesus is the Christ of Culture unless one can confess much more than this."

[84] David B. Barrett, Schism and Renewal in Africa (London: n.p., 1968), p. 66.

[85] Ibid., p. 79.

[86] Frazier's The Negro Church in America is still the best published outline of U.S. black church history. Its bias is contradicted by articles in the Journal of Negro History. Arthur Huff Fausset's Black Gods of the Metropolis (Philadelphia: University of Pennsylvania Press, 1944) is helpful when compared with similar descriptions of African and West Indies churches.

In addition to my own experiences in the U.S., I have also used Arthur Piepkorn's files describing black denominations to write this paragraph on U.S. black churches.

[87] F. B. Welbourne and B. A. Ogot, A Place to Feel at Home: A Study of Two Independent Churches in Western Kenya (London: Oxford University Press, 1966). They suggest this as a motive for indigenous East African churches.

[88] Herskovits first pointed to this connection in The Myth of the Negro Past, pp. 232-233. He weakened his case by adding his speculation that this water symbolism became more important in the new world because many river priests who were deported as slaves.

[89] This subject is treated in detail by LeRoi Jones, Blues People: Negro Music in White America (New York: William Morrow & Co., Inc., 1963). In our opinion, this is the best book on U.S. black culture published.

[90] David Beckman, "Trance: From Africa to Pentecostalism," Concordia Theological Monthly, XLV (January 1974), 11-26. Harold W. Turner, African Independent Church: The Life and Faith of the Church of the Lord (Aladura), (Oxford: The London Press, 1967), 11, 301, and 309.

[91] Joseph R. Washington, Jr., in "How Black is Black Religion?" Quest for a Black Theology, edited by James J. Gardiner and J. Deotis Roberts, Sr. (Philadelphia: Pilgrim Press, 1971), pp. 22-43, is one of several who makes this comparison.

[92] James Baldwin, The Fire Next Time (New York: Dial Press, 1963), pp. 47-48.

[93] This experiential foundation was central to the Reformation. Luther found comfort not in the external authority of popes or councils, but in the experience of the gospel. Wenzel Lohff, "Rechtfertigung und Anthropologie," Kerygma and Dogma, IV (October-December 1971), 227, refers to the timportance of experience in the Reformation concept of justification and its relationship to anthropology: "Kennzeichnend fur das Geminte ist vor allem der Satz in CAXXX, 17; tota haec doctrina ad illud certamen perterrefactae conscientiae referenda est, nec sine illo certamine intelligi potest (BSLK, 75). Die enthscheidende Leistung der theologischen Lehre Besteht darin, dass, der Glaubende das Evangelium Hort, des Heils gewiss wird und seine Identaitat erfahrt." Lohff also speaks of the need to recover the experiential matrix of the gospel: "Kan did Aufgabe christlicher Verkundigung und ihrer Theologie nur so gelost werden, dass eine Vermittlung geleistet wird, die diese Polarisierung (between anthropology and justification) producktiv uberwindet (T. Rendtorff), damit das was die Reformation als Evangelium bezeugte, inder Lebenswirklichkeit heute gehort werden kann." The article is in English translation, see "Justification and Anthropology," Concordia Theological Monthly, XLIV (January 1973), 31-47. The sentences quoted are translated on page 33.

[94] The illusions men live by and by which they defend themselves are poetically described by C. S. Lewis in The Great Divorce (New York: Macmillan

Co., 1946), where men build houses that don't protect them, defenses that don't really defend, securities that don't make secure and in the midst of their illusions are in hell, out of touch with reality. Another powerful statement of the human predicament is portrayed by Hannah Green in I Never Promised You a Rose Garden (New York: Holt, Rinehart and Winston, 1967), in which a psychiatrist can only finally offer his patient reality with all its hardness and brutality, but which is still preferable to the illusory dream world of mental illness.

Werner Elert, The Christian Ethos (Philadelphia: Fortress Press, 1957), pp. 158, 159, and Law and Gospel (Philadelphia: Fortress Press, 1967), pp. 16-25, does a theological analysis of "as if" existence whereby men seek to avoid the threat by denying the truth about themselves.

Perhaps the most radical recent statement of behavioristic determinism is B. F. Skinner's Beyond Freedom and Dignity (New York: knoph, 1971).

Gilkey, Part II, Chapters 3 and 4, has an extensive analysis of the secular experience of God as threat. See also Helmut Thielicke Death and Life (Philadelphia: Fortress Press, 1970), p. 105.

See Thomas Oden's concise analysis of the structure of idolatry (absolutizing the relative) in The Structure of Awareness (Nashville, Tenn.: Abingdon Press, 1969), pp. 235-241. See also Walter R. Bouman, "The Gospel and The Smacald Articles," Concordia Theological Monthly XL (June, July-August 1969), p. 415; Paul Tournier, Guild and Grace: A Psychological Study (London: Hodder and Stoughton, 1962), pp. 80-88, who sees self-justification as the universal problem, both social and religious, of mankind; Augsburg Confessions, Art. II, p. 29: "Our churches also teach that since the fall of Adam all men who are propagated according to nature are born in sin. That is to say, they are without fear of God, are without trust in God, and are concupiscent."

[95] Supra, p. 219.

[96] Harold Ditmanson, "New Themes in Christian Social Ethics," Lutheran World, XV, No. 1 (1968), 33.

[97] Supra, p. 218.

[98] Major J. Jones, Christian Ethics for Black Theology (Nashville: Abingdon Press, 1974), pp. 15-16.

[99] Unconditional love means exactly that – loving without imposing conditions. Although Jesus Christ is the only human being we know who was able to live this ideal fully, we also recognize that our very humanity prevents us from being able to live the same type of life as Jesus. All we can do is strive to fulfill this ideal by "putting on the new man" (sic) everyday; and by remembering those occasions on which one human being was able to manifest unconditional love.

[100] While biblical time appears to be linear, our knowledge of human existence is but one point in the on-going life of the universe. Western society

consistently attempts to set itself apart from and above the entire creation by insisting on a linear model of time, beginning with the creation in the biblical scheme of history. What is perhaps more significant is the fact that 75% of the world's population as well as the animal and plant kingdoms operates in a cyclical time scheme.

[101] Walter Brueggemann, The Land (Philadelphia: Fortress Press, 1977), p. 14.

[102] This quotation is taken from a taped interview with Dr. Albert Pero of the Lutheran School of Theology at Chicago and is on file at the Dvision for Mission in North America.

[103] Study Document on Christian Action in Racial and Ethnic Relations: Its Biblical and Theological Basis (New York: Board of Social Ministry, 1965).

[104] Paulo Friere, Pedagogy of the Oppressed, Chapters 1 & 2.

ABOUT THE EDITOR

Richard J. Perry, Jr. is associate professor of church and society/urban ministry at the Lutheran School of Theology at Chicago. He received his Ph.D. in Theology from the Lutheran School of Theology at Chicago.

He has served as a parish pastor, director of inclusive ministry in North Carolina, and Director of Black Ministries on the Commission for Multicultural Ministries of the ELCA.

He has authored several essays and a chapter on African American Lutheran ethical thought. More recently, he co-authored an essay with Jose David Rodriguez in the book *Faithful Conversations* (Fortress Press). He is a member of the Conference of International Black Lutherans (CIBL). He serves on the Planning Committee of the 2004 Transcultural Seminar.